JAMES A. RHODES
OHIO COLOSSUS

The bronze statue of James A. Rhodes guards the front entrance of the state office building named for the former four-term Ohio governor. It was moved there in 1991 after spending nine years on a corner of the Statehouse lawn.

JAMES A. RHODES
OHIO COLOSSUS

Tom Diemer
Lee Leonard
Richard G. Zimmerman

The Kent State
University Press
Kent, Ohio

Copyright © 2014 by The Kent State University Press, Kent, Ohio 44242
All rights reserved
Library of Congress Catalog Card Number 2014012499
ISBN 978-1-60635-215-1
Manufactured in the United States of America

Every effort has been made to obtain the permission of persons interviewed
by the authors to be quoted in this book.

Library of Congress Cataloging-in-Publication Data
Diemer, Tom.
James A. Rhodes : Ohio colossus / Tom Diemer, Lee Leonard, Richard G. Zimmerman.
pages cm
Includes bibliographical references and index.
ISBN 978-1-60635-215-1 (hardcover) ∞
1. Rhodes, James A. (James Allen), 1909–2001.
2. Governors—Ohio—Biography.
3. Ohio—Politics and government—20th century.
I. Leonard, Lee, 1939– II. Zimmerman, Richard G., 1934– III. Title.
F496.4.R46D54 2014
977.1′043092—dc23
[B]
2014012499

18   17   16   15   14   5   4   3   2   1

To my wife, Judith Zimmer, and my mother, the late Joan Diemer,
for their constant love and support.

To all those who knew James A. Rhodes and contributed the stories
that enliven this volume.

Colossus: 1. A statue of gigantic size, especially that of Apollo set at the entrance to the harbor at Rhodes c. 280 B.C., and considered among the seven wonders of the ancient world. 2. Any person or thing of extraordinary size or importance.

—*Webster's New Universal Unabridged Dictionary*

Contents

Foreword

GOVERNOR RICHARD CELESTE

TOM DIEMER, LEE LEONARD, and the late Rick Zimmerman do a masterful job of describing the life and achievements of a one-of-a-kind Ohioan—four-time governor James Allen Rhodes. I should know; I studied at his knee for most of twenty years.

This volume captures in nitty-gritty detail the rise of this quintessentially (a very non-Rhodes word!) self-invented political overachiever. From the rough days of his childhood in Coalton to the glory days of his remarkable service in the governor's office, the authors describe just how completely Jim Rhodes honed his sales skills (from working North High Street and the Ohio State University campus to wooing Soichiro Honda in a full-court press in Japan) and exercised leadership (from the Knothole Gang to the Ohio Statehouse).

In the process, Rhodes grew to embody the mythic tale he spun about himself and his rise. Diemer, Leonard, and Zimmerman convey how Rhodes and his handpicked chroniclers transformed a story that began with only a few fading black-and-white photos into a 3-D, full-color, larger-than-life spectacular.

Why was Jim Rhodes so successful? I believe it boils down to this: nobody loved Ohio, every nook and cranny, every bar and barbershop, every farm and factory, and every county fair, more than he did. He loved Ohio more than partisan politics or political ideology. If Ohio needed revenue, he put the State above his political promises and raised taxes. He loved Ohio more than Washington, D.C. He just kept coming back to his first and only love.

And he loved the ordinary people of Ohio—like his neighbors in Coalton and Springfield, and the voters of Columbus who gave him his first boost. He cared deeply about their problems. And from his perspective, the one solution to all of their problems—poverty, poor housing, ill health—was a job. That had been the medicine he sought as a young man—not one job, but any and all that he could wangle.

Jim Rhodes understood the importance of a job—for personal dignity and family security and for community stability. He also understood, perhaps from the outside looking in, that education opened fresh opportunities for young people. He also knew that education and "smart" were two different things. He said to me on the eve of my inauguration (presciently, it turned out), "You got too many PhDs in your cabinet."

Yet, no one did more than Jim Rhodes to promote higher education and put it within an easy commute of every Ohioan.

Jim Rhodes balanced genuine humility, never forgetting where he came from, with massive self-confidence, which enabled him to take on elections—primaries as well as generals—against the odds. I suspect that one reason he did not pay too much attention to people in his party's establishment is that he was certain that in his bones he knew Ohioans far better than they did. He was right, of course.

But as the authors point out, Rhodes also made a point of having experienced and capable people around him. And he usually listened to them. Here is one example that may help to explain the lack of death-row executions after the early part of the first of his four terms. One day as I was preparing to take office as governor in late 1982, I encountered John McElroy, the respected attorney and Rhodes confidant. He told me that making decisions on death-row cases would be one of the toughest challenges I would face.

When I asked him why, he said that Rhodes had sent him to witness an execution that took place shortly after he became governor. McElroy said it was the most shocking and traumatic experience of his life. The next morning, he marched into the governor's office and announced that he would resign if Rhodes ever sent him on that duty again. In fact, McElroy said, "I told him that he should go personally and witness the next execution so that he would truly understand what his decision entailed." Rhodes never let another death sentence be carried out.

There is no question that Jim Rhodes loved his family, even though he was torn, as many politicians are, by the demands that political ambition and public service put on family time. The authors do a fine job of conveying Rhodes's effort to be present for his family members—and protect them from the perils of life in the public eye. Rhodes knew how to dive "into the weeds" when he faced public controversy. He kept his family even more distant from the press with great success. When I stood in his office with him before the inauguration in 1983, he pointed to my wife and children and said: "Take a good look at them, Dick. After this is all over, they will be the only ones who still care about you."

Why did Jim Rhodes run one last time, against the wishes of his wife and many in his political party? I am sure that it was because he did not believe either of his primary opponents or me, for that matter, knew and loved Ohio as much as he did. It wasn't about ambition; he had nothing to prove. It was about his abiding love of his state and its people.

When he came to believe that I loved Ohio, from lake to river, and honored promises he made (but was not able to fund), like the Honda expansion in Marysville or the completion of the Jackson bypass in his backyard; when he saw me set up office at the Ohio State Fair and cheer side by side with him for the OSU Buckeyes; perhaps even when I went to the Kent State campus on a May 4th anniversary to apologize personally to the families of those killed and wounded on that tragic day, Rhodes knew that I loved Ohio as deeply as he did.

Jim Rhodes, without the benefit of a college degree, taught this Rhodes Scholar many lessons. He taught me how to lose. And he taught me how to win. But no lesson was more powerful than to get up every day and be grateful for the privilege of serving the people of Ohio.

Foreword

Governor Bob Taft

JIM RHODES WAS A COMMANDING FIGURE in Ohio politics for most of the second half of the twentieth century.

I was witness to many of those eventful years. In Toledo in early 1970, I gave my maiden political speech on behalf of my father, who was running against Rhodes for the Republican nomination for U.S. Senate. I was a twenty-eight-year-old rookie on stage, with the legendary governor looming before me as an "Ohio Colossus." To say I was intimidated would be an understatement.

I served in the Ohio House of Representatives during parts of Rhodes's final two terms as governor. I saw how he got Honda to choose Ohio for its first U.S. plant and Ford to locate a new transmission plant near my district in southern Ohio. I soon saw how he had built Ohio's transportation, education, and recreation systems.

In 1986, history took an odd turn. I ran for lieutenant governor on the ticket with Jim Rhodes—my dad's onetime opponent—in his ill-fated attempt to serve a fifth term. Then fifteen years rolled by. And in March 2001, during my first term as governor, I had the honor of participating in the final farewell to Governor Rhodes at his memorial and funeral service, interrupting a South American trade mission to do so.

There will never be another governor like Jim Rhodes. No leader has cast a longer shadow over Ohio's political landscape, influencing the tactics and policies of every governor, Democrat or Republican, who has followed him. We were all "Rhodes Scholars." It's remarkable that until this publication we have not had a thorough, balanced biography of this dominant political personality and amazing human being.

This book is important; it demonstrates how Rhodes became a political master. I learned a lot campaigning with him and serving as a legislator during his time as governor. He taught us all about the centrality of jobs, jobs, jobs—"The average Ohioan wants a job and wants to be left alone." His biographers recount how he urged Ronald Reagan to focus on jobs in his Ohio campaign, helping him carry the state and win the presidency.

From Rhodes, I learned to look forward and move on—he stayed positive and upbeat always, never looking back or getting derailed by setbacks. He encountered tough economic times, frustrations, and failures during his last two terms, but he always remained hopeful and optimistic about the future.

Rhodes had a keen sense of political timing; he knew when to take charge, as I watched him do during the "Great Blizzard of 1978." And he knew when to "lie in the weeds," as he did when one of his bond issues would go down to defeat.

He taught us to *listen* before *leading:* "find out what people want and give it to them" was his advice, though he sometimes gave communities projects whether they asked for them or not. He always seemed to be talking a blue streak and promoting something or other, yet he listened carefully to good political advice from all sources.

The book does a nice job of showing how Jim Rhodes courted the media—the Statehouse press corps when he was state auditor and big-city editors and publishers when he was governor—something any statewide candidate must learn. He was a master of humor and obfuscation when he didn't want to answer a reporter's question, as some of the most entertaining stories in the book illustrate. His unique, sometimes unintelligible manner of speaking was impossible to imitate—"We are not in a state of ego," he would say as a way of dismissing questions about his successes in life.

Rhodes never met a stranger—he could work with Democrats, Republicans, African American politicians, big-city business leaders, and farmers; he had an unusual background for a Republican, coming from humble origins, working his way up, connecting with all kinds of people along the way. His plainspoken ways appealed to average voters, and he never deviated from his "Jobs and Progress" mantra. He networked and built coalitions, realizing the importance of cultivating friends and allies all across the state.

Rhodes was an Ohio original. He loved the state and never stopped promoting it, doing more to create an Ohio identity than anyone before or since;

I so often heard him say, "Ohio has more things by accident than other states have on purpose." And he loved the Ohio State Fair because it showcased Ohio; he was always there with me and other governors on opening day, and he started the tradition of governors spending the night in the barns with 4-H farm families—a sleepless but memorable experience for me.

The Rhodes legacy was about much more than politics, as Diemer, Leonard, and Zimmerman make clear. He had a vision for progress in Ohio that matched the postwar boom years; this was especially clear during his first eight years as governor. He built the foundation for the state's future: parks, highways, career centers, and airports.

Without a college degree himself, Rhodes understood how critical higher education was to the state's prosperity. He was ahead of his time in his "Blueprint for Brainpower," adding state universities and building branch campuses and community and technical colleges in every corner of the state. He also pioneered the use of state bonds to accomplish his vision.

And finally, we can all learn from Jim Rhodes as we confront today's polarized and often poisonous political environment. The authors show how Rhodes was pragmatic rather than ideological—"People want answers, they already know the questions," he would say. When Democrats took over the legislature during much of his final two terms, he learned how to work with House Speaker Vern Riffe and Senate president Oliver Ocasek to get things done. In times of recession, after making deep cuts to state spending, he went along with tax increases to preserve funding for schools and colleges.

Jim Rhodes was a hustler, a promoter, a political artist, a lover of Ohio, and a self-made man. He was an extraordinary governor. He cared about struggling families and their aspirations. He was a builder for the future. He was a family man but also had an earthy sense of humor. He was truly one of a kind. We are fortunate we can experience his life and times immediately and personally, thanks to the authors of this timely biography.

Introduction

JAMES A. RHODES's long, productive, improbable, and at times bewildering life led one Ohio newspaper to declare that the "state had its own 'colossus' in Rhodes."[1] Some Ohioans probably thought he would never go away—like that comfortable, homely old shoe in the corner of the closet.

He forever will be remembered as the great promoter. His critics, and they were always lurking, might prefer the more pejorative term "common huckster," or "carnival pitchman." But his admirers, and they were legion—enough to elect him three times mayor of Columbus, four times Ohio's chief executive—recall him as the man who so loved his job and his city and state that he never tired of promoting himself, his many personal and political issues, and what he would call "The Wonderful World of Ohio."[2]

Before James Allen Rhodes arrived at the Statehouse, first as state auditor and then governor, Ohio had never experienced the likes of him. And it is unlikely to experience anyone like him again.

Born proudly poor and underprivileged in Ohio's dreary, southern coal-mining region, Rhodes methodically clawed his way up the political ladder from Coalton to Columbus, first a ward committeeman, then mayor, then state auditor, and finally governor. He had a few boosts along the way, but mostly he pulled himself up by his own bootstraps, clinging to his own coat-tails. Certainly, he made mistakes and miscalculations during his climb, and more after he reached his ultimate goal as governor—most notably his role in the tragedy at Kent State where four students were killed in a hail of National Guard gunfire. Yet his severest critics might now concede that he far outdistanced his less colorful, more sedate, and usually duller predecessors and successors through a combination of foresight, intuitive political adroitness, panache, and plain hard work.

"He absolutely loved and understood people," his last executive assistant, Robert Howarth said of the chief reason for Rhodes's political success.[3] Ohio Supreme Court justice Paul Pfeifer, whom Rhodes outpointed in the 1986 Republican gubernatorial primary, said simply, "I still regard him as the most instinctive politician that I came to know."[4]

In this biography, the authors show how an ineloquent, modestly educated son of the Ohio hills rose to the top in Republican politics, served as governor of his state longer than anyone else, squired Sir Winston Churchill around Columbus, befriended Bob Hope, and gave expert advice to Ronald Reagan on carrying Ohio in 1980. Three former Columbus-based journalists—each of whom reported extensively and daily on his political career and thus grew to know him, his staff, family, and his contemporaries, friend and foe alike—tell his remarkable story here. Thus, it is only fair to share with readers how his biographers got along with Rhodes and to examine his relations with the press generally, both the working Statehouse reporters and their more remote superiors. In an attempt to shed light on the antics of this colorful public official, the authors have drawn on their own recollection of anecdotes, some of which were never recorded or reported for public consumption.

The idea for this book—the first full published account of Rhodes's life and career—originated with the late Richard Zimmerman. Rick covered Rhodes's final months as state auditor, the rough-and-tumble 1962 campaign that elevated him to the executive suite, his first two terms as governor, and his rather reluctant and ultimately failed 1970 primary effort to move to the U.S. Senate. Zimmerman was a legend in journalistic circles in the state capital. He was known as a critic of Rhodes, yet he usually enjoyed an easy rapport with him. Zimmerman eventually became the *Plain Dealer*'s Washington bureau chief.

Lee Leonard covered Rhodes for United Press International from the middle of his second term through his last two terms and failed 1986 attempt at a fifth term. He reported on Rhodes in private life for the *Columbus Dispatch* from 1990 through the former governor's death on March 4, 2001. Leonard showed no mercy in trying to break through Rhodes's attempts to buffalo and hide from reporters, but he grudgingly admired the man and the politician. He respected Rhodes's fondness for his family and for any children.

Tom Diemer arrived from New York City in time to report for the Columbus bureau of The Associated Press on Rhodes's comeback reelection to a third term as governor in 1974. He also covered the governor's 1978 reelection and subsequent term for the *Plain Dealer,* Ohio's largest newspaper, which editorially often supported Rhodes. Diemer then also left Columbus to join the Cleveland paper's Washington bureau.

Rhodes's working relationships with beat reporters, such as the authors, whose job it was to chart his daily activities, was a studied mix of guarded accommodation and suspicious evasion. Except during great political stress—as when voters rejected his pet Ohio Bond Commission constitutional amendment and following a well-publicized if somewhat vaguely documented exposé by *Life* magazine—Rhodes was available to Statehouse reporters, but usually on his terms. He never especially favored open, give-and-take formal news conferences and had a propensity to operate furtively, behind the scenes, as far from reporters' scrutiny and analysis as he could get. Rhodes even teased reporters about his avoidance of freewheeling, open news conferences and his propensity for secrecy. He once confided kiddingly to Diemer, "Off the record, we're having a press conference later today."

When an even mildly controversial bill originated in his office and was sent upstairs to the legislature with his private stamp of approval, Rhodes might publicly deny authorship or go so far as to deny knowing anything about the measure in question. "That's not *our* bill," he flatly claimed, using the royal plural pronoun, as he often did, in response to a question in the early years about a pending piece of civil service legislation. He made the assertion even though the inquiring reporter had witnessed the legislation being drafted in the governor's office and later was told by Republican legislative leaders, "This is an administration bill."[5]

Rhodes's aversion to public conflict was to become legendary. As one political columnist put it in 1963, his "desire to avoid controversy appears to be almost an obsession."[6] When asked about a rival or competing program, Rhodes invariably would reply, "We [note the royal "we"] have no objections"—even if he was working quietly to kill or severely limit the same program. While conflict and controversy remained the life's blood and favored theme of most political journalists, more often than not Rhodes's secrecy frustrated them.

But Rhodes needed the working press in his corner to communicate his message and his promotions to voters. These ranged from bond issues and the debt that went with them to fairs in general, the Ohio State Fair in particular; Ohio tomato juice; and Columbus-based Wendy's fast food hamburgers. He always seemed aware of that need and of his symbiotic relationship with the media. So he could be cooperative and accommodating up to a point, provided the reporters saw things as he did. Throughout his four terms as governor, Rhodes never gladly suffered critical, independent background analysis of his motives, such as references to his personal investment in Wendy's franchises.

Despite his protests that "we're not running for editor," Rhodes's relations with beat reporters' bosses—Ohio's editors and publishers—were generally smooth and pliant. With billions of dollars in voter-approved capital improvement bond funds, Rhodes wooed newspaper leaders and opinion-makers by backing their favorite community projects, whether the undertaking was a branch university campus, a new vocational or technical school, a new or upgraded state park facility, or an expedited highway project. His public policy rationale was consistent: "jobs, jobs, jobs." And he seduced not only those editors and publishers representing major news outlets. For example, Ken Woodman, editor of the *Mansfield News-Journal* had long dreamed of an Ohio State University branch at Mansfield, Ohio. Rhodes made Woodman's dream a reality, in partial fulfillment of his campaign pledge to locate some sort of state-approved institution of higher learning within an easy commute of every Ohioan. Consequently, that editor became a fervent Rhodes supporter.[7]

But Rhodes's close connections with several of Ohio's major publishers proved particularly and notably politically rewarding. He enjoyed largely uncritical support from his hometown newspaper, the *Columbus Evening Dispatch,* owned by the locally powerful Wolfe family of bankers and media moguls. He also cemented a close relationship with Paul Block, the hereditary and sometimes autocratic publisher of the *Toledo Blade.* In an editorial endorsing Rhodes for governor, Block dramatically and unalterably terminated his longstanding support of incumbent governor Michael DiSalle, a former Toledo mayor, whom Rhodes was to defeat in 1962. Block came to conclude that DiSalle wasn't paying sufficient homage to his benefactors in the Glass City, which included the *Blade* and, of course, Block. Soon after becoming governor and with passage of one of his earliest capital improvements, Rhodes repaid Block's editorial and kindness with a new, state-established medical school in Toledo.[8]

Perhaps Rhodes's most notable and advantageous rapport with an Ohio press lord led to his enduring alliance with Louis Seltzer, the elfin, egocentric, self-made, up-from-the-ranks publisher of the *Cleveland Press*. Seltzer came to exercise broad supervisory authority over not only the *Press* but also other Scripps-Howard properties in Ohio, including dailies in Columbus and Cincinnati and the Columbus-based Ohio Press Service (OPS), a small wire service that offered news stories for a fee to other Ohio newspapers. These included the Brush-Moore chain of smaller Ohio dailies, headquartered at the *Canton Repository*. Under Seltzer, the *Press* and OPS sometimes seemed to complement Rhodes's own well-oiled, state-supported propaganda machine, much to the dismay of some of OPS's more politically independent reporters. (Seltzer and Scripps-Howard also were responsible for promoting stories embarrassing to the DiSalle administration both during the latter part of the Democrat's controversial four-year term and in his losing 1962 reelection campaign.)

Rhodes expertly played on Seltzer's hubris for being known as "Mr. Cleveland," a title a national magazine bestowed on him. He made certain Seltzer was involved when the metropolitan Cleveland area won its share of state-backed projects, including a new state university, where the centerpiece building was named the Rhodes Tower.

But Rhodes didn't owe the favorable publicity during his years as state auditor and governor solely to seduced publishers and editors, or to a manipulated Statehouse press corps. He was an active, hard-driving, and innovative political leader who was to dominate Ohio Republican politics before, during, and, up to a point, even after his record sixteen years as governor. "He had an ability to make Ohioans happy they were Ohioans . . . more so than people do today," said Keith McNamara, a Columbus lawyer and state legislator who followed Rhodes's career from the prewar years through his last term as governor. "[Now] there isn't the pride in Ohio that he generated."[9]

No matter if one didn't always agree with his pragmatic, moderately conservative politics or his sometimes vainglorious self-serving promotions. Jim Rhodes made himself a highly visible governor and was simply impossible for either the press or public to ignore. "Some say he's laughed at outside Ohio. Maybe," *Columbus Dispatch* columnist Duane St. Clair wrote during Rhodes final term. But "his undisputed political instincts now seem more respected and admired since his days in the Statehouse definitely are numbered."[10] Political instincts? It wasn't complicated: find out what people want and then do it—or at least try. That was the Rhodes way, and it worked.

After Rhodes's death in 2001, reporter George E. Condon Jr. wrote, "It is safe to say that no politician ever so dominated the state for so long and left so much behind. Other Ohioans—McKinley, Taft, Hayes, Grant, Garfield, Harrison and Harding—made it to the White House. But none had anywhere near the impact on Ohio as this son of a coal miner in Coalton."[11] Rhodes was rarely reflective—"Nothing," he would say if asked what he wanted to be remembered for. But in 1979, in his last inaugural address, he credited the state and country he loved for his success. "It's only in America and only in Ohio where a coal miner's son could become the chief executive," he said. "That's what it's all about."[12]

CHAPTER 1

The Hustle from Coalton to Capitol

IF THERE WAS ONE CONSTANT THEME running through Jim Rhodes's life, it was his emphasis on his hardscrabble, humble beginnings. If there was a second, it was highlighting the sensitive, benevolent influence his widowed mother had in shaping his never-ending ambition "to be somebody."[1]

Most of what is known about Rhodes's formative years came from yarns the man spun about himself, sometimes confirmed by contemporaries—now long dead—when interviewed by political reporters and would-be biographers. Dean Jauchius, a former Columbus newspaperman, coauthor (or ghostwriter, as some critics have suggested) of Rhodes's three historical novels, a onetime Rhodes employee, and eventually a professor at Columbus's Franklin University, once candidly sighed, as he was completing research on his former boss's definitive but yet unpublished biography, "sifting legend from fact is some job."[2]

It can be reported with confidence that James Allen Rhodes, four-time governor of Ohio, was born on September 13, 1909, into a small but comfortable clapboard house located in the tiny village of Coalton, Jackson County, Ohio, the son of James L. and Susan Howe Rhodes. While born in a mostly poor coal-mining area of the southeastern Ohio Appalachian region ("I came closer to being born with a lump of coal in my hand than a silver spoon in my mouth," Rhodes once told an interviewer), Jim Rhodes and his family, which included three older sisters, Garnet, Catherine, and Ardella "Midge," were solidly middle class until the death of the elder Rhodes in November 1918. He was felled by spinal meningitis brought on by flu in the course of a national epidemic.[3]

His mother, Susan, whom friends called Susie, boasted a high school diploma. Young Jim's father, like many of his neighbors, came from Welsh coalmining stock but had taken business college courses and worked his way out of the dangerous, deep shafts to become a mine superintendent. The senior James Rhodes, "Big Jim," also was interested in politics and for a time served as a Republican precinct committeeman. Many of the Welsh immigrants who settled in Jackson County were coal miners and Republicans. Big Jim had split with his father, a mine owner, over the value of union representation. The son favored the new United Mine Workers of America, because it fought for higher wages and health and safety standards. Big Jim remained a staunch Republican, which apparently rubbed off on the future governor.[4]

With the death of the family's breadwinner, young Jimmy Rhodes saw a turning point for the family: "We had a different status in life," he later told Jauchius. "We were on the giving end before, helping a lot of people, and then we were on the receiving end."[5] Years later, Hortense Rhodes Hall, the future governor's aged aunt, said, "If we were poor, we didn't notice it," but Rhodes and many of his contemporaries recalled otherwise.[6] Rhodes proudly asserted that following his father's death he was "never known not to have a job." He claimed that as male head of a fatherless household, he delivered newspapers, caddied, cut grass, ran errands, delivered groceries, and took other odd jobs "to make a nickel." Nonetheless, he recalled his childhood with great fondness. He told Jauchius: "I had probably the most enlightening boyhood of any boy. I had a mother [who] believed in discipline and obedience. My mother had one thing she taught us all. It was to pray every morning and every night, and the prayer was this: 'Oh, God, help me to *be* somebody.' That was her whole theme; that anybody can be what they want to be if they work at it."[7]

In later years, Rhodes often told about his mother calling the family together on the Christmas Eve following his father's death. She gave the children some fruit and nuts—their Christmas gifts. "Divide it up," Susan Rhodes said tersely. "There is no Santa Claus, and we're together against the world. When you come home and close that door behind you, all of your loved ones are in this house."[8] He repeated this whenever he wanted to emphasize the importance of his family: "Your family's all you've got," he'd say.

The Rhodes family lived for a time in Jasonville, Indiana, a village in the southern part of the state. After seven or eight years, Susie and the kids moved back to Jackson County, Ohio, perhaps to a modified chicken coop, but without the elder Rhodes, who died in Indiana.[9]

In a 1986 description of his childhood, Jim Rhodes said, "I lived at 123 Water Street, rear, in Jackson. It was a chicken coop. My mother cleaned it out real well."[10] A reporter checked the Water Street address in July 2012 and found a vacant lot at 123, but the inspection revealed a vintage bungalow with an appendage the size of a chicken coop jutting out from the rear next door at 121.[11] Jauchius wrote that Susie and her children lived at 432 Water Street in a "ramshackle one-floor cottage most recently used as a chicken house" and furnished with orange crates. In winter, Jim and his older sister Garnet filched coal from a passing rail car to stoke the living room fireplace, the only source of heat.[12]

The family probably moved from Coalton to southern Indiana because Indiana's mines were more active and productive than the deep mines of Ohio, which were playing out. Jauchius said the family moved in July 1910, when Rhodes would have been nine months old. He also wrote that Indiana had safer regulations for miners and that Big Jim had labor-management issues with his own father, who owned the Coalton mine.[13]

Following her husband's death in 1918, Susan Rhodes reportedly remarried, to a man recalled only as "Barrett." Even Aunt Hortense couldn't summon up his first name when reporters asked her years later. She remembered only that this fellow died a few years after his brief marriage to Rhodes's mother. Jauchius, however, wrote that Susie married John C. Barrett, a telegrapher with the Detroit Toledo & Ironton Railroad, who had struck up a "platonic" friendship with her. The wedding took place in Barrett's hometown of Napoleon, Ohio, in June 1924. The family moved to Springfield, where both Barrett and Susie had ties; in Susie's 1950 obituary it was noted that she had a brother then living in Springfield. Jauchius wrote that both Susie and her new husband wanted to go to Springfield, for employment and family reasons. The Rhodes children, including Jim, then fourteen, didn't accept Barrett as a stepfather and answered only to Susie. In the summer of 1930, early in the Depression, after the railroad laid Barrett off, he took his belongings and vanished for good.[14]

Also somewhat at variance are details concerning the demise of one of Rhodes's sisters, Catherine, who died at about six years old, apparently of natural causes, and his little brother, Carl Kendal Rhodes, who died at about six months of age, apparently while the family was living in Indiana.[15] Jauchius reported that Catherine died of heart failure brought on by a "vicious attack of pneumonia," in June 1910 while Big Jim was commuting to Jasonville before the family's move.[16] Rhodes's sister Garnet confirmed Catherine's childhood death but insisted there never was a younger brother.[17] According to Jauchius, though, Carl Kendal Rhodes, named after a good friend of Big Jim's, was born dangerously prematurely with a weak heart on December 10, 1910, and died November 19, 1911.[18]

The reconfigured Rhodes family departed Jackson County a second time, settling in Springfield, a west-central Ohio city of mostly small industries, about the time Jim was approaching high school age. While he was vague about when he arrived in Springfield (a biographical sketch suggested it was "probably about 1923"), Rhodes vividly explained to Jauchius, and to almost anyone else who would listen, why the family moved away from the hills of Jackson County for good:

> The county people [Rhodes likely was referring to Jackson County child welfare authorities] came out to our house to get the kids, to take us to a home. My mother grabbed a broom and chased those people clear out through the front gate. She shook that broom at them, and told them not to come back; never to come back, that this was a family, and by God, it was going to stay a family. So we moved away from there, and went to Springfield, and I was hustling all kinds of jobs. And we never looked back, and we never had any—any level of support at all—from any government.[19]

Rhodes was never recorded as explaining in detail why "the county people" tried to place him and his siblings in some sort of "home." Perhaps his hard-working, widowed mother—first a cook, then proprietor of a restaurant and boardinghouse catering to miners and railroaders—did not have time and/or money enough, in the opinion of local bureaucrats, to properly care for her kids. Rhodes's recollection of this unhappy experience, along with other childhood memories of economic deprivation, mixed in with his mother's grit and fierce independence, help explain why he never had a high opinion of welfare programs. Instead, he chose to emphasize the obligation of state and local governments to promote vocational and post–high school educa-

Jim Rhodes as a toddler with big sister Garnet in Jackson County, Ohio. Photo courtesy of Suzanne and Richard Moore.

tion generally, while also fostering an atmosphere creating decent-paying jobs for well-trained heads of household.

"Dusty" Rhodes, as he came to be known, made his mark at Springfield High School, then the city's sole public high school (the name was later changed to Springfield South). When he started getting elected to higher and higher political office in Columbus, a plethora of former high school friends, teachers, coaches, and a veteran principal always came forward with tales of young Dusty Rhodes's career at Springfield High. He was best remembered as an athlete (primarily basketball), a promoter, hustler, and all-around "big man on campus," even if he wasn't invited to join the National Honor Society.

"Everyone in class knew him and liked him," Charles Fox, longtime principal at Springfield High, remembered. "He was a good school citizen. He was a promoter. Even then he always had something in the fire." Fox later was to recall that even in high school Rhodes harbored dreams of becoming an important public official. Both Fox and Elwood Pitzer, a Rhodes classmate who later would become a coach and art (sculpture) instructor at both Springfield South and then at a newly opened second high school, Springfield North, said Rhodes was a "pretty good all-around athlete" and a "born leader."[20]

Rhodes was a good football player, a triple-threat who could run, throw, and kick the football. He organized his own team in Jackson and as an eighth-grader quarterbacked his squad to a six-point win over the Jackson High varsity, only to have his mother whip him and send him to bed without supper because he was an hour late. On the basketball court, Rhodes was a high-scoring guard, eventually leading his high school team in scoring.[21] Jauchius reported that Rhodes had a macho, somewhat profane streak. In fact, the future governor was expelled from high school for calling his basketball coach a son-of-a-bitch to his face when, as a sophomore and budding star, he asked the coach to help him juggle his classwork, basketball practice, and a night job at a factory. The coach was unsympathetic. His high school records indicate he was out of school for more than a year, between October 1926 and January 1928.[22] During those fifteen months, Rhodes managed a grocery store, among other jobs. He had a chance to enter Springfield Central Catholic High School, but his mother vetoed that idea, since the family was not Catholic.[23]

Her strapping, energetic son also had a health issue, though it didn't appear to slow him down. Rhodes had suffered from a never fully explained chest ailment that caused one of his lungs to fill with pus. The affected organ was first drained of fluid when Rhodes was six years old. Garnet recalled that a doctor came to the house and operated on the impaired right lung on the kitchen table while family members and neighbors assisted and Garnet watched. The doctor said the boy would not live ten years.[24] Jauchius noted the death sentence as just six weeks. Three weeks after the kitchen-table procedure, Rhodes was sent to Terre Haute, Indiana, where a doctor removed part of

Portrait of a handsome young man—Jim Rhodes as a young adult. Photo courtesy of Suzanne and Richard Moore.

his right lung, according to Jauchius's account. He then spent a week near death while his mother ministered to him around the clock. Doctors later advised him to "cough and spit"—a practice he carried into adulthood—to clear his lung. And they counseled him to take catnaps—a habit that became legendary while he was governor—to conserve his energy. He jokingly called it his "heart medicine."[25]

While his one-functioning-lung status may have explained why he was rejected for military service at the start of World War II, it did not interfere with his athletic ability. He graduated from Springfield High with an offer of a modest basketball scholarship for tuition from Ohio State, and he continued his interest in athletics throughout his adult life.[26] As a public official, he would expertly sink basketballs through hoops at dusty midway stands at county fairs, where he enjoyed campaigning. His up-close-and-personal approach delighted fairgoers (voters, hopefully, or at least the children of voters, including the kids who often received the stuffed animals Rhodes invariably won) and also the concessionaires who began recognizing him.[27] He continued to play a competitive, low-handicap golf game almost until the end of his life.[28]

Armed with a high school diploma (obtained in June 1930) and some talent for basketball, Rhodes nosed around several campuses, including the Lutheran-affiliated Wittenberg College in Springfield. Friends said he was never particularly enthusiastic about going to college but enrolled at Ohio State University in Columbus, just an hour east of Springfield.[29] Garnet said their mother moved the Rhodes brood to Columbus at the depth of the Great Depression in 1932 so they would be close to Jim.[30] Jauchius wrote that the family moved in November 1931 because Jim was wearing himself out driving from Springfield to Columbus and back each night to protect Susie and his two sisters.[31] The family eventually put down deep roots in Columbus, a city Rhodes would cherish and eventually preside over as mayor. He lived in Columbus or its suburbs for the rest of his life.

In September 1930, before enrolling at Ohio State, Rhodes hitchhiked to Columbus to survey campus life on the Oval and explore the social roadmap. He ended up spending a year in the area, meeting OSU athletes, university officials, and merchants on North High Street and ingratiating himself with them by doing favors. He also plotted his career path, which by now involved becoming governor of Ohio.

To earn money, he booked bands, as he had in Springfield. Now his territory included not only the campus and Columbus but the nearby towns of Granville, Newark, Buckeye Lake, Circleville, Chillicothe, and Lancaster. He gained access to big band giants Lionel Hampton, Benny Goodman, the Dorsey brothers, and Guy Lombardo. He also was a broker for agencies that rented caps and gowns for high school and college graduations.[32]

As he drove back and forth to Springfield and saw firsthand the ravages of the Depression—"bearded men in ragged clothes huddled around flickering campfires" and clusters of tarpaper shacks, Hoovervilles—Rhodes vowed that when he became a public servant he would use his leverage not for partisan political gain but to help people. The seed of "Jobs and Progress"—his theme for the rest of his political life—was planted during this time. Rhodes accumulated enough money to buy a four-door Model A Ford. He also rented a live-in office and took an option on an adjacent unit for the rest of his family.[33]

Rhodes never claimed to have graduated from Ohio State, but his official biographies almost invariably said he was a "student at Ohio State University," without stating exactly when or for how long. When asked, Rhodes always repeated his standard answer: he was forced to drop out when his mother contracted cancer and he had to work to support her. "I had to make a choice," he told Jauchius. "This was my mother. It costs a lot of money to fight cancer."[34] For a full-time student in the early 1930s, tuition and textbooks would have come to a little under $50 per quarter at Ohio State, plus housing and meals.

In late October 1969, when Rhodes was completing his second term as governor and was gearing up to run for the U.S. Senate—which involved issuing an updated biography with the familiar phrase concerning his career at Ohio State—the *Cleveland Plain Dealer* obtained a long-suppressed copy of his university records. These revealed he was enrolled for only one quarter and was on academic probation when he dropped out of college, having carried only a thirteen-hour course load. He was failing hygiene, physical education, and military science (ROTC) and receiving Ds in English and geography.[35] To have done that poorly in such easy courses as phys ed and ROTC, Rhodes would have likely skipped most of the classes. He was busy promoting himself, playing some freshman basketball, and holding down several jobs.[36]

Garnet had a different take on Rhodes's departure from OSU: an English teacher had assigned students to write a paper about the strangest person they ever met. Rhodes, who had a wry sense of humor, wrote about the English teacher. "They kicked him out," she said.[37] Rhodes's daughter Suzanne also said her father flunked English as a result of the assigned paper and was summoned before a "board of discipline." He refused to go. "He said, 'Hell with that, I can make some money." That's when he started booking bands."[38] But Jauchius noted that Rhodes already had been doing bookings. He attributed the withdrawal to a blend of academic difficulties (had he continued, Rhodes would have been on academic probation for the spring quarter), his mother's cancer, and his relentless grind to support the family. He withdrew from the university on January 28, 1932. On the registrar's withdrawal slip was written, "for financial reasons."[39]

Rhodes claimed to have continued to monitor some college classes without credit or paying tuition: "I would just go from class to class, especially law classes, and sit in."[40] According to OSU law student Glenn Detling, who later became a prosecutor and judge in Springfield, the future governor even briefly considered law school, though he lacked the patience for law and opted for a career in politics.[41]

During the early 1930s, an event occurred that would change Rhodes's life. He came to the attention of Grant Ward, also a native of Wellston, neighbor to Rhodes's hometown in Jackson County, at the time a state senator representing a Columbus-area district and an Ohio State sports radio broadcaster, the radio "Voice of the [football] Buckeyes." Ward, according to friends, mentored Rhodes and set him up in business at Jim's Place, a small hamburger and donut joint at 17th Avenue and High Street across from Ohio State's main campus. Rhodes's reputation as a colorful campus-area character became well established during this period. Among other activities, he organized turtle races outside his restaurant and founded both a street-corner fraternity—Si U (Sidewalk U, a takeoff on the Greek national fraternity Psi Upsilon)—and a youth sports group known as the Knothole Gang. And then, at the urging of both Ward and his mother, whose cancer apparently was in remission, Rhodes became active in local Republican politics. He organized a campus Young Republicans Club, even though he was no longer a student, and then ran for GOP ward committeeman, an unpaid post.

"I bought $6 worth of campaign cards [with money contributed by his mother] and walked every street in the ward and knocked on every door," Rhodes recalled. He beat a veteran incumbent, a now-forgotten Clyde Kearns, in the 1934 Republican primary, ran unopposed two years later and, also through Grant Ward, obtained a part-time patronage job as a $10-a-day journal clerk in the Ohio House of Representatives.[42]

Jim Rhodes was on his way. He was becoming somebody.

CHAPTER 2

Up Broad Street,
Step by Careful Step

EXCEPT FOR ONE SERIOUS MISSTEP, perhaps two, Jim Rhodes's rise from Columbus ward committeeman to state elected official was a methodical, step-by-step climb up the political ladder. As he said years later, "When I got into politics, I decided that I would become governor of Ohio. So I picked a path."[1]

Grant Ward, Rhodes's early mentor, recommended to Rhodes that he pick a path. Like a sponge, Rhodes absorbed Ward's advice and learned many of the stratagems that would carry him through the political minefields for the rest of his legendary career.

Rhodes wanted to run for a state office right away, but Ward wisely steered him toward a Republican Party position—ward committeeman—that would serve as a power base. Then he should pick a path of "stepping stones," Ward said, leading to ever-higher office.[2] The older man also schooled the younger in the finer points of politics. He wanted Rhodes to identify and listen to his natural constituents. Much later, as governor, Rhodes translated this: "Find out what the people want, and give it to them." He was great at promising people what they wanted. Sometimes he delivered.

Ward counseled Rhodes to hold his temper: "Don't ever get so angry with somebody that you can't sit down the next morning and talk it out." Rhodes followed this to a T. He seldom let his anger show, including with reporters. He got revenge, if he wanted it, quietly and sometimes when least expected. In campaigning, Ward advised, "the first rule of attack is timing."[3] Rhodes prided himself on timing. He knew when to strike and when to refrain, when to comment and when to be quiet, when to command attention and when to "lay in the weeds." When running for reelection against Democrat Richard F. Celeste in 1978, Rhodes upbraided one of his aides who was tired of Celeste's attacks on his boss and urged retaliation. "Be patient," Rhodes said. "You gotta let the rabbit get away from his hole before you hit him over the head." He would only retort when Celeste had gone too far and had no retreat. But later, campaigning in 1982 for Republican gubernatorial nominee Clarence J. Brown Jr., Rhodes would not criticize Brown's apparent lack of political savvy. "I only know timing for me," he told reporters.

One of Ward's big rules was "never run for editor." He showed Rhodes how some Democrats spent too much time attacking the *Columbus Evening Dispatch* publishers. "If the press finds something wrong," Ward said, "and if it is wrong, fix it. If it isn't wrong, prove it. In either case, blow your own horn. Get that ink. But by all means, never, never run for editor."[4]

During his years as governor, at the first hint of scandal, he would call in the respected Ohio Highway Patrol and announce, "We're gonna get to the bottom of this." If a crook got caught within his administration, he wouldn't deny or stonewall. Rather, he would crow that he caught the guy. He got the ink when he wanted it and frequently assured newsmen, "We're not running for editor." Many times, however, he would go behind reporters' backs and do business directly with editors, promising projects for their areas.

Ward also advised Rhodes to stick to the middle of the road and not get too far out on the right wing; he said the "swing" vote was most important. Thus, Rhodes, though conservative on some issues, never swerved too far right and, in fact, shunned Republican ideology, sometimes to the consternation of GOP leaders. He was not known as a strong party man.

Rhodes had no trouble following two other Ward tenets: be proficient at buttonholing—shaking hands with voters and holding their attention—and be regular and punctual in attending political meetings.[5] Rhodes was always early for meetings and critical of latecomers. Once he called a press conference for 3:30 P.M., and when a reporter arrived (unusually early) at 3:25, the governor was not impressed. "I been here since 3:15," he scolded. Some might have thought the governor didn't have enough to do.

Armed with Grant Ward's political wisdom, Rhodes was elected in 1934, at age twenty-five, to the first of a brace of two-year terms as a Republican ward committeeman. Next, his mother, Ward, and others urged him to seek higher municipal office. So in 1937, the college dropout, who as Ohio governor would practically reinvent his state's system of higher education, looked over the political landscape and decided to run in a five-way race for three openings on the Columbus school board the next year. After another typically energetic, press-the-flesh, door-to-door campaign, he finished first (probably due to his Republican connections, the *Evening Dispatch* suggested, and also possibly because of quiet support from the local Democratic machine) and became the youngest person ever elected to the Columbus school board.

About the same time, he was appointed to a fifty-cents-an-hour patronage job as a laborer with the city's water department, thanks in part to William Schneider, chairman of the Franklin County Republican organization, who for decades would continue to play a positive role in Rhodes's political career.[6] It obviously wasn't much of a job, but during the Great Depression any job was a good one.

While on the school board, sports fan Rhodes got a call from Branch Rickey, general manager of the St. Louis Cardinals, owner of the Columbus Redbirds, one of the big club's Triple-A affiliates.[7] Rickey wanted a Knothole Gang, which would give kids of a certain age free access to Redbirds' games, much like the namesake holes in outfield fences youngsters looked through to watch games. The young fans would, of course, be accompanied by their paying parents and thus swell attendance.

Why approach Rhodes on such an issue? His interests in youth and sports were well known, and he had connections in the education community. Rhodes was against outright freebies, so he asked the city superintendent to allow teachers to sell baseball tickets for ten cents, with the money going to the Columbus Division of Recreation. The Columbus Teachers Association refused to allow the teachers to participate. So Rhodes bided his time. Six months passed, and a pay raise proposal for teachers came before the board. Rhodes asked the superintendent and the board members if he could take the document home to study it. Somehow, it got "misplaced," which delayed a vote. When the head of the teachers' association approached Rhodes, he was ready. He said the increase would be considered "when the teachers sell the Knothole Gang passes." He got his wish, and so did the teachers; this tactic would serve Rhodes well during his political career: don't argue, bide your time and make all parties to the dispute winners. The Redbirds led the league in attendance that year, and the Columbus Knothole Gang became the largest in the nation.[8]

Much later, Rhodes would use his influence as governor to entice tight-fisted Cincinnati city fathers to spring for a modern stadium overlooking the Ohio River. While Riverfront Stadium was to replace Crosley Field, home of the baseball Reds, there was another objective beneath the surface: Cincinnati was in the running for a National Football League expansion franchise, and the new Bengals (named to recognize the prized Bengal tigers at the Cincinnati Zoo) would need a place to play. Rhodes was a friend of Paul Brown, who had helped found the Cleveland Browns but was dismissed by subsequent owner Art Modell. "Rhodes promised Paul Brown he was gonna get that stadium," recalled Jim Duerk, the governor's aide. "Rhodes called all the top business leaders Downtown," said Duerk, who later would be Rhodes's development director and then his private business partner. "They said, 'Well, governor, we don't know if we can support this.' Rhodes retorted, 'We're gonna do it whether you're on board or not.'" The stadium was built, and in 1967 Cincinnati landed the NFL franchise over Seattle. The Bengals moved to Riverfront in 1970—sharing the stadium with the Reds—after two seasons at Nippert Stadium on the University of Cincinnati campus.[9]

In 1938, Jim Rhodes got himself elected mayor of University City, a purely honorific title, since University City was just an OSU neighborhood of perhaps twenty thousand souls. Yet this rather meaningless popular election further whetted Rhodes's appetite for politics and public office. In 1939 he ran for Columbus auditor and was elected to the $4,000-a-year post by nearly five thousand votes, easily beating the Democratic incumbent who had been appointed to fill a vacancy. In announcing him as city auditor, the *Dispatch* described Rhodes as "an energetic young citizen" who had "attended" Ohio State University.[10] He was reelected in 1941.

Following Pearl Harbor, claiming to have been rejected by all branches of the military service—"They don't take people with one lung"—Rhodes married Helen Rawlins on December 18, 1941.[11] Perhaps he felt it was past time for a politician on the rise to settle down. Helen, also a native of Jackson County, regularly described in press releases and by Rhodes as his "childhood sweetheart." Helen Rawlins Rhodes—attractive and rather shy—never seemed cut out to be the wife of a public figure. In 1972, in a rare interview, she recalled first meeting her future husband sometime in the 1930s, while he was proprietor of Jim's Place. She said Grant Ward encouraged the marriage with the pointed comment to Rhodes, then older than thirty, that "Helen has waited long enough."[12]

Mary Lou Crumley, Helen's niece, said in 2012 that the couple met on the Ohio State campus, when Helen was living with Mary Lou and her parents. Crumley's father, James Paul Reardon, was manager of the Ohio State Bank branch at 11th Avenue and High Street, and Rhodes came in seeking a loan to start his restaurant. Reardon happened to mention Helen as someone Rhodes might want to meet, and he introduced them, according to Crumley.[13] But Rhodes had a more romantic recollection. He told writer Dean Jauchius, in vivid detail, how he met Helen when he went to Olentangy Park to collect his fee from a band he'd booked for a high school Halloween dance party. There he met the "vivacious" high school senior and danced with her "as if they were all alone in the world." One of the tunes was "You Were Meant for Me," and evidently she was. He escorted her home (forgetting to collect his band fee), where he immediately received her mother's approval. They dated steadily thereafter but didn't marry for another ten years.[14] Years later, Rhodes told his housekeeper, Carol Cooper, it was love at first sight. "I stood still. I looked into her eyes and I loved her, heart and soul."

During the 1940s, the union of Helen Rawlins and Jim Rhodes produced three daughters, Suzanne "Sue," Saundra "Saunie," and Sharon "Sherry." With the exception of whispered, yet persistent, rumors that Helen Rhodes drank too much, Rhodes's family life appears to have been without blemish.[15] Carol Cooper challenged even those rumors. "I worked for her for twenty-seven years and I never saw her take a drink," she said in a 2013 interview. "The only thing that woman ever drank was iced tea—four pitchers a day."[16]

In his public life, Helen Rhodes's husband was often on the road both as a statewide candidate and officeholder, but the devoted family man tried to get home by nightfall whenever possible. He liked to sleep in his own bed. And though hard-bitten Statehouse reporters took his repeated pronouncements about the importance of "family" with a grain of salt, there was a private tenderness in his relationship with Helen. He carried a yellow legal pad with him each day, on which he jotted down ideas and phone numbers. "Every morning, he'd tear a sheet off that yellow pad and write a note to Mom before he left for the office, telling her how sweet she was," said daughter Suzanne Moore. "And he signed it, 'I love you. Daddy.'"[17]

Rhodes didn't use stationary and had no journal, so he would compose notes to his wife on envelopes and the cardboard shirt supports from the cleaners. After Helen Rhodes's death in 1987, the family gathered twenty-seven paper grocery bags filled with the little love letters, according to Carol

Cooper. "You are so beautiful when you are asleep," said one. Another read: "Thank you for being there for the kids." And another: "Helen, those beans you cooked last night are the most delicious beans you ever cooked."[18]

After serving twin two-year terms as city auditor and learning how City Hall functioned, in 1943 Rhodes successfully ran for mayor of Columbus, a $6,000-a-year-post for which he ran as a self-appointed reform candidate, opposing Franklin County sheriff Jacob Sandusky, who Rhodes darkly hinted might be partly responsible for the city's then-rampant gambling and vice problems. He also challenged Sandusky to publicly produce his income tax returns, an indirect way of suggesting that his foe might be receiving undisclosed money. It was a rough, nasty campaign, though Rhodes also ran on a positive platform promising good government and more and better jobs (an issue which would serve him well in campaigns to come). On Election Day, he easily defeated Sandusky, 40,383 to 28,026, and at thirty-four, he became one of the youngest mayors in the history of any major city in Ohio.[19]

Rhodes was reelected twice—in 1947 and 1951. In 1950, during his second term as mayor he made one of the few miscalculations related to his march toward the Statehouse on Capitol Square. Desiring "statewide exposure and [to] learn the rounds," Rhodes foolishly entered a four-way Republican primary for governor, without the endorsement of his state party.[20] He was soundly defeated, 338,390 to 157,346, by then-Ohio treasurer Don Ebright, the state Republican Party's endorsed candidate. (Ebright, a five-term state treasurer, was beaten in the subsequent general election by the popular, independent-minded Democratic incumbent, Frank Lausche.) Rhodes had learned his lesson: be patient and pick your spot when the timing is right. While he had won his first election as ward committeeman running against an established candidate, he would avoid running without party support for twenty years—in 1970 he narrowly lost an open primary for the U.S. Senate.

Adding to Rhodes's woes the same year was the death of his beloved mother, Susan, who succumbed to a recurrence of cancer at a reported age of sixty-four on November 23, 1950, following her son's defeat in the May Republican gubernatorial primary. Rhodes was said to be at his mother's bedside when she died following a cancer operation. Her obituary said she was survived by her son and two daughters and had been preceded in death by her husband and by a daughter and son but did not mention her reported brief second marriage. It was noted that her surviving son, the mayor, often referred to his mother as his "chief political advisor" and "campaign manager." Rhodes continued to display his mother's photograph in his various offices and spoke lovingly of her throughout his life. While many of his civic activities centered on amateur sports, including the Amateur Athletic Union (president), the United States Olympic Committee (member), and the Pan-American games (a founder), following his mother's death Rhodes also became an active supporter of the American Cancer Society.[21]

As mayor, Rhodes is remembered as a good administrator who could delegate authority well and also as a colorful promoter (some viewed him as a cornpone huckster) of himself and his city. He loved being a ceremonial and working mayor. During his second term, he was pragmatic enough to put Columbus on the road to financial solvency. Soon after his reelection, Rhodes, without protest, signed into law a modest .5 percent municipal income tax ordinance, unanimously passed by a GOP-controlled city council that he greatly influenced. It was only the second time such a controversial municipal tax had been imposed in Ohio.

Columbus mayor James A. Rhodes greets Winston Churchill at Union Station. During his lengthy political career, Rhodes met many famous people. As a boy, he even met Henry Ford. But he never forgot his Jackson County roots. *Columbus Dispatch* file photo, March 6, 1946.

As a spokesman for a confederation of cities complaining that the state had usurped most major tax sources and demanding that the Ohio legislature share state revenues with municipalities, Rhodes was hardly in a position to oppose an ordinance permitting Columbus to raise its own revenue in one tax field not yet co-opted by the state. Also, as a former city auditor, Rhodes knew full well that his city was woefully short of funds. In early June 1940, as auditor, he had reluctantly announced that more than eight hundred police-men and firefighters would have to wait for their pay for the second half of May because of a general-revenue-fund cash shortage.

Mayor Rhodes made no secret of his support of the Columbus income tax ordinance in the run-up to a June 8, 1948, referendum on the tax, forced by an antitax petition drive led by the Congress of Industrial Organizations (CIO). The then-competing labor group, the American Federation of Labor (AFL), supported the tax.

A month before the referendum vote, Rhodes announced the appoint-ment of a "Civic Progress Committee" with a mission to support retention of Columbus's municipal income tax. The conservative, Rhodes-friendly *Columbus Evening Dispatch* also threw its considerable editorial weight behind keeping the municipal income tax. When not flogging Democratic president Harry S. Truman and "socialist" Britain or promoting the cause of conservative presidential candidate Senator Robert Taft, the paper found time to run articles backing the new city income tax and heartily endorse its retention, with a page 1 editorial on the eve of the referendum. During the campaign, the *Dispatch* even featured a June 2 front-page story about Toledo's Democratic mayor Michael DiSalle, whose city already had an income tax. Eventually DiSalle would become Rhodes's political rival, but in 1948 the newspaper described him as "recognized throughout Ohio for his abilities." DiSalle touted Toledo's 1 percent payroll tax as bringing about a "rebirth of civic pride." On Wednesday, June 9, 1948, the *Dispatch* happily announced that Columbus was "rooted to firm financial ground for the first time since Depression days," since voters had supported retaining the Rhodes-backed income tax by almost 59 percent, nearly 2 percent more than Toledo voters had given their municipal income tax two years earlier.[22]

In any event, Rhodes is remembered as a pretty good mayor. That he could delegate authority was underscored in June 1948 when Columbus faced a crisis, with younger members of both the police and fire departments threatening to resign en masse over a pay and uniform allowance dispute. While this went on, sans critical comment, the *Dispatch* reported Mayor Rhodes to have been blissfully visiting California for an AAU women's swim meet.[23]

As mayor of a growing city, Rhodes remained popular with voters. After his 1951 reelection, the *Columbus Citizen* noted, "James A. Rhodes today became the first mayor to win a third term here in 24 years."[24] Yes, he was a successful mayor. But how honest? When Rhodes served, big-city politics were rough-and-tumble almost everywhere and at every level. Under Rhodes, Columbus City Hall was awash with the usual tales of involuntary employee salary kickbacks that financed unaudited political "flower funds," an unlimited and uncontrolled spoils system, payroll skimming, and under-the-table deals with powerful businessmen and special interest groups. But if Rhodes was directly involved in any questionable activities, he was discreet enough that none of his future political rivals discovered much of anything substantive or specific enough to successfully use against him. One opponent, Democrat DiSalle, whom Rhodes would run against for governor in 1962, either sponsored or at least had in his possession a rather thorough background investigation of Rhodes's entire personal and political life through his time as mayor.[25] (Rhodes's own federal income tax problems apparently occurred after he had completed his three terms as mayor, during his stint as state auditor.)

Columbus, unlike Cleveland, Toledo, and Youngstown, was never really "mobbed up." What vice there was—gambling, prostitution, violent street crime—was mostly local in nature and not linked to Mafia families. The closest Rhodes came to associating with people linked to organized crime was his chumminess with Bill and Jackie Presser, the Cleveland-based father-and-son leaders of the International Brotherhood of Teamsters in Ohio. Jackie—"Big Bill's" son—served as president of the international union, headquartered in Washington, D.C., in the 1980s. But according to James Neff's definitive biography of the Pressers, Rhodes's involvement was generally limited to showing up at Presser-related testimonials or funerals or writing letters on their behalf. This was not deemed unusual conduct for a Republican who normally got the union's endorsement in political campaigns.

Rhodes also had a foreign policy of sorts, or, rather, he knew how to get what he wanted for his city when overseas guests came calling. The Italian consul, based in Cleveland, diplomat Egidio Ortona, got burned by a parking ticket on a day trip to Columbus in the late 1940s. Furious, he demanded to know where the mayor's office was. Once there, he informed Rhodes, "I have diplomatic immunity. I'm not paying this fine." After some negotiating—one wonders what each man thought of the other's English—Rhodes agreed to reduce the ticket to $1. But it didn't end there. "Now," the young mayor said, "what are you going to do for me?" Ortona had no immediate answer, so Rhodes thought of one: "How about a statue of Christopher Columbus to put outside of City Hall?" Ortona agreed, and on October 10, 1955, Ohio's capital got its statue—a handsome, bronze full-size likeness of the man, a gift to the city—the largest in the United States named after the explorer—from the citizens of Genoa, Italy. It was designed by Edoardo Alfieri and cast at the Michelucci foundry in Pistoia, Italy. Two days after it was uncrated and put in place twenty feet high on a pedestal, thousands flocked to the downtown for its dedication. The statue is still there. (Years later, Governor Rhodes encountered Ortona—by then the Italian ambassador to the United States—at a public event. After a moment, they recalled their first meeting and had a good laugh.[26])

While mayor, Rhodes began to assemble a cadre of loyal employees and influential cronies who stood by him and often would benefit from his upward-bound political career. Among the latter were two stalwarts. Emma Scholz, Rhodes's fiercely loyal private secretary and administrative assistant from his time as mayor, followed her boss to the Statehouse first when he was elected state auditor and then governor, where she was the major gatekeeper in the governor's office during Rhodes's first two terms. Rhodes appointed her to the Air Quality Development Authority before he left the office in 1971. Elmer Keller also followed Rhodes from the mayor's office to the Statehouse. He held a number of executive positions at both locations, but primarily was suspected of being Rhodes's chief "bag man," that is, the collector and overseer of flower funds. These cash stashes were usually supported at least in part by public employees' salary kickbacks and maintained primarily to underwrite elected officials' sundry political expenses, including flowers for funerals, weddings, and other occasions—hence the term flower fund. Keller ended his career by being made a full-time, salaried member of the powerful Public Utilities Commission of Ohio, which regulated power companies.

After Rhodes moved from Columbus City Hall to the Ohio Statehouse as auditor, he added others to his crew, including R. Dean Jauchius, previously known to readers of the *Columbus Evening Dispatch* under the byline Ronnie

Jauchius; his full name was Rollin Dean Jauchius. Jauchius served as Rhodes's literary guru, press secretary, and speechwriter during his early days at the Statehouse. He was Rhodes's biographer and best known as coauthor—and considered the actual author of Rhodes's three historical novels and two nonfiction books. Roy Martin, a tough, former small-time Republican county chairman served as Rhodes's chief of patronage (that is, he was charged with sorting out who among supporters and party faithful would be appointed to full-time state jobs or made part-time members of various boards and commissions) in both the auditor's and governor's offices.

The list of business, financial, and political cronies and supporters Rhodes collected is practically endless. These folks often prospered during his long political career. A few of the most notable include:

Preston Wolfe of Columbus, somewhat of a recluse, who headed the Wolfe family's powerful communications and banking empire during much of Rhodes's career. From the time Rhodes was mayor, the Wolfe-owned *Columbus Evening Dispatch* was his unabashed supporter, both on the editorial page and in its news columns. Wolfe family–controlled banks also often lent Rhodes money for personal and business uses. The Wolfe family empire, which included a Columbus radio and television station, prospered during Rhodes's time in public office.

Don Hilliker of Bellefontaine, an investor with Rhodes in, among other ventures, the Wendy's hamburger chain, Howard Johnson motel franchises, and a K-Mart. Hilliker became a director of Wendy's International, the franchising enterprise established by Rhodes's friend and booster Dave Thomas. Rhodes subsequently appointed Hilliker to the Ohio State University Board of Trustees.

Ralph Stolle of Lebanon, Hilliker's brother-in-law and a Cincinnati industrialist-investor. A longtime contributor to Rhodes's campaigns, Stolle owned land near Marysville, where Rhodes located the Transportation Research Center, and he sold a portion of the test ground to the Honda Motor Company, which established a plant nearby.

Len Immke of Columbus, a well-known owner of a Buick dealership, another long-time Rhodes friend and supporter. Immke was an investor in and became a director of Wendy's International. Though he was not a college graduate, Rhodes later named him to the Ohio State University Board of Trustees.[27]

Earl Barnes of Cincinnati, a Rhodes political protégé who became chairman of the Ohio Republican Party. The jaunty, press-friendly Barnes was a part-owner of land in Clermont County, Ohio, which was greatly enhanced during the Rhodes administration by its proximity to a Ford Motor Company transmission plant.

Hal Schott of Cleveland, a businessman and major Rhodes campaign contributor who reportedly lent Rhodes almost half a million dollars to invest in Wendy's stock and who became a partner with Rhodes in Wendy's franchises in New York.[28]

By the early 1950s, Rhodes was ready to move up Broad Street to the Statehouse. The conventional wisdom was that the best path to the governor's office was to first be elected either state auditor or state attorney general. Each post offers a built-in, statewide patronage network of workers who stand ready to become an instant campaign apparatus for an ambitious boss. And each post, if properly handled, can become highly visible and commanding. As Rhodes did not boast a law degree but had served as a city auditor, his choice was obvious. This time, with a nod of approval from the provincial princes of his party, he was the Republican Party's unopposed nominee to take on incumbent Democratic state auditor Joseph Ferguson in the 1952 general election.

Ferguson was a popular Democrat, but a bit of a clown who butchered the English language and had made a fool of himself in 1950 when he presumed to run for the U.S. Senate against "Mr. Republican"—incumbent Robert Taft—and was beaten by a humiliating 58 percent to 42 percent. During that campaign, Ferguson was the butt of several jokes, including his alleged boast, "I'll carry them both [counties] at this election" when asked to comment on the issue of Quemoy and Matsu, Chinese Nationalist–held offshore islands being shelled by mainland Chinese Communist forces. His major foreign policy plank, it was jested, was "Beat Michigan!" While these stories may well have been apocryphal, they rather typified the voters' perception of "Jumpin' Joe" Ferguson, who acquired the nickname for the way he bounced up and down when speaking to anyone taller than himself. And he was quite short.[29] He was known to send out bushels of Christmas cards to keep his name before the public, yet he was considered vulnerable against a seasoned campaigner like Rhodes, especially with popular Republican presidential candidate

Dwight Eisenhower heading the national GOP ticket. This was expected to be a Republican year in Ohio and was, with the exception of the reelection of Governor Frank Lausche.

During the 1950 Democratic senatorial primary, Ferguson had beaten the much-endorsed and favored Michael DiSalle, along with five others, to oppose Taft. Ferguson won mainly due to strong support from organized labor. Rhodes sensed union backing would not be especially helpful for Ferguson in a general election campaign in a Republican year. He considered Ferguson an incompetent union lackey and made no secret of it. Rhodes ran his usual intense, mostly positive campaign and defeated Ferguson in the 1952 general election by more than three hundred thousand votes.[30]

Rhodes was now sitting in the catbird seat, a position that allowed him to monitor and audit all state and local officials and their offices. He was paid $12,000 a year for what was then the only four-year state elective administrative office in Ohio. (Terms of other state administrative officials would be extended from two to four years in 1954, when voters also approved a two-consecutive-term limit on governors, pressed by Republicans to get rid of Lausche.) Rhodes easily beat Joe Ferguson for auditor again for another four-year term in 1956 and then trounced Ferguson's son James in 1960, by about seven hundred thousand votes for a short, two-year duration, devised to bring the auditor's term into sync with those of other elected administrative state officials. Thereafter, all state administrative officials were to be elected to four-year terms in even-numbered years between presidential elections.[31]

At the midpoint of his first term as Ohio auditor, Rhodes made what some consider his second misstep on his determined march to the governor's office. Perhaps it was a miscalculation, but then, maybe Rhodes was shrewdly sacrificing himself as the Republicans' standard bearer—taking one for the team—while also gaining statewide exposure on the GOP's tab. In 1954, no Republican was especially eager to run against Frank Lausche, heavily favored to win a fifth two-year term. Rhodes, in the middle of a four-year term and therefore with little to lose, stepped forward ("Who else wanted to go against Big Frank?") and was nominated, unopposed, to stand that November. As expected, he lost by more than two hundred thousand votes, while all other Republican state officials held or won their respective offices.[32]

Rhodes claimed to have learned much from his rather strident, if hopeless, campaign. Lausche, who grew up in a Slovenian enclave on Cleveland's

East Side, was only a nominal Democrat, an avowed fiscal conservative, an ardent anti-Communist and one hell of a public speaker. "I liked Frank Lausche, and I didn't like my [negative] campaign," Rhodes later confided to Jauchius. "It wasn't like me. The thing people want is answers. They already know the questions. So I set out to find some answers, and to really study the governor's job."[33]

In the meantime, Rhodes made his mark as state auditor. He appointed many of his loyal city hall retainers as heads of departments within the auditor's office but made sure each was backed up by a competent, apolitical career bureaucrat. So Rhodes had time enough to set himself up as a kind of self-promoting, one-man speaker's bureau, ready and willing to talk anytime throughout Ohio about the auditor's office. He also spoke about the historic events that inspired the three novels he claimed to have written while auditor—with the help of Jauchius—*The Trial of Mary Todd Lincoln, Johnny Shiloh* (both published in 1959), and *The Court Martial of Commodore Perry* (1961). Rhodes also would add his name to two short nonfiction books: *Teenage Hall of Fame* (1960), concerning youngsters who began making their marks before they reached age of twenty—which he promoted with a permanent photo display in his Statehouse office suite—and *Alternative to a Decadent Society,* a serious work promoting vocational education, published in 1969, while Rhodes was governor.[34]

Denizens of the Statehouse found it hard to believe Rhodes read many books, let alone wrote them. But he loved reading history. His father, Big Jim, was also a serious reader. Jauchius did the actual writing: "Jim would tell him what he wanted and Jauchius did it," said longtime aide Jim Duerk.[35] "He [Rhodes] reads everything," Duerk said in 1986. "It's amazing how much stuff. But he favors biographies. He liked to study other leaders. He just finished *Iacocca.* He then adapts things he likes to himself."[36] When did Rhodes find time to read during his busy days as a public official? "He only slept a couple of hours at a time," said daughter Suzanne. "He read at night when he couldn't sleep."[37] Rhodes was a bit of an insomniac, but he made up for lost sleep with frequent catnaps, friends said.

Although *he* didn't use caffeine, Rhodes courted the statewide working press corps by throwing open his employees' coffee and donut shop, located in the Statehouse basement, to the large contingent of reporters assigned to cover the legislature, governor, and other state officials. As a city official,

State Auditor James A. Rhodes and family pose atop a combine harvester at the 1960 Franklin County Fair at Hilliard. Left to right are Rhodes, daughters Sue and Sherry, wife Helen, and daughter Saundra. *Columbus Dispatch,* August 17, 1960.

Rhodes had had a fairly easy ride with reporters, since they mostly represented local Columbus newspapers generally friendly to him. But he courted even these reporters with gifts of Christmas hams and booze.

Rhodes faced a more sophisticated, independent, and critical bunch in the statewide press corps. He successfully seduced some members with not only free coffee and a friendly, ready-made meeting place but also news tips and political gossip supplied by his retinue of locally based state auditor's inspectors. And Rhodes was often available for usually off-the-record coffee shop appearances. He might entertain the reporters with such folksy aphorisms as "Down in Jackson County, a seven-course dinner is a six-pack and a possum." While Rhodes massaged the Ohio press corps, especially editors and publishers, he remained a realist about working reporters. He once allegedly warned an aide, "The press are like dogs in heat. If you stand still, you get screwed. If you run away, they chase after you and bite you in the ass."[38]

In 1956, Rhodes toyed with running for governor when Lausche decided to run for the U.S. Senate, but he deferred to C. William O'Neill, his Republican colleague and political friend of convenience whom, completing his second term as attorney general, party bosses considered next in line to run for what would be Ohio's last two-year governor term. In that gubernatorial election, O'Neill handily defeated Democrat Michael DiSalle, and Rhodes successfully ran for a second full term as auditor.

O'Neill, despite his enviable background and record as a popular, youthful speaker of the Ohio House of Representatives and an aggressive attorney general, was an indecisive governor and somewhat of a disappointment to many voters. Yet Rhodes again stood aside in 1958 so O'Neill could seek reelection as Ohio's first four-year governor. Not on the ballot because he was halfway through his own four-year term, Rhodes watched from the sidelines as a desperate O'Neill foolishly embraced a controversial antiunion, right-to-work proposed constitutional amendment, placed on the ballot over Republican professionals' objections. This time, organized labor turned out in droves. The Democrats, led by DiSalle, trounced O'Neill and most Republican state officials.

In 1962, when controversial "Tax Hike Mike" DiSalle came up for reelection, Jim Rhodes, who had dutifully waited his turn, was ready. O'Neill was now an Ohio Supreme Court justice, and Rhodes was free of any taint of the right-to-work issue. Against a single, gadfly opponent, he easily won the Republican gubernatorial primary nomination. Rhodes now stood at the threshold of accomplishing his lifelong ambition.[39]

CHAPTER 3

The Telling and Fulfilling
Campaign of 1962

If State Auditor James Rhodes and his 1962 gubernatorial opponent, Governor Michael DiSalle, agreed on anything during their only one-on-one debate, held at the Cleveland City Club the Saturday before the November 6 election, it was that their weeks-long struggle had become one of the "most vicious" ever witnessed in the history of Ohio politics.[1]

This single debate turned out to be characteristic of the campaign generally. This sole meeting of Rhodes and DiSalle was an icily formal affair; the candidates did not shake hands before or after the debate, even avoiding each other's glances during most of the verbal fencing. Rhodes, by then considered comfortably ahead, could well afford to open the debate on a coolly impersonal, positive note with a repetition of the "Jobs and Progress" spiel he had pitched from the start of his campaign. During this opening round, it was difficult to tell Rhodes even had an opponent in the same room.

The most notably negative aspect of Rhodes's campaign to that date had been his wail that, given Ohio's soft economy and declining job market (both national trends over which state government had little control), DiSalle's newly created Department of Industrial and Economic Development (tagged, especially by Rhodes, with the unfortunate acronym "DIED") was "dead—dead as a dodo."[2] Rhodes's continued pledge to avoid additional taxes, if possible, by better managing state government was interpreted as a subtle attack on the new taxes "Tax Hike Mike" DiSalle had asked for and mostly received when his party briefly controlled the legislature in 1959–60. So DiSalle approached the City Club podium very much on the defensive, prepared for combat, having been frustrated by Rhodes's practiced bob-and-weave campaign tactics.

(DiSalle had been widely quoted as complaining that campaigning against Rhodes was like trying to "play Ping-Pong on a Pogo stick."[3])

After opening with a repetition of his own basic campaign pitch, DiSalle began throwing Rhodes curve balls, including that during his ill-fated general election battle with Democrat Frank Lausche in the 1954 gubernatorial race, Rhodes had waged a particularly nasty, negative, and personal campaign. DiSalle complained that while Rhodes "has attempted to demonstrate he is no longer the candidate of 1954 . . . he has engaged in the same sort of diatribe, the same kind of personal attack. . . . The difference has been that when I make charges I make them myself and don't require fronts and friendly newspapers to do them for me."

DiSalle might have been referring to any number of the political enemies and unfriendly newspapers taking potshots at him but most likely was alluding to editor Louis Seltzer and his *Cleveland Press*. Early in September, the *Press* published, and continued to rehash, charges by a Chicago distiller named Joseph Mackler who said he had to deal with shadowy Democratic Party–connected influence peddlers to get and keep his rather obscure brand of bourbon listed for sale in Ohio's monopoly liquor stores. Except for a few veiled references to what the *Press* and other newspapers now were referring to as the "DiSalle liquor department scandal," Rhodes himself had not made the disgruntled distiller's allegations a major issue during the campaign. But then he didn't have to—the *Press* and most other Ohio newspapers were doing it for him.[4] DiSalle always suspected Rhodes and Seltzer had secretly connived to promote the distiller's accusations and then arranged for their source to disappear and remain unavailable to other reporters for further questioning.

DiSalle's aggressive attack on Rhodes distracted the challenger from keeping the debate centered on "Jobs and Progress." And so the two candidates swapped petty personal insults during the rebuttal stages of their confrontation in downtown Cleveland. When DiSalle alluded to Rhodes dropping out of Ohio State University after only one quarter, Rhodes, visibly angered, retorted, "[My] father died when I was eight . . . you always had someone to support you"—as if Rhodes didn't know DiSalle had had almost no financial support from his poor, immigrant parents while he struggled to put himself through Georgetown University and Georgetown Law.

Rhodes, who accused DiSalle of using a team of investigators to probe his life, even to follow his children, hotly added he was willing to match "integrity" with DiSalle and that such a match could "start with your home life first." Rhodes promptly backed off, promising not to get "in the gutter with insinuation," having just done so. As practically everyone in this audience of political junkies knew, Rhodes was referring to widespread and persistent rumors that DiSalle's relations with his wife, Myrtle, and their children were being strained by whispered but mostly unproven accounts of the governor's alleged extramarital dalliances, especially with his personal secretary, Mildred Cunningham. What even those who turned out for City Club debates may not have known was that Rhodes often privately joked about the rumors and so helped perpetuate them. He also appeared to have been genuinely outraged after learning that an investigation of his own life, prepared for DiSalle, included some mostly inconsequential material concerning his mother and wife and children, all of whom Rhodes considered above reproach and unfair targets.[5] Happily for voters, the candidates' home lives never rose to a substantive, open issue during the campaign. Regardless, when this debate was over, most independent observers were at a loss to declare a clear winner. But even a draw meant Rhodes held his lead over DiSalle in the now-lopsided race.

When the 1962 campaign had begun by tradition on Labor Day, Rhodes was a few days shy of fifty-three years old. He had settled in Columbus about thirty years before, and this campaign was his thirteenth since he first successfully ran for Columbus ward committeeman in 1934. In the interim, he had lost only two elections. But this year, 1962, appeared to be the one Rhodes would finally achieve his ultimate goal.[6]

DiSalle was running for reelection severely wounded by his own party: after some weeks of equivocation, once declaring he would not run for reelection—the better to work for passage of portions of his agenda still stalled in the now-Republican dominated legislature—he suddenly changed his mind and announced he would seek another term after all. But when it looked like DiSalle might not run again, Ohio attorney general Mark McElroy of Cleveland, who had been swept into office on the same 1958 Democratic anti–right-to-work wave that helped elect DiSalle by a record margin, announced his candidacy. He then belligerently refused to stand aside after incumbent DiSalle changed his mind. A bitterly contested Democratic primary ensued, further complicated by the candidacy of a third Democratic candidate, Alexander Metrakos—this one off-the-wall, distracting, and in favor of legalized gambling. With McElroy receiving the backing of the Cuyahoga County

Democratic organization—always out to embarrass DiSalle and support one of its own—DiSalle, even as an incumbent, emerged from the primary a wobbly winner, with barely 50 percent of the vote.[7]

In addition, short, fat, and peppery Mike DiSalle had been a controversial, combative governor, raising taxes and raising hell about the conditions in state mental institutions he found during well-publicized but unannounced tours of these long-neglected warehouses of human despair and suffering. DiSalle also stubbornly and dramatically opposed capital punishment, much to the chagrin of many in the Ohio law enforcement establishment, including locally influential county sheriffs, judges, and prosecutors.

By contrast, Rhodes, as the only endorsed GOP candidate in 1962, had come out of his gubernatorial primary with an almost 90 percent approval rating. His only opponent had been a rather eccentric Mt. Vernon rabbit-breeder, a lone, perennial, self-styled environmentalist named William White. Rhodes hardly had to campaign—though he was always doing so anyway.

Also by contrast, Rhodes had enjoyed a quite successful and mostly uncontroversial ten-year reign as state auditor. He had made his name practically a household word by his tireless speech making, the publicity he generated as coauthor of three historical novels, and other self-promoting gambits. Rhodes also enjoyed the support of many newspaper publishers and editors.

As state auditor Rhodes also was able to closely monitor the DiSalle administration. In at least one instance, Rhodes played a largely unreported role in creating a controversy that dogged DiSalle for weeks during what would be his only term as governor. Rhodes's office quietly had issued a report critical of the Department of Mental Hygiene and Corrections' lack of diligence in collecting legally mandated fees from families financially able to help cover the costs of their mentally disabled relatives' state care. It well may have been a legitimate criticism, yet when DiSalle set about remedying this inherited situation, he was criticized, especially by Louie Seltzer's *Cleveland Press* and other influential Scripps-Howard newspapers in Ohio (notably the *Cincinnati Post* and *Columbus Citizen*). The *Press* ran a series of sob-sisterish, heavily hyped stories, reinforced by indignant editorials and political cartoons, concerning destitute relatives of the mentally disabled being mercilessly dunned for fees they couldn't afford to pay. As complaints about DiSalle's collection campaign mounted, Rhodes mostly avoided regularly being identified as the state official who had prompted these collection efforts.[8]

Rhodes also wisely resisted being dragged into the partisan argument between DiSalle and legislative Republicans over the need for new and/or increased taxes. As state auditor, he was in a perfect position to evaluate DiSalle's contention that under the administrations of his tight-fisted predecessors, notably Democrat Frank Lausche and Republican John Bricker, the state had avoided major tax increases in large part by living off now nearly depleted surpluses. The state treasury had grown during World War II, when the war effort severely limited expenditures, especially for new highways and other capital improvements. But Rhodes steadfastly refused to take sides in the tax flap and during his first administration was able to pledge "No New Taxes," thanks in large measure to the increases DiSalle had bulldozed through the legislature, none of which Rhodes or his mostly compliant Republican-controlled legislatures ever seriously considered rescinding.[9]

By the time he announced his intent to run for governor, Rhodes had learned how to look very much like a governor, if not always to sound like one. Tall, a bit jowly, but fit from regular rounds of golf, with graying hair combed into a well-oiled pompadour, Rhodes had adopted a wardrobe in which he always looked nattily gubernatorial. His conservative dress code became a sort of uniform for Republican state officials of his era. Rhodes wore well-tailored dark suits, light blue or white shirts with tightly pinned collars, and tastefully subdued, narrow ties.

But as soon as he opened his mouth, a listener knew he still was dealing with good ol' Jim Rhodes, late of Jackson County and former operator of a campus hamburger joint. Rhodes never lost his southern Ohio twang and probably never tried to. He pronounced "Ohio" as "Ah-hi-ah," "Columbus" as "Klump-bus," "push" as "poosh," and "bush" as "boosh." His sentences often started in the middle, the subject left for the end. He might, for instance, tell a reporter, paraphrasing here, "Leave me just say, the Ohio State Fair, we may go up later this afternoon. But that's off the record." Rhodes also delighted in telling and retelling rustic tales; for instance, he called gin rummy, which he often played, "Jackson County bridge," and his favorite joke continued to be an off-color, mythical tale concerning an oversexed Jackson County coonhound named "Old Blue." Rhodes's down-home personal style didn't always sit well with more erudite Ohio Republicans, but it seemed to appeal to the rank-and-file, many populist independents, and even many registered Democrats. Except for their humble beginnings and having served as mayors of their respective adopted Ohio hometowns, Rhodes and DiSalle starkly contrasted each other. Rhodes favored processed cheese, bologna, popcorn, and other pedestrian dishes, washed down with soft drinks or—on rare occasions—domestic beer, usually eaten and gulped on the run. DiSalle fancied himself a gourmet Italian cook and lover of imported wines and liquors, savored at elegant, liveried sit-down dinners. While Rhodes seemed almost to relish murdering the English language, DiSalle, who spoke only Italian until he entered grade school in Toledo, now spoke polished, usually grammatically correct English without a trace of an Italian or regional accent. Both were history buffs, but Rhodes in a salty, down-to-earth, popular historical novel way, DiSalle in the more scholarly, aristocratic manner of one of his political heroes, Thomas Jefferson.

These opposites did not attract. Above and beyond philosophical and political differences, the two men seemed to neither respect nor even like one another very much. While usually polite in public, except perhaps during the heat of the gubernatorial campaign, they often expressed negative views about one another during more private moments. Rhodes represented everything DiSalle disliked about politics and politicians. Privately, DiSalle considered Rhodes a crude, evasive, vulgar ward-heeler who thought nothing of shaking down his own employees for contributions to his political slush funds. By the same token, Rhodes never tired of analyzing for reporters and his staff, in the off-the-record confines of his Statehouse coffee shop, what he considered DiSalle's haughty disdain for the egos of others, especially members of the state legislature, and the ugly public confrontations this arrogant attitude often provoked. Rhodes viewed DiSalle as an overemotional, bleeding-heart liberal who appeared to relish, rather than avoid, useless confrontation.

An early and ugly facet of the campaign surfaced not as an issue between these two antagonistic candidates, however, but rather as a front-page *Cleveland Press* story. In late September, papers subscribing to the Scripps-Howard statewide news wire service were supplied copies of letters written by Joseph Mackler, president of the Waterfill and Frazier Distilling Company of Chicago. Mackler asserted that he had to pay influence peddlers so he could "do business in Ohio," that is, to have his little-known brand of bourbon listed and sold in state-operated liquor stores. He further alleged his bourbon was delisted and banished when he refused to continue payments to the same band of influence peddlers.[10] State officials maintained Waterfill and Frazier's bourbon was delisted simply because of low sales.

(Ohio's system of state-controlled liquor stores, in place well before DiSalle took office, was ripe for abuse by anyone claiming special knowledge of or influence with the Ohio Department of Liquor Control. Legitimate distillers routinely retained agents in Columbus to look after their business interests. To give this system a semblance of legitimacy, most such agents registered themselves with the Department of Liquor Control, but they were not well policed, if policed at all. The influence peddlers Mackler said he retained in order to "do business in Ohio" were not registered agents but gave him the impression they were well connected with the Ohio Democratic Party, he wrote.)

As scandals go, this one was pretty slim pickings; Mackler did not name DiSalle or any official of the liquor control agency as party to the alleged scam. Yet, the Ohio press made the most of Mackler's charges, and DiSalle further legitimized and prolonged the affair when he authorized a special grand jury to investigate it. It will probably never be clear whether Rhodes played a role in Mackler's opening his files to *Press* and Scripps-Howard reporters. But given Rhodes's close relationship with Seltzer, who had turned on DiSalle after initially supporting him for election in 1958, it's a safe bet that Rhodes knew about Mackler's tale well in advance of its publication. To his credit, Rhodes cannot be accused of taking unfair advantage of the hyped "exposé," other than occasionally alluding to it during the course of the campaign.[11] As noted, Rhodes didn't have to make the Mackler affair a campaign issue—the Ohio press was doing that for him.

(Following publication of Mackler's complaints, Waterfill and Frazier bourbon again became available—like other brands, in plain brown paper bags—in Ohio's dreary liquor stores. In fact, perhaps as a sly joke, Rhodes offered it to reporters at the first press party he threw at the executive mansion after becoming governor. The bourbon subsequently was again delisted for poor sales.[12])

Next it was DiSalle's turn to dirty up the campaign. After weeks of mysteriously referring to the "$54,000 Question," DiSalle, who carefully absented himself from Columbus in early October at the moment of revelation, arranged for his shill, Democratic state chairman William Coleman, to charge at a Columbus news conference that Rhodes had been allowed to amend his income tax returns in the 1950s. The negotiated amendments, he said, were to settle a tax dispute with the Internal Revenue Service over his conversion of more than $54,000 in political funds to personal use and personal loans.

These conversions presumably permitted Rhodes to maintain a more-than-comfortable lifestyle for himself and his family, including the purchase of a dream home on Scenic Drive in a posh north-side Columbus neighborhood and the acquisition of several late-model cars, despite his comparatively modest mayor and state auditor salaries.[13] Rhodes apparently had broken no federal law by dipping into political funds for personal use—as long as he declared and paid federal taxes on the conversions, which apparently he later did.

After an initial panic attack, Rhodes issued a formal, carefully worded statement, insisting, "I categorically deny I owe the government of the United States any money" and went on to charge DiSalle with covering him with "globs of slime and vicious fictions." But, of course, Coleman had not charged that Rhodes *still* owed back taxes and, as the *Cleveland Plain Dealer*, among others, correctly noted, "There was no denial in [Rhodes's] statement that he had diverted campaign funds to his personal use."[14]

The $54,000 Question never seemed to jell as a viable, lasting campaign issue. A politician being caught converting political flower funds to his personal use was hardly unheard of, and the typical Ohioan apparently didn't find negotiating with the generally disliked IRS over disputed income taxes all that unusual or disreputable. Later, during a well-received speech before a group of generously applauding Republican women, Rhodes felt the need to offer a rather lame but more detailed explanation of his income tax problems. The issue never seemed to become all that consequential with the general voting public.

But DiSalle had only begun his attacks. According to a former aide, he, probably illegally, assembled a cadre of State Highway Department employees in a basement room of the Statehouse, with orders to "get something on Rhodes." This group came up with complicated documentation that it believed indicated Rhodes was arranging for local governments to acquire, under lease-purchase agreements, adding machines used by auditor's examiners during local audits; yet the state already owned these adding machines, and payments on the agreements subsequently had been swallowed up, allegedly unaccounted for, somewhere in Rhodes's office. In short, DiSalle's group was maintaining that Rhodes was forcing local governments to lease and then purchase state-owned adding machines, with the resulting income not used to buy new adding machines but rather remaining basically unaccounted for, that is, probably ending up in someone's (Rhodes's?) pocket.[15]

In mid-October, DiSalle summoned Statehouse reporters to a news conference at which he unveiled reams of documents, mostly complex ledger pages of adding machine serial numbers, which he said proved Rhodes was forcing local governments to buy state-owned adding machines, with the proceeds remaining unaccounted for. DiSalle's evidence was complicated and difficult for many reporters to fathom, so Rhodes saw no great need to directly answer the charges in detail or explain his convoluted lease-purchase agreements. Rather, his minions eventually, and rather offhandedly, produced their own equally complex set of documents, which they claimed proved DiSalle was all wet.[16] These complex charges and countercharges ended in a draw for most reporters and voters alike. Like the income tax issue, the adding machine controversy never really caught the fancy of the voting public or the press.

DiSalle, still desperately trying to salvage his political career, had not yet finished with Rhodes. In addition to endlessly urging, practically begging, reporters to interview a retired Columbus vice cop who claimed to have once arrested Rhodes for accepting numbers slips while running Jim's Place, DiSalle repeated charges Rhodes's short-term Democratic opponent James Ferguson had earlier leveled, to the effect that the auditor-author had used at least two additional auditor's employees, along with Dean Jauchius, to help him produce his three historical novels.[17]

DiSalle also came up with another complicated charge, documenting, but poorly, that his rival had used political influence to obtain a $325,000 federal Small Business Administration loan to bail out a Columbus firm facing bankruptcy. The owner of the firm, which eventually went bankrupt anyway, apparently owed money to both Rhodes and the Wolfe family's banking interests, according to DiSalle.[18] That issue didn't attract much attention either.

As for Rhodes, during all this bitterness he blithely appeared to pay little attention to DiSalle's charges. Except for the $54,000 Question, to which he did at least respond, he mostly continued to dance merrily along his own path, tirelessly repeating his positive "Jobs and Progress" campaign pitch, apparently having become convinced during his disastrous 1954 campaign against Lausche that negative campaigning is counterproductive, especially if you're already ahead.

Several stories underscored the single-mindedness of Rhodes's continued, unswerving, positive emphasis on the importance of creating a business-friendly, job-oriented climate in Ohio, which he rather simplistically preached also would solve such other pressing problems as welfare, unemployment compensation, and even mental health. Rhodes's intimate, John Andrews of Toledo, who was to become Rhodes's Republican state party chairman later told one of these tales. Andrews said Rhodes once excused himself from his dinner table by explaining he had an appointment to make his three hundredth speech of the campaign. According to Andrews, Rhodes's wife, Helen, wryly replied, "No, Jim, you're going to make the same speech for the three hundredth time."[19]

The second concerned reporters assigned to follow Rhodes on his tireless speech-making rounds. As most political reporters come to learn, candidates deliver essentially the same speech time and time again, maybe two or three times a day, but before different audiences. Rhodes followed this to the extreme, delivering almost exactly the same "Jobs and Progress" pitch over and over again, sometimes five or six times a day, ad nauseam. To relieve their boredom, reporters turned to organizing a cash pool based on how often Rhodes would use the word "jobs" during any given appearance. Those who bet on the high side usually stood the best chance of winning the pool.[20]

In addition to spreading his "Jobs and Progress" and "Profit Is Not a Dirty Word in Ohio" gospel, Rhodes also presented voters with a series of more detailed position papers, prepared by his personal retainers and the skilled professionals at GOP state headquarters, always under his direction and with his final approval. These covered almost every aspect of state government, from highways to mental health.

One of Rhodes's most intriguing proposals was the "Blueprint for Brainpower," which turned out to be one of the most successfully implemented of his plans, thanks mainly to a series of debt-incurring capital-improvement bond issues he persuaded voters to approve after he became governor. In his blueprint, he pushed the proposition that some sort of a state-supported or municipally run institution of higher learning, be it an expanded or new university, an added branch campus of an existing institution, or a vocational education facility, be located within an easy commute of every Ohioan. Also, from his catbird seat as auditor, Rhodes had observed the disorganized, pandering way university presidents appeared individually before legislative committees to seek money for their respective institutions. He proposed the creation of a governor-appointed nine-member Board of Regents to oversee this newly expanded higher education system. By dangling promises of new building funds in front of these usually fiercely competitive princes of academe, Rhodes eventually convinced university presidents to go along with his centralized concept, which the legislature eventually approved.[21] All this from a college dropout!

In addition to coming up with such substantive programs, Rhodes was thinking up clever gimmicks to promote his candidacy. For example, he might make a pitch for his expedited highway program while standing at a lonely podium in a windswept, empty field at the end of a stalled DiSalle highway project.[22]

Faced with such a nearly flawless campaign and campaigner, DiSalle could only defensively justify his own record and offensively attack Rhodes. The outcome almost was a foregone conclusion, with perhaps only DiSalle believing to the very end that he had a slim chance to win a second term.

On the evening of November 6, 1962, those reporting statewide election returns from the Ohio secretary of state's office in Columbus had an early night of it. Rhodes jumped ahead early and stayed ahead, defeating DiSalle with almost 59 percent of the vote in a state where 55 percent was considered a near landslide. Rhodes finally had achieved his goal, winning with more than 1.8 million votes to his opponent's fewer than 1.3 million.[23]

The next morning DiSalle, surrounded by a representative number of sleepy, disheartened but not especially surprised staff and cabinet members, delivered an uncommonly bellicose concession statement. Traditionally, a politician's concession is filled with remembrances of a tough but well-fought campaign, followed by best-of-luck wishes to the winner. But DiSalle had grown to so dislike Rhodes that he would have none of this. Instead, in a candid, indecorous, statement he obviously personally composed and dictated, DiSalle promised to continue in his legal efforts to put Rhodes behind bars. (Nothing ever came of that threat, as none of the special grand juries or special prosecutors who became involved in the very dirty campaign of 1962 ever charged either Rhodes nor DiSalle, or anyone on either side, with criminal conduct.)

DiSalle also said, "[I] feel no different today than I did yesterday about my opponent. I have never had an opponent for whom I have less respect and whom I feel is less qualified to serve the people of this state. During the campaign I questioned his integrity. . . . The fact that my opponent has won the election does not change my beliefs."[24] As usual, Rhodes had no public comment on

DiSalle's bitter concession speech. Privately, however, Rhodes later was to refer to his 1962 opponent as "that fat little Eye-talian son-of-a-bitch."

So no love lost. But no matter. James Allen Rhodes, the coal miner's son from Coalton, Jackson County, Ohio, was on the way to his first year as governor of Ohio without his predecessor's blessing. He would go on to serve Ohio for a record sixteen years, as probably its best-remembered chief executive.

CHAPTER 4

First Term—
Four Mostly Smooth Years

JAMES ALLEN RHODES was inaugurated governor of Ohio on January 14, 1963, during a deliberately simple, austere ceremony held in the rotunda of the unadorned Doric-columned state capitol building. Outside, the temperature had dipped to near zero. At the last minute, departing governor Michael DiSalle agreed grudgingly to attend the ceremony to hand over the warrant of office to the successor he so thoroughly disliked. If several split-term governors—Rutherford B. Hayes, James Cox, Frank Lausche, Allen Trimble, and Wilson Shannon—are counted separately for each time they assumed and then reassumed office, Rhodes was sworn in as Ohio's sixty-first chief executive since the state's constitution was adopted in 1803.[1]

In his brief inaugural address (doctors had been treating his hoarseness, brought on by a cold, almost up to the time of his speech), Rhodes said, "I do not intend to take much of your time . . . this administration means promptly to get to work—I mean today!" He went on to identify unemployment as Ohio's greatest problem and pledged to "use every available tool . . . to create jobs so our unproductive segment will melt away to only those unable to care for themselves." Taking a cue from president John F. Kennedy, whose charisma, if not politics, Rhodes admired and envied and who had arranged to have poet Robert Frost appear at his 1961 presidential inaugural, Rhodes quoted from a Frost poem as he neared the end of his address—"I have promises to keep, and miles to go before I sleep."

As expected, Rhodes brought with him to the executive suite and various departments of state government a bevy of his most trusted retainers from Columbus City Hall and/or the state auditor's office, just across the State-house rotunda, among them Emma Scholz, Elmer Keller, Roy Martin, and

Dean Jauchius. Scholz had become much more than a personal secretary and enjoyed at least executive assistant status by this time. Keller, whatever his official title, presumably continued his primary role as keeper of the political flower funds. Martin was installed in a large front office in the governor's wing of the Statehouse, where he quietly continued to oversee a much-expanded patronage network, including even more prestigious part-time appointments to various boards and commissions. Jauchius carried on as Rhodes's public affairs advisor and literary muse, although his title was now "coordinator of programming and financing."

Rhodes also recruited several outsiders as key members of his new executive entourage. Foremost among the newcomers was his new chief of staff, John McElroy (no relation of former Democratic attorney general Mark McElroy), soon to become the governor's acknowledged assistant for detail and legal affairs. A middle-aged, articulate, balding, bespectacled, bachelor lawyer, John McElroy was a protégé of John Bricker, former Republican governor and U.S. senator, and had previously served as minority counsel on the Senate Commerce Committee in Washington, D.C. McElroy's usually paper-strewn, tiny office adjoined Rhodes's more sumptuous and orderly chambers (Rhodes was a "clean desk" man), which meant McElroy had direct access to Rhodes's office without having to get past Scholz, who usually stood guard at the main entrance to the governor's inner sanctum.

McElroy soon became a primary source in the governor's office for most reporters. Almost always available, if he couldn't or didn't want to discuss a subject, he always said so up front. But when he could speak freely, he normally was frank, informative, and articulate. In other words, he was somewhat the opposite of Rhodes, who still could be secretive, evasive, vague, and verbally obfuscating, especially if it meant avoiding unnecessary controversy. Among other myriad duties, McElroy handled most commutation matters for Rhodes, but in a quiet, low-key way, in contrast to DiSalle's public agonizing over entreaties to commute a death sentence to life, that is, usually a minimum of twenty years in prison. Like Rhodes, McElroy seldom, if ever, publicly discussed his personal views on capital punishment or the details of the commutation cases he handled. But with one exception, a holdover case from the DiSalle administration, no executions were carried out during any of Rhodes's four terms as governor.[2])

Another recruited outsider who became a visible, active member of Rhodes's newly assembled executive team was Finance Director Richard

Krabach (CRAY-baw), an appropriately lean and hungry-looking Cincinnati lawyer who had served as comptroller of the Virgin Islands during the Eisenhower administration. Krabach, his face tanned and wrinkled from vacations in sunny climes, had a cordial relationship with Statehouse reporters, one of whom liked to joke, "every time he tells a lie, he gets another wrinkle." Because the theme of Rhodes's first term was fiscal austerity, Krabach would play a pivotal role in promoting the administration's agenda.

But despite Rhodes's talent for delegating authority and for choosing a compliant but highly competent staff to carry out his wishes, they still were *his* wishes and *he* always was governor. And so Rhodes set the tone for his administrations. During his inaugural address, following up on campaign promises, Rhodes had pledged to institute "rigid economics and prudent spending." A few days later, thirty-five hundred state employees were laid off, ostensibly as part of Rhodes's announced 9 percent, across-the-board cut in state spending. Whether this was an honest attempt to deal with the budget deficit Rhodes claimed to have inherited or the reconstitution of a spoils system, as Democrats charged, is a matter of opinion. But the new administration also readied legislation to remove as many as nineteen thousand additional workers from civil service protection, the better to manage state government. But this reorganization also made sure these now-unprotected employees who remained on the state payroll knew they owed their continued employment to James Rhodes.[3]

In due course, Rhodes and Krabach submitted their austerity budget to a receptive 105th General Assembly, which comfortable Republican majorities controlled in both House and Senate. This political dominance came about in part due to Rhodes's popularity as head of the GOP ticket the previous November and his efforts on behalf of individual legislative candidates. Although it proposed record spending (as new budgets invariably do) of $1.3 billion, Rhodes's first budget was austere as far as major increased outlays were concerned and remained more or less balanced, with no conspicuous tax increases. One of the reasons Rhodes could balance his first budget was that in addition to projecting increased revenues from natural growth, it contained no provisions for major capital improvements, for example, construction projects such as highways, university buildings, and additional state park recreational facilities. Rhodes had other, soon-to-be-disclosed plans to fund the massive construction work for which he would be long remembered.

Associates and other observers later suggested that Rhodes's propensity to ask Ohio voters to approve debt-incurring, tax-supported capital improvement bond issues—by which, among other things, he vastly expanded the state's system of higher education—may well have been inspired by the example of his fellow governor and friend, Nelson Rockefeller. First elected governor of New York in 1958, then reelected in 1962, 1966, and 1970, Rockefeller was known to use bond issues to finance his capital improvements programs. That this to-the-manner-born, well-schooled, sometimes liberal Brahmin heir to his grandfather's oil-refining fortune and Ohio's blunt-spoken, college-dropout, up-from-the-wards, once dirt-poor governor would form a mutual admiration society seemed, indeed, a case of opposites attracting.[4]

Whatever his inspiration, beginning one year after his election Rhodes successfully asked Ohio voters to approve three capital improvements bond issues: in 1963 for general improvement construction funds, predominantly for higher education facilities ($250 million), then in 1964 specifically for highway construction ($500 million), and again in 1965 for highway construction and other development ($290 million).[5]

Rhodes easily convinced the General Assembly to place his bond issues on the statewide ballot, demonstrating how well he had mastered the art of legislative management. During his first term, Rhodes got most of what he wanted from the legislature by a combination of smooth and wily tactics. To begin with, he carefully and with great foresight actively supported the candidacy of many of the Republicans who now served in both houses of the legislature. He also made it a rule for himself and his minions to avoid public quarrels with lawmakers of either party; he had obviously formulated this while watching his combative predecessor so often openly and needlessly brawl with the legislature to no constructive end. Third, members of Rhodes's staff sent upstairs to represent his administration before the legislature were mostly experienced hands who were cognizant of legislators' tender sensibilities. Or, as House Speaker Charles Kurfess, Republican of Bowling Green, once admiringly put it, "There were no young bucks [sent to represent Rhodes before the legislature] who offended old timers . . . who forgot they were dealing with a lot of egos."[6]

With a wealth of goodies from his bond issues to pass out, Rhodes also became a master of the pork-barrel school of persuasion. Need a vote? Need a bill introduced? Need to silence a critic? What better way than to find out what a particular member of the legislature most wanted for his or her home district? A new branch campus or vocational school? A new state park facility? An expedited highway project? No matter the member's party affiliation, promise (within reason) whatever he or she most desired. Rhodes also was mindful to have local members of the legislature present when he performed three of his favorite ceremonial duties—ground-breakings, ribbon-cuttings, and building dedications.

He proved to be a master of the legislature in a negative way as well. He did not especially like to exercise his veto power, as it represented the sort of public confrontation he liked to avoid. He preferred heading off and killing bills he didn't like before they reached his desk, using any one or several of the above-described tactics—agreeing to a pet project, for instance, to make a bad bill go away—or the quiet threat of a veto. If he had to, of course, Rhodes could play hardball, too, but almost always quietly, behind the scenes.

Former Democratic House member Carl Stokes, later mayor of Cleveland, eventually became a Rhodes admirer. But as a brash young freshman legislator, Stokes often was quite critical of Ohio's Republican governor. In his memoirs, he gives a rare account of Rhodes playing hardball behind the scenes. McElroy contacted Stokes early in his House career to tell him Rhodes had vetoed a pet Stokes bill, one that would have clarified and codified an arrested person's right to promptly consult with a lawyer. It was not a major piece of legislation, but it was important to Stokes's fledgling political career and to the mostly African American constituents in his Cleveland district. McElroy agreed to arrange a meeting between Rhodes and Stokes.

During their sit-down, the governor asked McElroy to bring him a file that contained a bundle of newspaper clippings relating to Stokes's public criticism of Rhodes. According to Stokes, Rhodes began reciting the headlines: "Stokes Slams Rhodes on Education," "Stokes Says Rhodes Programs Ruining State," and so on. "You know, you've been giving me hell all over this state," Rhodes said next. "And you never heard me say anything, did you? Well, now it's my turn," he continued, explaining his veto. "I've been laying in the weeds for you."

Stokes concluded in *Promises of Power:* "My political education took a great leap forward. When the legislature resumed its session the next spring, the Republican governor and the second-term black Democrat from Cleveland began to find areas where they could agree. And when the legislator gave speeches, he was much more, shall we say, issue oriented. He attacked the terrible problems that existed in Ohio. He did not descend to petty name calling, or even name mentioning."[7]

On a more positive note, Rhodes expertly doled out capital improvement rewards from his bond issues to woo non-legislators as well. Newspaper publishers and editors whose communities just had gained branch universities or state park chalets found it hard to be overly critical of the governor who had been responsible for spiffy, up-to-date facilities. And, of course, the promise of money for expanding college campuses persuaded university presidents, though they did not favor centralized power, at least to not vigorously oppose creation of a badly needed state agency to bring order to an otherwise chaotic state system of higher education.

Rhodes's handling of legislation creating the Ohio Board of Regents in 1963 and the post of chancellor to be powerful czars of higher education (all his appointees, of course), stands as a prime example of how he expertly, and often patiently, worked behind the scenes to smooth the way for passage of his more controversial legislation with a minimum of public outcry. In addition to creating the Board of Regents and successfully backing three bond issues during his first term, Rhodes gained approval of an enlarged industrial development agency, a new Transportation Research Center (TRC) near Marysville, and the Ohio Youth Commission to streamline the juvenile justice system.

This is not to suggest that everything he did during his first term as governor was a smashing success. By stubbornly avoiding major tax increases to retire his bond issues, but rather linking the existing taxes or the full faith and credit of Ohio to the retirement of the bonds, Rhodes doomed Ohio's public schools—along with the state's penal, mental hygiene, and welfare systems—to continued existence as underfunded mediocrities. His bond issues also resulted in a desperate need for additional taxes, to both operate the new facilities and retire the bonds that built them. The situation eventually led to the state's first income tax, passed while he was out of office between his two eight-year stints as governor. Outside of attracting some expanded auto manufacturing plants, in part due to the new Transportation Research Center, his leadership of teams of businesspeople raiding other states and foreign countries for new industry met with only modest success.[8]

In 1966, Rhodes proposed building a bridge over Lake Erie to connect northern Ohio with Canada. The widely ridiculed project went nowhere but haunted the governor's legacy, an emblem of his over-the-top schemes. His Golden Age Village concept—moving elderly patients not suffering debilitating mental illness out of state mental hospitals to housing complexes financed by revenue bonds—never got very far off the launchpad, either. Arguably, what Rhodes had in mind conceptually was the kind of housing that would later be called "independent" or "assisted" living.

On the national political front, Rhodes and state Republican chairman Ray Bliss were unsuccessful in their efforts to keep Ohio neutral during Arizona senator Barry Goldwater's determined 1964 march toward the nomination as Republican presidential candidate. They did so not because they necessarily disagreed with Goldwater's hardcore conservatism, although Rhodes steered away from any philosophy that seemed rigidly doctrinaire, but rather because Bliss's private polls showed Goldwater losing Ohio so disastrously that his candidacy threatened to pull down other Republican candidates with him (including Robert Taft Jr., a candidate to follow his famous father, "Mr. Republican," to the U.S. Senate). As the impartial host governor at the 1964 National Governors Association Conference, held in Cleveland that June (primarily due to his lobbying for Cleveland at the 1963 conference), Rhodes mostly ignored a "stop Goldwater" movement privately discussed by more moderate Republican governors.

But as Ohio's "favorite son" candidate, Rhodes supposedly controlled the state's fifty-eight delegates as the national Republican convention approached that July. And he no longer could remain aloof and avoid the controversy created by Goldwater's apparent lock on the nomination. Following Bliss's urgent counsel and bucking pressure from Goldwater supporters, notably former U.S. senator John Bricker and Johnstown congressman John Ashbrook, Rhodes reiterated his wish to keep Ohio out of the fray by insisting his delegates hold to their pledge to vote for him as favorite son through the first ballot.

But during a Chicago stopover on his flight to the San Francisco convention, Rhodes was pounced on by a howling pack of reporters, demanding to know how Ohio would vote on the first ballot. More than likely just to put off the annoying newsies, Rhodes mentioned that the Ohio delegation planned to caucus just prior to the opening ballot. It remains open to dispute whether he intended his statement to be interpreted as a release of his delegates to vote for whomever they wished on the first ballot. But that's exactly the way most of the noisy, pushy press read his evasive, perhaps flustered, statement,

and that's what they was transmitted to San Francisco. So the already sput-
tering, last-ditch effort to stop Goldwater was effectively doomed, as many
in the Ohio delegation were known to support the Arizona senator.

By the time Rhodes reached San Francisco, the die had been cast, the
"stop Goldwater" movement was dead. So he had no choice but to release
his delegates, most of whom joined the politically suicidal stampede to
nominate Goldwater on the first ballot. During the ensuing presidential
campaign, Rhodes was polite but noticeably cool toward Goldwater, keeping his distance from the GOP standard-bearer whenever possible during
the latter's campaign forays into Ohio. As Bliss's projections were indicating,
the following November Goldwater lost Ohio to Lyndon Johnson by more
than a million votes. And, as Rhodes and Bliss had feared, Taft also lost to
Democrat Steve Young, but in a much closer contest. In the process, Ohio
Republicans forfeited their ironclad grip on the state legislature.[9]

Yet, despite this and other occasional miscues, many Ohio voters seemed
to relish having Rhodes as their governor as much as he loved the job. In addition to expanding and streamlining the state's system of higher education,
Rhodes may be best remembered for promoting anything and everything
Buckeye and of course, in the process, himself. While hustling new industry
in far-off Japan, Rhodes was even reported to have boasted of Ohio's contribution to manned flight, relating to his mostly bemused Japanese hosts the
story of Dayton's Wright brothers and their early heavier-than-air aeronautical
experiments, while wildly croaking and flapping his arms like wings.[10]

Rhodes also seemed to genuinely love all fairs, county fairs to begin with,
but eventually and particularly the annual Ohio State Fair in Columbus.
Trailed by much younger but soon exhausted reporters, Rhodes happily
and tirelessly swept through the state fairgrounds just north of downtown
almost every day the exposition was open. He personally arranged for the
appearance of top-flight entertainers. Attendance soared.

But perhaps Rhodes's best remembered promotion resulted from his having
learned that northwestern Ohio was a major producer of canned tomato juice.
Rhodes ordered a fully functioning carousel installed in the rotunda of the
statehouse, loaded it with cans of Ohio tomato juice, while crowing, "If every
Ohioan drank an extra 16-ounce can of tomato juice a year, 2,000 jobs would
be created."[11] He also hosted a luncheon in his executive suite featuring large,

Governor Rhodes poses with the 1966 Republican team for statewide offices before the campaign bus departs for northwest Ohio. Rhodes went to every county and often traveled by bus, regaling Statehouse reporters with stories. *Columbus Dispatch* file photo, September 11, 1966.

chilled pitchers of tomato juice. It didn't seem to bother him at all when a snoopy reporter discovered the luncheon's caterer was serving California tomato juice.[12]

His insensitive caterer and Goldwater's disastrous nomination aside, it seemed most of whatever Rhodes was doing, he was doing right. When 1966 rolled around, he was the odds-on favorite to win. The Ohio Republican Party enthusiastically endorsed and renominated him. Dispirited Democrats went through the mostly empty motion of nominating for governor a strikingly handsome, if bland, state senator named Frazier Reams Jr. The Toledo Democrat was the son of a once well-known and highly respected crusading Depression-era Lucas County prosecutor, who by 1966 was mostly forgotten. Rhodes, who never really stopped campaigning but barely deigned to acknowledge Reams's nominal candidacy, was reelected to a second term on November 8, 1966, by an astounding and record-setting margin of more than seven hundred thousand votes out of about 2.9 million cast.[13]

Popular, independent-minded Democrat Frank Lausche, running without constitutional restraints, had served a postcolonial record of five (two-year) terms as governor. Republican Rhodes, although now constitutionally limited to two consecutive four-year terms, largely due to his own party's shortsighted efforts to be rid of Lausche, nonetheless eventually would best Lausche's record for total years served. His easy, slam-dunk first reelection was just the beginning.

CHAPTER 5

Four More Years,
with a Few Bumps

H AVING SERVED a successful, busy and productive four-year term as governor, Jim Rhodes was likely to have a more mixed record in his second term. And he was to make some vainglorious miscalculations.

First, however, Rhodes's second inauguration ceremony, held Monday, January 9, 1967, was as simple and austere as his first, with the exception of performances by high school choirs from his own native Jackson County and his adopted hometown of Springfield. Rhodes was sworn in at 8:40 A.M., then delivered a brief (just over eight minutes) address, and was said to have been back behind his desk by 9 A.M. Wouldn't we applaud such brevity now?

Rhodes reiterated his pledge to "stand between the tax spenders and the taxpayers" and announced he would reconstitute his "Little Hoover Commission" (so named after an efficiency-oriented federal commission headed by former president Herbert Hoover) to study ways to further streamline state government. In a not-too-convincing reference to the growing political gossip that he might be interested in higher office, such as the vice presidency or even the presidency, Rhodes stated that, God willing, he would serve out his term as governor.

Encouraged both by voters' approval of his first three bond issues and his practically uncontested reelection, Rhodes made his first major misstep a few months later. At a May 2, 1967, special election, he asked voters to approve a revolutionary state constitutional amendment, making it faster and easier to raise the capital improvement funds that he had grown so fond of doling out. Rhodes was a borrow-and-spend conservative, and he made no apologies.

He had devised the plan with the help of the bond lawyers who stood to make money from it. Rhodes proposed that instead of being required to seek voter approval of individual bond issues, he and his successors (both gubernatorial and legislative) be authorized to appoint an Ohio Bond Commission (OBC). It would have continuing authority to issue, within a few designated limits, capital improvement bonds backed by Ohio's general revenue funds—essentially the state treasury. Put another way, Rhodes was asking voters to endorse the creation of a kind of gubernatorial-controlled development bank with authority periodically to raise, without a further vote of the people, capital improvement funds using long-term mortgage financing.[1] The program already was operating in other states, such as Pennsylvania.

This time, Rhodes's salesmanship abilities failed him. He personally campaigned tirelessly for passage of his pet amendment, calling it "the most important piece of legislation I've [seen] since I've been in public life."[2] But a coalition of Rhodes's traditional opponents—primarily partisan Democrats and the leadership of organized labor—combined to defeat the complex OBC amendment by more than two to one—1,022,078 to 508,364.[3] Many other interests—including several influential newspaper publishers and editors, who viewed the OBC scheme as an overreaching, unmitigated power grab—united with Democrats and labor in opposition.

In the same election, the Ohio Republican establishment suffered a setback, probably because of the unexpectedly decisive defeat of the bond commission amendment. An unconscionably complex Republican-backed legislative reapportionment amendment also went down. It was ostensibly devised to address the recent U.S. Supreme Court's "one-man, one-vote" decision, which linked legislative representation to population, not geography. But the GOP plan, craftily designed to salvage as many incumbent Republican seats in the Ohio legislature as possible, was placed on the ballot at the same time as the OBC proposal. A thoroughly confused electorate rejected it, too, 850,068 to 699,021.

Rhodes had played only a marginal role in drafting the Republicans' complicated reapportionment map, but as leader of his party and benefactor of a Republican-controlled legislature, he supported it, although his main interest centered on the campaign for the bond panel. With the guidance of his staff, using up-to-date demographic information, Ohio attorney general William Saxbe had concocted separately a more comprehensible and evenhanded, single-member district reapportionment proposal. Saxbe, a Republican, had become exasperated with his party's efforts to save its legislative seats by trying to sell voters an overly complex reapportionment map. Democrats had already challenged his plan in state court, and the attorney general feared the federal court, which had directed the one-man, one-vote guideline, might not accept it. On November 7, 1967, voters approved Saxbe's much-easier-to-understand, more equitable reapportionment by a margin of 1,315,736 to 908,010. Further state court challenges to reapportionment were rendered moot.[4]

Asked on the evening of the overwhelming defeat of the OBC amendment what Rhodes would do next, his new finance director, the rotund Howard Collier wryly replied with a typically Rhodesian comment: "Head for the weeds!"[5] And indeed, the governor's confidence seemed shaken by his first defeat at the polls since 1954; he did appear to head for the weeds following this defeat. Usually readily available for public appearances, invited or not, he often sulked alone in his inner office suite, behind doors newly equipped with buzzer-controlled, automatic locks. Never very keen on open press conferences to begin with—he typically would appear before reporters at rare news events flanked by members of his staff and cabinet, to whom he would toss the particularly tough questions—Rhodes now became even less accessible. Chief of Staff John McElroy often was reporters' only knowledgeable contact in the governor's office. Whenever Rhodes said something worthy of note (or it was attributed to him), the quotation was circled with a cartoon-style balloon, pinned on the press room bulletin board over a rough drawing of a clump of tall weeds, labeled "Report from the Weed Patch" or, more simply, "Weed Patch Report."

At the next year's general election, on November 5, 1968, Ohio voters approved a more conventional highway and general capital improvements bond issue for a whopping $759 million. While Rhodes was required to seek legislative approval to put this fourth bond issue on the ballot, his campaign on its behalf was much more subdued than for the bond commission amendment and his previous three bond issues. Rhodes also quietly supported, or at least acquiesced to, legislative approval of several tax increases, including a $300 million boost in sales and corporate franchise taxes passed in late 1967.[6]

His tacit approval of tax increases may well have been prompted by the likes of such loyal supporters as the *Cleveland Plain Dealer*. Ohio's largest newspaper had endorsed the Ohio Bond Commission, but now, in the wake of OBC's overwhelming defeat, it editorially expressed the view that while "the tax stability which Governor Rhodes brought to Ohio when he was first inaugurated was good for the economic health of this state . . . there has come a time when the effect could be the opposite. Neglect of the state's support of such essentials as public education can result in harm rather than help for the state as a whole."[7] Rhodes's once solid "No New Tax" mantra appeared to be eroding along with his self-confidence.

But as titular head of the Ohio Republican Party, Rhodes could remain reclusive for just so long. When the time for the Republican National Convention rolled around that summer, he popped up from the weed patch long enough once again to control the Ohio GOP convention delegation. Actually, Rhodes was Ohio's favorite son as head of the delegation. He had run in the Ohio primary as favorite son, and when all the nation's Republican presidential primary votes had been counted, Rhodes came in third, on Ohio's tally alone, with 614,492 votes, behind only Nixon and Ronald Reagan.[8] So when the Ohio delegation arrived in Florida, the governor ordered Jim Duerk, his aide, to prepare materials for the Buckeye delegation to display at the convention hall. Duerk ordered "Rhodes for President" signs on eight-by-thirteen-inch cards to be sent to every Ohio delegate's hotel room.

He also ordered signs to be attached to sticks, which delegates would carry and wave in a demonstration of support when Rhodes's name was placed in nomination at the convention hall. Those blue placards bore color head shots of Rhodes and the words "Rhodes for President" and "New Leadership Now." The slogan, Duerk said, came from a late-night conversation with a bartender at the Doral Hotel lounge. Duerk told the bartender, who had come in from New York on a temporary assignment, that he worked for a governor who was running on a platform of leadership. Duerk quoted the barkeep: "If ever we needed new leadership, it's now." Duerk said Rhodes, relaxing in a chair in his hotel room, for a few moments allowed his mind to be wrapped around all the preparations for a presidential candidacy. "Long way from Jackson County," Rhodes mused.[9]

Richard Nixon, the former vice president, was poised to win the 1968 Republican nomination on the first ballot. But Rhodes never warmed to Nixon, for reasons he never fully disclosed. And so when Ohio's name was called during the convention's first roll call, Rhodes passed his state, even though many in the delegation were visibly anxious to vote for Nixon. When Ohio's name was called again, Rhodes again stated: "Ohio passes." Many frustrated pro-Nixon Republicans presumed that Rhodes was hoping his friend Nelson

Rockefeller might emerge to head off Nixon. But Nixon was nominated on the first ballot as expected, with Ohio impotently sitting on its fifty-five votes.

When Nixon went to pick his running mate, Rhodes was on the list with some other governors of large states that were key to a Republican victory, along with prominent senators and a few others, twenty-one in all. Former Ohio House assistant minority leader Ben Rose says a young man who later became a House Republican staffer, in the hotel room because he was the son of the chairman of the Florida Republican Party, reported that Nixon had a legal pad and his brain trust assessed each name for pros and cons. As they went around the room, Nixon would scratch off a name when the liabilities outweighed the benefits. After awhile, five names remained, and Rhodes's was one of them.[10]

Now, accounts differ as to how close Rhodes came to being vice president. Hal Duryea, a staffer with the Ohio Republican Party at the time, says, "Rhodes got a call, and we think it was from Nixon or one of his people. They offered him vice president, and he turned it down, mainly on the basis that he didn't have the education or the sophistication to be the vice president." Duerk said that could have happened, but he doesn't think so.[11] He agrees with Duryea's account of what happened when Nixon announced he had chosen Maryland governor Spiro T. Agnew as his running mate.

"We were all sitting in front of the TV at the hotel [Doral] when the choice was announced," Duryea said. "[Republican State Chairman John] Andrews was there, and Roy Martin and Duerk. Rhodes said, 'Come on with me,' and he and I rode up in the freight elevator to his room. He said, 'Spiro Agnew has been in Columbus more than anybody knows. He comes in and plays golf and picks my brain. I can tell you, he hasn't got it.'"[12] Much later, after Nixon's near impeachment and resignation, Rhodes reportedly told a business associate he was glad not to have been chosen Nixon's running mate. "Hell, I'd probably still be in jail," he laughingly observed.[13]

Following the convention, relations between Rhodes and Nixon remained proper, if coolly restrained. The next November, Nixon narrowly won Ohio's crucial electoral votes (and the national election over Hubert Humphrey) without Rhodes as his running mate. But the popular vote in Ohio was close enough that Nixon might well have lost the Buckeye State, had it not been for the third-party candidacy of segregationist Alabama governor George Wallace. The state's final tabulation showed Nixon with 1,791,014, Democrat Humphrey at 1,700,586, and Wallace with 467,495. Wallace and his running mate, Ohio native and former Air Force chief of staff Curtis LeMay, ran especially well in several traditionally Democratic northeastern blue-collar enclaves.[14]

The comparatively poor showing of Republican presidential candidates in Ohio during both 1964's total blowout and 1968's narrow victory raised questions as to how effectively Rhodes could lead the Ohio Republican Party. Granted, the rather shabby treatment he had accorded both Goldwater and Nixon, along with his friendship with the often maverick, sometimes liberal Nelson Rockefeller, already had raised doubts among the sizeable and vocal right wing of the party as to whether he was a strong enough conservative. But aside from the reactions of this predictably doctrinaire crowd, opinions as to his party stewardship were mixed.

Bliss was said to have been concerned about Rhodes's dependence on his own patronage network rather than on the regular Republican Party's statewide organization. Yet Bliss and Rhodes always seemed to get along well enough superficially, at least. John Andrews, the former Lucas County (Toledo) Republican chairman, chosen to succeed Bliss when the latter was summoned to Washington as national chairman to heal the GOP's wounds in the wake of the 1964 Goldwater disaster, offered a positive opinion of Rhodes's party leadership abilities.

Andrews noted that Rhodes tirelessly campaigned on behalf of other Ohio Republican candidates and, along with First Lady Helen Rhodes, always stood ready to welcome groups of visiting Republicans at the executive mansion in suburban Columbus. Andrews observed, practically, "I never tried to run the state and [Rhodes] never tried to run the party."[15] Andrews obviously liked having a known winner at the top of the ticket—a winner who also happened to be one of his patrons.

Former House speaker Charles Kurfess, a moderate Republican lawyer who unsuccessfully opposed Rhodes in the 1978 primary for governor, offered a far less charitable view of Rhodes's party leadership; he likened it to Frank Lausche's openly indifferent stewardship of the Ohio Democratic Party: "I always had a certain disdain for Lausche, and Rhodes ended up doing the same thing. We [regular organization Republicans] had lost everything by the time Rhodes lost."[16] Many dispassionate observers might agree more with Kurfess than Andrews. Rhodes's political philosophy had been more practical than ideological, and he usually was ready to make book with Democrats, independents, or anyone else, if he needed their support.

While perhaps never as aloof from his state party's organization as Lausche was from his, Rhodes often angled to set his own political agenda and keep it apart from party interference. As Bliss correctly perceived, Rhodes sought to cultivate his own cadre of personal loyalists outside the GOP's statewide patronage machine. While he appeared aware of his responsibilities as party leader by virtue of being a sitting governor, Rhodes seldom seemed interested in fully exercising this noblesse oblige.

As his second term drew to a close, Rhodes emerged from his weed patch to become an activist governor once again. He crisscrossed Ohio in his vintage, but comfortably refitted and still airworthy, state-owned DC-3, to resell himself and his administration to voters. Constitutionally barred from running for the third consecutive term his intimates believed he would have preferred, Rhodes was gearing up to run for the only elective office of a comparatively equal status then open to him—the U.S. Senate.

The road ahead would prove much more than just bumpy, involving major detours—such as a somewhat half-baked, yet embarrassing exposé by a national magazine; the tragic Kent State shootings; and mainly a roadblock in the person of a Republican rival for the Senate named Robert Taft Jr.

CHAPTER 6

Kent State
and the Day After

As 1970 DAWNED, Ohio Republican leaders looked forward with excitement to mounting a dream ticket for the fall general election. It would be headed by two-term outgoing Governor James A. Rhodes, running for the U.S. Senate, and well-known Congressman Robert Taft Jr., of Cincinnati, the Ivy League–educated scion of a respected political dynasty, running for governor. Both men, it was assumed, would run as party-endorsed candidates in the GOP primary with no formidable opposition.

But Taft decided against running for governor, and the Ohio Constitution barred Rhodes from seeking a third straight term. Instead Taft announced he would seek to follow his famous father, the late three-term senator Robert A. Taft, into the U.S. Senate, as he had tried to do in 1964, the year conservative presidential nominee Barry Goldwater dragged down many GOP office-seekers and almost the entire Republican Party.[1] (Technically, Robert or Bob Taft Jr., fifty-three, wasn't a "junior" at all, as he didn't share his famous father's middle name, "Alphonso." But he always was known as "Jr.," to set himself apart from his more prominent "Mr. Republican" father, who three times had been considered as a top contender for president.)

So these Republican heavyweights were competing for the same prize, to the chagrin of party leaders and activists. Neither candidate would yield. By conventional measures, Taft was the more qualified, owing in part to his experience in the give and take hurly-burly of the U.S. House of Representatives. He was a graduate of Yale University and received a law degree from Harvard before serving as a naval officer in World War II. Rhodes had attended college for less than a year, never held a legislative office, and did not serve in the armed forces.

Yet, many Republicans—including, it was said, Rhodes himself—believed

Taft would have been satisfied to run for governor and would not have challenged Rhodes for the Republican senatorial nomination, had it not been for an exposé of Rhodes that appeared in *Life* magazine, available in late April 1969. Not so, insists Taft's then–campaign manager, John Kelley, a Cincinnati lawyer: "That article had no influence on Bob's decision" to oppose Rhodes for the U.S. Senate. "The overriding issue was [Taft] was a legislator, not an administrator. He didn't want to be governor. I urged him to run for governor, I said we'd surround him with good people." Kelley also thought Taft would be in a better position to influence Republican presidential politics as governor, "but he wanted to be senator."[2] Kelley did not mention that if Taft ever wanted to sit in the Senate, time was running out. Even in the unlikely event he served just one term as governor, he'd be almost sixty before he could next run for the Senate. That hardly would leave him time enough to become an influential voice in the Senate, as had been his father, only forty-nine when he was first elected.

Whatever its influence on Taft's decision, the *Life* article, a cover story in the magazine's May 2, 1969, edition, marked one of the rough spots in Rhodes's mostly smooth sail during his first two terms as governor. Except for the ballot defeat of his 1967 Ohio Bond Commission amendment and the criticism generated by his withholding of the Ohio delegation's votes at the 1968 Republican National Convention, Rhodes had suffered few serious setbacks since his successful 1962 campaign against incumbent governor Michael DiSalle. More turbulence was ahead on a midsized campus in northeast Ohio, but Rhodes went into the primary campaign in pretty good shape.

Without benefit of exit polls, it is uncertain what role the article may have played in the 1970 senate primary, in which Rhodes narrowly lost to Taft. After all, the fatal shootings of four students during an antiwar protest at Kent State University the day before the election also have to be factored into the outcome of the primary. But as feeble as the magazine exposé was in the eyes of Statehouse beat reporters, it certainly didn't help Rhodes's image; rather, it may have served to augment the vague impression many, more sophisticated, Ohio Republicans held—that Rhodes, while a populist vote getter, was also a crude, down-home huckster politico who somehow was putting something over on them and getting away with it.

By the mid-1960s, *Life,* once the flagship of American national weekly magazines, was undergoing severe circulation and advertising losses. In defense of its turf, it had metamorphosed into a rather pathetic exponent of the cheap celebrity exposé. In the late 1960s, the Ohio Statehouse press corps caught wind that one of *Life*'s better-known muckraking reporters was nosing around asking about Rhodes. Rhodes and the press gang in Columbus held their collective breaths. The Ohio reporters were concerned that *Life* might come up with something they'd missed. Rhodes was simply concerned.

By one account, on the day in late April when portions of the article first became available, Rhodes canceled his dedication of a state park golf course and waited in his office for three hours for highlights to be faxed to the Columbus-based press corps.[3] The article itself, promoted in full-page ads, titled "The Governor and the Mobster," turned out to be fairly innocuous.

Essentially, the article was divided into two parts: the "mobster" in the title referred to Rhodes's parole of Thomas "Yonnie" Licavoli, an aging, nearly blind, and ailing but still incarcerated former Toledo Mafia boss; the second part was not much more than a rehash of the "$54,000 Question" involving Rhodes's past income tax problems with the Internal Revenue Service, which DiSalle and the Democrats first revealed during the 1962 gubernatorial campaign.

According to Toledo gangland lore, Yonnie Licavoli's older brother Pete, one of the ruling dons of Detroit's infamous Depression-era Purple Gang, dispatched him to Toledo in the 1930s to take over its indigenous mob activities. (A cousin, James Licavoli, aka "Jack White," later became boss of Cleveland's La Cosa Nostra.) During the course of the takeover, Yonnie had ordered a number of gangland slayings of recalcitrant mobsters, so said the case Lucas County Prosecutor Frazier Reams made against him. Thanks primarily to Reams, Yonnie and four of his henchmen were convicted of first-degree murder. But Yonnie's conviction, oddly, carried a jury's recommendation of mercy, and two others later had their death sentences commuted to life by various governors, to equalize punishments. So the gang members, having served their minimum mandatory twenty years for murder one, were eligible for parole consideration by the 1950s. But a succession of parole boards and governors, including Mike DiSalle, had turned them down. As an Italian American from Toledo, DiSalle was not about to release Yonnie Licavoli or any of his crew, for obvious reasons. (As governor, he was once parodied in a Columbus-area Fourth of July parade as "Big Daddio from Toledo.")

So when Yonnie Licavoli's case reached Rhodes, the governor was not obliged to reduce Yonnie's sentence to second-degree murder to "make him eligible for parole," as was widely reported. Licavoli, having served more than his mandated term, was already eligible. What Rhodes did was to actually *parole* him, that is, order the old man released from state custody. It was a parole, pure and simple, although in the process Rhodes apparently reduced Licavoli's sentence from first- to second-degree murder.

In Ohio, as in most states, while a pardon and parole commission may make recommendations to a governor, it is the governor who actually grants a parole or pardon. The reporters covering Rhodes dutifully took some, but not much, note of the aged Licavoli's parole and release. After all, the case involved mobsters having killed other mobsters thirty years before, and anyway, John McElroy, Rhodes's accessible, compassionate, first-rate, and highly respected executive assistant likely handled the parole request. Besides, the most that many younger reporters knew of the Purple Gang era was that Jacob "Firetop" Sulkin, the alleged "finger man" of the Yonnie Licavoli gang, once under a death sentence, before his much-earlier commutation, had become a stooped, graying prison trustee who silently padded about the Statehouse delivering mail to Rhodes's office, among others.

In its article, *Life* retold the hoary, possibly apocryphal, tale that organized crime had established a $250,000 "free Yonnie" fund to be paid in cash, no questions asked, to anyone who could arrange the aging mobster's release. It went on to claim that former governor Michael DiSalle had been offered such a bribe. If so, DiSalle did not mention the offer to others, nor did he write of it in his 1965 book *The Power of Life or Death,* although he devoted several pages to Licavoli and his gang's efforts to win paroles.[4] *Life* broadly hinted, but offered absolutely no evidence, that Rhodes or someone close to him had been paid to assure Licavoli's parole. If McElroy received any money, it wasn't evident from the spartan bachelor's life he continued to live.

The article went on to charge that Rhodes had paid almost $100,000 in back taxes, interest, and penalties on unreported personal income—not just taxes on a mere $54,000 in income, as earlier charged by DiSalle. The unreported income mostly involved political funds Rhodes allegedly had converted to personal use to maintain a very comfortable lifestyle while serving as state auditor.

Rhodes flatly denied that he had been offered or had accepted any money on behalf of Licavoli, and he not-so-flatly denied the income tax charges. "I have never been assessed or paid a *penalty* for either failure to report or failure to pay any federal income tax," he said in a prepared statement.[5] In short, just as he had done with the $54,000 Question in 1962, Rhodes did not deny he was required to pay back taxes, simply that he ever was assessed a penalty. Both press and public generally accepted Rhodes's emphatic denial of the Licavoli bribe; *Life* had only implied, but offered no real proof, that a bribe prompted the Toledo hoodlum's parole. Rhodes's answer to the income tax charges, however, again seemed carefully hedged, incomplete, and unsatisfactory, as several newspapers editorially noted.[6]

The question remains as to who tattled on Rhodes to both DiSalle and later to *Life*. Rhodes always thought the Internal Revenue Service was to blame. At the time of the $54,000 Question, DiSalle claimed a former disgruntled auditor's employee had been his source. But in later private conversations he hinted that while such an employee may have alerted him that Rhodes had tax problems, the details surreptitiously were leaked by President Kennedy's IRS. *Life*'s reporters no doubt first heard about the matter via DiSalle's well-reported earlier charges and later obtained confirmation and updated information from their Washington sources.[7] Whoever the source or sources, Rhodes became less available to the news media and public following publication of the *Life* article, just as he had following the defeat of his OBC amendment. He retreated behind his buzzer-and-lock-controlled office doors and the shield of his protective staff.

As a candidate for high office, however, Rhodes could remain reclusive for just so long, and he reluctantly agreed to four Senate primary campaign debates with Taft. Until their final meeting in Cleveland, the debates were ho-hum affairs, as both candidates were moderates and had few quarrels over substantive political issues. Early in the campaign, Rhodes was embarrassed by reports that fish in Lake Erie were found to contain unacceptable levels of mercury. Taft darkly hinted that thanks to Rhodes's lack of concern for pollution control, the lake was turning into a swamp. Rhodes blamed its sorry condition on Canada.

Taft did not bring up the *Life* article per se but slyly mentioned "integrity" enough times that voters understood his reference. As for Rhodes, he could mention issues such as Taft's rather spotty congressional attendance record and his failure to recuse himself from voting on congressional issues that directly affected corporations in which the Taft family held substantial interest.[8]

Otherwise, their campaign mostly involved Taft's name and lineage (son of a senator, grandson of a president) versus the many chits politico Rhodes could and would claim in exchange for the many political favors he had doled out over the course of almost two full gubernatorial terms. Until the Kent State shootings the day before the primary election, the Rhodes-Taft contest for the most part was a typically dull, Ohio Republican primary, except for presenting faithful Republican voters with a tough choice.

* * * * *

Those Ohioans who closely followed the 1970 Republican primary campaign, especially the final debate at the Cleveland City Club on Saturday, May 2, should not have been surprised when later the same day Rhodes authorized the Ohio National Guard to protect the terrorized little college town of Kent. There, thirty-three miles southeast of Cleveland, groups of a comparatively few radical students, joined by local protesters and vandals and outside agitators, roamed the city's modest business district—breaking store windows, looting, and throwing stones at police. Rhodes later approved sending the Guard onto the Kent State University campus itself, ignoring the pleas of Portage County prosecutor Ronald Kane and other Kent officials to simply close down the university.

The campus unrest at Kent State during the late 1960s and early 1970s, as elsewhere, primarily was prompted by growing opposition to the protracted Vietnam War. The situation was greatly exacerbated on April 30, 1970, when President Richard Nixon, even though pledged to wind down hostilities, announced he was ordering U.S. troops and bombers to Cambodia to flush out sanctuaries he claimed were harboring America's wartime enemies.[9]

Long before he formally launched his Republican primary campaign, Rhodes had taken what he perceived was a generally popular, no-holds-barred hardline stance on campus disturbances. While never a doctrinaire, militant right-winger, he seemed to regard state university facilities almost as his personal property. Indeed many of the newer buildings on Ohio's established campuses and newly created state institutions were built with money raised by Rhodes-instigated bond issues. A college dropout himself, Rhodes could be almost anti-intellectual, a reverse snob of sorts. He seemed especially annoyed that—in his view—some state-paid, effete college professors, along with a scattering of their often privileged, tax-assisted wards, seemed dedicated to disrupting university life for all students. And, as a Republican officeholder, Rhodes obediently, if offhandedly, supported Nixon's Vietnam War policies, whatever they were at the moment.

As early as the fall of 1969, Rhodes emphasized his hard line on campus unrest—during a tour of Cleveland State University, an institution he had practically created and built from scratch. Accompanied by John Millett, the Rhodes-appointed chancellor of the Rhodes-created Ohio Board of Regents, the governor belligerently warned, "These buildings were built by the taxpayers and I have a duty to see they are not damaged or destroyed. Public opinion in this state will not tolerate takeovers or any such thing. If students have been led to think disruption and violence will bring about change, they have been misinformed. It can only bring about the destruction of higher education."[10]

The following February, Rhodes ordered well-disciplined state highway patrolmen in riot gear to Ohio University in Athens, an academic Eden flowering in the mostly poor, southern Appalachian region, when students rioted, ostensibly over a $10 increase in tuition fees for an academic term. Rhodes reiterated his stance against campus unrest, this time flanked by Maj. Gen. Sylvester Del Corso, head of the Ohio National Guard, whose presence underscored Rhodes's pledge to "use every force possible to maintain peace on the campus." In April 1970 Rhodes alerted the Guard for action when students at Miami University, in bucolic Oxford, acted up, explaining, "We're not going to have a Harvard or an MIT or Columbia in the state of Ohio"—a reference to scenes of other campus uprisings. He also ordered the Guard to the main campus of his beloved Ohio State University to quell sporadic student demonstrations there.

But not until the Cleveland City Club debate did Rhodes clearly make his no-nonsense, stern response to campus unrest a major issue in his flagging battle with Taft. Perhaps the contest between these two mostly moderate icons of Ohio Republicanism was proving frustratingly short on substantive issues. "The way I have handled [campus unrest] points up the sharp difference of opinion and philosophy between my opponent and myself," Rhodes argued, as some of his handlers either visibly winced or smiled approvingly off-camera. "He said he would have gone much more slowly and obtained a court injunction against the rioters. By the time an injunction is obtained, campus buildings could be burned to the ground and people maimed or killed. My opponent's soft attitude on campus violence is not surprising, since in 1968 he voted against an amendment to the [federal] higher education bill requiring colleges to deny federal funds to students who participate in campus disorders." Rhodes's charge that Taft was soft on campus unrest was reported in many of the same Sunday morning newspapers that also carried stories of torching of the ROTC building on the Kent State campus on the night of Saturday, May 2.[11]

Early the next morning, awakened by news of the still smoldering fire, Prosecutor Kane toured Kent State and noticed guardsmen were stationed on campus. Many were the same troops Rhodes had activated earlier to patrol interstate highways when a Teamsters' strike in northern Ohio had led to shooting and serious rock-throwing incidents. Kane thought some of them looked red-eyed, tired, and jittery.

About 10:00 A.M. Sunday, Rhodes arrived by plane and held a news conference at a Kent fire station. Red-faced and angry, he pounded the table and stormed, "These people just move from one campus to the other and terrorize the community. They are worse than the Brown Shirt and the communist element and also the nightriders and the vigilantes. They're the worst type of people that we harbor in America." Del Corso, somewhat more calmly but no less resolutely added, "We have sufficient force in the area, we will apply whatever force is necessary to provide protection for the lives of our citizens and his [*sic*] property." Later, in support of Kent police chief Roy Thompson, he added threateningly, if not prophetically, "As the Ohio law says, we use any force even to the point of shooting. We don't want to get into that, but the law says we can if necessary."[12]

Unlike many of those actually present to hear Rhodes, popular novelist James Michener in his later nonfiction book on the shootings took pains to note that the governor applied the terms "Brown Shirt"—referring to Nazi storm troopers—and "communist element" only to "the few who were determined to destroy the university," not to all university students. But, as even the establishment's apologist Michener admitted, "The damage was done. Word was flashed throughout Kent and across America that the governor of Ohio had castigated students as being worse than Brown Shirts; accused young people conducting legal protests against the war as being nightriders and vigilantes. . . . Rhodes had never said that, but to this day people everywhere believe that one of the principal reasons for the deterioration of affairs at Kent and elsewhere was the Rhodes rhetoric." The *Cleveland Plain Dealer,* among others, also editorially wondered if Rhodes's "tough talk" may not have contributed to the tense situation.[13]

What happened at Kent State at about noon the next day, Monday, May 4, has been well documented by a flurry of contemporaneous investigations. Why it happened still is the subject of continued debate. At about 12:20 P.M. Monday, a relatively small band of jeering, rock-throwing students confronted guardsmen patrolling the university's open-air Commons area, where an antiwar rally was scheduled to take place. Larger groups of students also were in and around the area either to peaceably take part in the rally or simply because they were going to or from classes. The beleaguered guardsmen began retreating, maneuvering up a hill overlooking the Commons, and suddenly, very likely without specific orders, whirled and indiscriminately began firing their M-l rifles into the throng of students for a terrible thirteen seconds. Four students were instantly killed, and nine were wounded, two very seriously. Apparently, none of those killed, all bona fide Kent students, were a part of the militant group directly confronting the guardsmen. The closest corpse was determined to have been 265 feet from where the shots were fired, the furthest, 390 feet.[14]

The day after, Rhodes lost the senate primary to Robert Taft by less than 1 percent of 940,000 votes.

This chapter's purpose is not so much to reexamine the Kent State events as to discuss what part the tragedy played in the outcome of the Rhodes-Taft primary the next day and to examine how and why each of the candidates handled the unhappy situation as he did. The snap, conventional wisdom was that the Kent State tragedy cost Rhodes the election. But a retrospective review indicates Rhodes's hard-line stance at Kent State and even the resulting killings actually helped him, narrowing the wide gap.

In an analysis later corroborated by John Kelley, Taft's state campaign manager, Taft's private polls—taken up to a week or so before the election by Cincinnati's respected Burke Marketing Research firm, Procter & Gamble's pollster—were projecting Taft beating Rhodes by a healthy 7–8 percent. Yet, a day following Kent State, Rhodes lost by less than 1 percent.[15]

"Between the polls that showed Taft far ahead and Election Day, something had to [have] happen[ed]," an anonymous Republican county chairman said. "I think it was the Governor's move to keep order on campus. . . . Remember, there were a hell of a lot of people who have had it with these kids."[16] It should be remembered that this was a Republican primary, not a general election; off-year GOP primaries tend to bring out regular

Republicans and party activists, who in the Ohio of the early 1970s were predominately conservative law-and-order types.

Clearly having made his give-no-quarter stand an issue in the primary contest, Rhodes had limited his options and had little choice but to send the Ohio Guard to the city of Kent, then to Kent State, and later to defend the Guard's panicked, fatal response on the Kent State campus. He would also, of course, express sadness over the killings.

The always cautious Taft, Kelley recounts, interviewed two witnesses to the Kent shootings soon after the tragedy but was unable "to make any sense out of what had transpired." Accordingly, Kelley remembers "with a senate seat hanging in the balance, the decision I made was to overrule our brain trust from Southern Ohio, who was urging applause for the National Guard for keeping order, [and] our brain trust from Northern Ohio, who were urging that we blister Rhodes and the National Guard with a scathing release against them both. . . . [I] decided to express the sincere shock and sympathy which Bob Taft personally felt and say nothing to prejudge either side for the events that occurred. It worked, barely."[17]

Rhodes was an instinctive, intuitive politician. Given his comments during the Cleveland City Club debate, by alerting troops to the civil unrest at Kent and Kent State, he was simply following through on what he had said he would do, which was also what he thought his constituency wanted. This is not to suggest Rhodes acted out of sheer cynicism and rank political opportunism by cracking down on dissidents in a desperate, last-ditch effort to save his senate bid, even though he probably knew he was running well behind Taft. Perhaps some such motivation prompted Rhodes's debate remarks, but there is no reason to think his outrage over threats to *his* campus facilities was anything but genuine. Rather, by thoughtlessly calling on overwrought, tired, homesick, and improperly trained young troops to restore order—over the objections of Kent authorities—and then spooked by what turned out to be spurious rumors of deadly sniper fire, Rhodes was just being Rhodes.

Local, state, and federal investigators seemed to think so, too. The spate of mostly flawed and biased investigations that followed the shootings prompted much finger-pointing and recrimination, but it seldom directly or even indirectly involved Rhodes's part in the affair. Rather, the local investigations briefly involved guardsmen but centered on the university administration and most often on students and professors.

The Guard generally was held blameless, and a special grand jury indicted no guardsmen. The twenty-five county-level indictments returned involved students, including two of the wounded, and a professor. It was almost as if the governor who had played such an active role in stirring things up no longer existed, although some time later, he was named as a defendant in a civil action brought by the parents of some of the students, and his actions prior to the shootings were examined during a subsequent federal investigation. Nothing much came of the investigation; the civil suit was settled out of court in 1979, with a $675,000 award going to the families of the dead and wounded students. Rhodes and National Guard commanders also signed a "statement of regret."

Nearing the end of his second term, Rhodes soldiered on, albeit as a defeated Senate candidate and lame-duck governor with no new public office in sight. He served out his term, and in January 1971, John J. Gilligan succeeded him. The Cincinnati Democrat was elected in part because of a scandal involving the investment of state money in questionable financial instruments by several Republican officials and candidates.

But the so-called Crofters scandal, which Rhodes personally dodged, had no impact on the Senate primary campaign. So why was Rhodes so far behind Taft a week before the 1970 primary that even the added support he probably gained by his firm action at Kent State failed to save his candidacy? Many might agree with former Republican Ohio House speaker Kurfess, who knew both candidates and had a ringside seat at the primary, that "it was a matter of [the] level of expectation." Or, as another Rhodes watcher was to observe: Rhodes "fit the classical mode of the hawking, bawling politico. . . . [Voters] could wave off his imperfections with an exasperated gasp, 'Hell, he's just a politician.'"[18] Both of these observers essentially were saying Republican voters might support Rhodes as governor but not as a U.S. senator, especially when offered the choice between a folksy, self-promoting politico and a more erudite, highborn, bookish grandson of a president and Supreme Court chief justice, William Howard Taft, and son of Robert A. Taft, "Mr. Republican."

Ohio's political landscape is littered with the corpses of otherwise popular politicians taken down when voters perceived their ambition was exceeding their competence. A typical example is the case of Ted Brown, the oft-elected Republican Ohio secretary of state, so popular and so well known that he alone among Republican statewide officeholders survived the 1958 anti–Right-to-Work law Democratic sweep. Yet six years later, when Brown presumed to run in the GOP senatorial primary against Robert Taft Jr., he was defeated by a staggering 606,000 votes to 160,000.[19]

That Rhodes would twice again be elected governor seems to prove voters were quite willing to send him to the Statehouse in Columbus again and again but balked at sending him to Washington even once. In this same vein, in 1970, more sophisticated voters, wise to the ways of Washington, must have wondered if Jim Rhodes at sixty, accustomed to impatiently and imperiously running his own shop as governor, was temperamentally suited to the constraints of starting over as a mere freshman senator in an arena noted for its slow, deliberate pace and seniority system. He perhaps failed to convince these more thoughtful Republican voters he really wanted to leave Columbus for Washington and was not running for the Senate only because the term limit prohibited him from running for reelection, which he probably would have preferred. Taft, a Washingtonian by birth with brief service in the U.S. House, by contrast, may have seemed destined to follow his father to sit in the U.S. Senate.

Regardless, for the first time since his days running a hamburger joint near the Ohio State University campus, Jim Rhodes faced life out of public office. But he would survive to successfully run again and again for governor.

CHAPTER 7

Chasing Smokestacks, Dodging Democrats

AFTER SIXTEEN CAMPAIGNS, and eight years in the governor's office, Jim Rhodes involuntarily entered private life in 1971 at an age when many men begin thinking of retirement. He was sixty-one years old, and a career politician out of a job. But he would be busy during his interlude from government. After all, he had a wife and three daughters (Saundra, Suzanne, and Sharon) to help support and a comfortable lifestyle to maintain. He had a new home on Tremont Road in affluent Upper Arlington, bordering a country club fairway, and also a Florida rental. He made $40,000 annually serving as governor, and in 1969 his reported net worth was only $65,000. By the time he returned to politics he would be a multimillionaire.

Rhodes began prepping for private life before he left the Governor's Mansion. With four days left in his term, he obtained a real estate license, by way of a highly unusual forty-five-minute oral exam, which the Ohio Real Estate Commission gave him in his office. Conveniently enough, the commission's three members were his appointees and willing to forgo the customary written examination. Four of his top aides—including Development Director Fred Neuenschwander and Commerce Director Gordon Peltier—also got preferential treatment from the accommodating panel. A few months later, Rhodes went into business with Neuenschwander.

Backed by generous loans from friendly banks, the two men jump-started a Columbus-based real estate business with projects in Florida, Illinois, Georgia, Indiana, and Ohio. "There's money to be made," Rhodes cackled. In 1970, another partner, his onetime campaign treasurer, Don Hilliker of Bellefontaine, Ohio, bought undeveloped land near the under-construction

Walt Disney World in Orlando. Soon Rhodes joined Hilliker—the firm was called H and R Development Co.—in investing in a planned complex of shopping centers, hotels, condominiums, and commercial projects in central Florida. The firm he formed with Neuenschwander, James A. Rhodes and Associates, was hired as a development consultant for the project, the brainchild of R. F. Raidle of Orlando. Rhodes and his partners soon put up two high-rise Howard Johnson's hotels near Orlando and built a third at O'Hare International Airport in Chicago. Soon more HoJos were sprouting, near the new Atlanta airport, and in Indianapolis, also close to an airport.[1]

His Florida investments were aided not only by Hilliker, who had the foresight to buy land near Orlando when Disney World was being built, but also by Florida developer Raidle, who did business with a bank that included Rhodes on its board of directors. Rhodes and Hilliker eventually built two hotels in Raidle's Major Center project near Orlando. For the first, H and R Development obtained a $5 million mortgage from Cincinnati's Western and Southern Life Insurance Company, then headed by William Safford (whom Rhodes as governor had appointed to the Ohio State University Board of Trustees). A Columbus bank helped with a second Florida hotel and also with a motel and restaurant at Atlanta International Airport.

Rhodes was on his way. He had two companies, James A. Rhodes and Associates—Neuenschwander was the key associate—and H and R Development, which he formed with Hilliker. He also owned land near Bucyrus, which he hoped to develop, and a twenty-two-acre island in the middle of a small lake in his native Jackson County.

Rhodes also picked up a "small amount of stock" in Wendy's International, a fast-food chain started in 1969, acquired in exchange for his James A. Rhodes and Associates consulting work. The founder, Dave Thomas (the restaurants were named after his daughter), had little education but a powerful, if simple, idea. His slightly more expensive burgers would be bigger than McDonald's and its imitators, and his customers could order whatever fixings they wanted—ketchup, onion, mustard, pickle, lettuce. In addition, Wendy's produced decent chili and an inexpensive milkshake: the Frosty. Columbus car dealer Len Immke, a Rhodes golfing buddy, had a big early stake in Wendy's.

In 1975, Rhodes bought nearly $500,000 worth of Wendy's stock at about $16 per share, using a $495,000 loan from Cleveland businessman Harold

Schott, a campaign contributor. The stock went public that year and soon doubled in value. Rhodes and Hilliker quickly acquired exclusive franchise rights to build more than a hundred hamburger joints. Dave Thomas, an affable, plainspoken man whose genius for marketing ground beef pulled him up from working-class roots (and who got many of his ideas about the fast-food business by working for Colonel Sanders at Kentucky Fried Chicken), soon became a political supporter of his new investor named Rhodes.

No question, Rhodes worked hard, took risks, and had an entrepreneurial spirit. But he wasn't circumspect about his key to financial success. "Use other people's money," he told a reporter.[2] And more than a few were anxious to help an influential politician get rich, especially when that same politician—a once and future governor—might return the favor. Elmer Keller, a longtime associate, said bluntly, "Jim Rhodes has something very essential if you are going to make money. That's credit from friends."[3] Reporter Joseph D. Rice, who covered Rhodes for the *Plain Dealer,* said the rumors of shady financial deals were "always there," hanging over Rhodes. "He knew people who gave him entrée. He made his money in real estate. He was a guy who knew people who could make things happen."[4]

When the extraordinary circumstances of his real estate license became public in 1973, Rhodes insisted nothing improper had taken place and said he had never even used the license. Eventually, he returned it to the state, but only after a Democrat-appointed Real Estate Commission threatened revocation. Rhodes wasn't one to brood over bumps in the road; besides, he had already made his grubstake. And with financial security assured, he wanted to be governor again—so much so that he went to court to get a shot at it. Ending months of speculation that he'd try for a comeback, Rhodes called in his sidekick, Jim Duerk, his partner in the development office.

"Gonna run against Gilligan," the two-term governor told Duerk.

"What do you want to do that for? You got a good business going. You can make money and play golf at the same time."

"Whattaya want me to do, die?" Rhodes asked, with a serious look on his face.[5]

Many old supporters thought a comeback was a mistake; Rhodes should step aside for another generation of Republican leaders. A move was under way to draft former senator and U.S. attorney general William B. Saxbe, a moderate with a strong independent streak. "The arm-twisting began in the spring of 1973 and continued that fall," Saxbe said. Harry K. "Bud" Crowl, a state GOP executive committee member from Dayton, was blunt in his assessment of Rhodes's candidacy. "Hopefully these [Republican] leaders," he said in a letter to potential Saxbe backers, "can be motivated to get a 'grassroots' opinion, which might bring Jim Rhodes to his senses."

In an October 26, 1973, letter to Rhodes, Crowl was even more direct: "I sincerely feel strongly that you cannot win next November. Not only do I feel you cannot win, I further believe your candidacy in today's political climate is so impractical that its end result will be disastrous for the whole state ticket. Pragmatically, it could be disastrous enough to initiate the demise of the Ohio Republican Party. . . . For everyone, there is a time to come on stage, a time to stay on stage, and then a time to leave it."[6] Rhodes ignored the unsolicited advice, but he didn't forget how Crowl and other party stalwarts had treated him. And this was not the last time others would urge him to leave the stage.

In January 1973, nearly two years ahead of the election, Rhodes filed petitions of candidacy—to force a court case after election officials rejected the signatures as invalid, based on the term limit law as it was understood. In the ensuing litigation, Rhodes's lawyers convinced the Republican-dominated Ohio Supreme Court that the state's constitutional limit on two terms for a governor meant *two consecutive terms*—not two terms total. Since he was sitting out four years, he was eligible, the attorneys argued. The court agreed on May 10, 1973. Rhodes was off and running, ostensibly against a well-financed but overconfident incumbent, Democrat John J. Gilligan. Gilligan's staff salivated at the prospect of running against a fellow they regarded as a buffoon and whose time they thought had passed.

The Saxbe threat didn't materialize; Saxbe had little interest in the job and no stomach for a primary fight with Rhodes. "Rhodes had no intention of giving up his candidacy, and I just was not willing to fight him for the nomination, despite what the polls said. I know I disappointed a lot of people, . . . but I just didn't have the desire. You've got to have the fire in your gut if you want to go on in Ohio politics."[7]

Saxbe was right about Rhodes. He had the fire.

* * * * *

First, though, Rhodes had to dispose of two Republican primary challengers—State Representative Charles Fry of Springfield and a minor candidate, Bert Dawson Jr., the Columbiana County engineer. He looked right past both of them and fired away at Gilligan as if the general election campaign were under way. Fry accused Rhodes of having a "public be damned attitude"; he would not engage his opponent. When Rhodes refused to make public his income tax records and brushed aside entreaties for a debate, Fry declared: "I believe the people want and deserve a much higher level of openness and accountability from their public officials. The day of the backslapping politician with his propensity for cronyism is passé."[8]

Passé, eh? Rhodes, unfazed, was surrounded by many of his old cronies. He went right on ignoring his primary election opponents and kept his focus on Democratic governor Gilligan's administration. He began in January 1974 by declaring he was being investigated by "the greatest set of plumbers we've ever had in the state of Ohio," playing off of the term applied to the Watergate burglars in Washington.[9] Gilligan could have turned the accusation on Rhodes, who had his own moles still employed in state agencies, but he didn't.

Rhodes was shaken a few days before the primary when one of his best friends, Jackson County native Fred Rice, collapsed and died after driving him to a campaign event in Cincinnati. Rice, who was sixty-two and worked for Rhodes's development firm, had driven him down from Columbus for a speech. Rhodes said Rice was "like a brother, probably my closest friend and confidant. I've known him all my life."[10]

A punch to the gut, but it didn't stop him. On May 7, 1974, Rhodes flicked Fry off his shoulder and rolled to a two-hundred-thousand-vote primary victory—385,669 to Fry's 183,889. Dawson polled 44,938. Gilligan showed vulnerability in the Democratic primary. He defeated a little-known Cleveland nursing home operator named James Nolan, but the conservative gadfly nicked the incumbent. Nolan picked up 29 percent of the vote, spending only $16,000. Further, Gilligan's appointee to Saxbe's vacated U.S. Senate seat, Howard Metzenbaum, lost a primary to John Glenn in a bitterly fought contest that split the Democratic Party.

Even so, as the general election campaign opened, Gilligan had a strong record to run on. He had created Ohio's first environmental protection agency, imposed the first income tax to bolster underfunded state services, and made strides in care of the mentally ill. Plus, he was running in the aftermath of the Watergate scandal—this election year would bring into public office a slew of Democrats, dubbed "Watergate babies." With a strong reelection showing, Gilligan might even get mentioned as a vice presidential candidate in 1976.

His twenty-six-year-old daughter, Kathy, joked to the *Ohio University Post* that her dad's "ego was too big to be vice president"—he'd probably prefer the top job.[11] Gilligan and his inner circle found it hard to believe he could lose to a foe they viewed as an aging country bumpkin—a man who called his state "Ahaya" and was tainted by the Kent State tragedy. His staff members, at least, already had visions of Washington in the backs of their minds.

But Jack Gilligan was far from lovable. Patrician in manner and quick with a snide remark, the redhead from Cincinnati sharply contrasted with his jowly, silver-haired rival. For sure, Gilligan was no backslapper. Rhodes, who turned sixty-five during the campaign, seemed more rooted in the flatlands and rolling hills of Ohio than Gilligan, who vacationed (gasp!) in Michigan.

Rhodes also knew that many in Ohio were smarting from the aftershocks of the excesses of the late 1960s. He ridiculed Gilligan for offering support to United Farm Workers Union leader Cesar Chavez's boycott of iceberg lettuce—a stand that cost him the Teamsters Union's support. Rhodes had "no objections" to iceberg; if Rhodes became governor, by gosh, Ohioans would be able to eat iceberg lettuce.

In a dissertation probing the Rhodes psyche, Ohio State University philosophy doctoral candidate William Russell Coil described how Rhodes spoke to blue-collar Ohioans.

> Rhodes and his political aides played to the anger of working class people and the desire to escape the control of reformers. . . . The trick, however, was to present Rhodes authentically as possible. Rhodes would have sounded stiff and unnatural had he tried to deliver a speech like [George C.] Wallace. Rhodes by nature was not an angry man and . . . did not possess the theatrical skill to fake it. . . .
>
> Rhodes attacked Gilligan's intellectual, cosmopolitan image, slyly connecting that to the negative perception of liberal Democrats as effete, out of touch reformers who knew nothing of the world of working-class men.[12]

The "average Ohioan," Rhodes said, with no small insight, "wants a job and wants to be left alone."

In his seventeenth campaign, Rhodes played rough from the outset. It wasn't personal; the first rule of a campaign is to attack when the time is right, and that was always his strategy in close contests. Operating from his real estate development office a block from the Statehouse, Rhodes put out a blizzard of press releases, at least one a day, to see which issues would stick. He harped on those for the rest of the campaign—they were mainly about government mismanagement, taxing, and spending but also included specific actions or inactions by the administration. For example, six months after a devastating tornado hit Xenia, he accused the administration of dawdling on state aid.

Rhodes put the Democrats on the defensive with bluster and hyperbole. They countered at staged news conferences called "Balloon Busters," with analytical, point-by-point refutations, complete with charts, graphs, and comparative tables. For every "myth" Rhodes devised, a Gilligan campaign functionary would pop a red balloon.

The Rhodes and Gilligan campaigns, backed by their respective political party officials, fenced with one another over which administration created more jobs for Ohioans and which deserved more blame for school closings. Without any evidence, Rhodes claimed Gilligan would double the income tax to pay for all of the spending programs he had dreamed up for a second term. He said his opponent wanted to tax everything "that walks, crawls or flies," later adding "smokes or drinks." He vowed he would never close the state parks the way Gilligan had during a standoff with the General Assembly over the state budget and the incipient income tax. Rhodes's media consultant, Robert Deardourff, produced an impressive television ad to make the point, showing distraught vacationers driving up to closed park gates. Another showed empty swings in a schoolyard.

"Deardourff was in their living room 15 times a day, beating hell out of them [his campaign organization] and it wasn't even a match," Gilligan said.[13] Rhodes was elusive, keeping pesky political reporters at bay and refusing to be pinned down on specifics of his own plans. "I'll tell you why I won't hold a press conference in Columbus," he told one reporter. "Because I'm runnin' two-to-one ahead in Columbus. That's why."[14]

Rhodes seized the offensive. "During the days when Gilligan was remaining 'above the struggle,' as governor, the Rhodes campaign aired five-minute, semi-autobiographical TV spots. The theme was 'Remember how good it was.'"[15]

Positives were turned into negatives. After scoffing at "speculation" that the state might have an $80 million budget surplus, Gilligan announced in early summer that such a surplus had indeed been discovered. The Rhodes team promptly ran a "shell game" commercial, refuting Gilligan's competence-in-government theme. Rhodes said the surplus, which later grew to $103 million, should be plowed back into the public schools; better yet, he promised if he was elected, every certified public schoolteacher would receive a $1,000 raise. The skeptical teachers' union, the Ohio Education Association, endorsed Gilligan anyway.

Rhodes even mocked Gilligan when he took a page from Jim Rhodes's own book and opened a new state park on Kelleys Island in Lake Erie, a short boat ride from Sandusky. In a speech at a United Auto Workers hall, Rhodes asked the workers how many of them owned a yacht, or a cabin cruiser, working his way down to canoes. "By then, about 10 hands were up," a reporter covering the event recalled. "'Ok,' he says, 'you ten guys can use the new state park on Kelleys Island, the rest of you are shit outta luck.' It's a union hall and so he knew he could talk like that. How better would you use that as a weapon against Gilligan," said the reporter, Chan Cochran, then of the *Columbus Dispatch*.[16] Gilligan had launched a satellite state office building in Cleveland; Rhodes, always ready for a game of one-upmanship, promised a feasibility study on state office buildings in ten more counties.

Gilligan outspent Rhodes, pouring more than $1 million into his reelection effort and employing a team of forty full-time campaign workers—about six times the size of Rhodes's full-time staff. Gilligan's staff eventually grew to a hundred full- and part-time workers. His opponent depended on a half dozen middle-aged men and one woman, a core group nicknamed the Over-the-Hill gang. Rhodes spent $857,000—much of it on his slick television commercials, most of them aired during the critical three final weeks of the campaign.

Missing from the Gilligan organization were pros like journalist Mark Shields and Cleveland lawyer James Friedman, who guided the successful 1970 gubernatorial campaign; they were crowded out by Gilligan's chief of staff John E. Hansan (who succeeded Friedman in the job), head of a governor's office palace guard that kept a tight rein on message and budgeted $280,000 for a grassroots field operation designed to bring sympathetic voters to the polls. The highly motivated canvassers and organizers—aided by as many as forty thousand volunteers—did their jobs. But Gilligan put too much faith in the ability of a traditional political organization to deliver on Election Day, when a compelling message would have served him better.

As Rhodes loudly challenged Gilligan's first-term record, he left the grass-roots fieldwork to the Ohio Republican Party and its respected chairman Kent B. McGough. For the GOP's ground war, McGough used party regulars and volunteers from all over the state—people he knew personally—to set up county-by-county organizations. Beneath a gruff exterior (he'd often respond to a friendly "how ya doin'?" with a terse, "never better"), McGough was a serious student of the game. Four years earlier, he had noted Gilligan's vulnerabilities, when the Democrat defeated a weak GOP candidate, Roger Cloud, with 54 percent of the vote, short of a landslide. In May 1973, McGough hired Market Opinion Research, a Michigan polling firm, and began sampling Ohio voters' views of Gilligan and Rhodes. The surveys, designed by Robert Teeter and Alex Gage, suggested the incumbent Democrat had problems with middle-class voters from his own party and also with young ticket-splitters. Gilligan was not polling as strong as expected with union households—all good signs for Rhodes, whose plainspoken appeals were aimed at blue-collar Ohioans.

In Columbus, Gilligan named a political professional—and fellow Irish American—Eugene "Pete" O'Grady, as his campaign manager. But O'Grady, who had served as the administration's highway safety director, had limited authority when it came to strategy and messaging. He took his orders from the governor's office. He also had to deal with a party deeply divided by the Glenn-Metzenbaum Senate primary. Glenn won the Democratic nomination but only after a battle that amounted to a political civil war. Gilligan backed the loser, Metzenbaum, a Cleveland millionaire who had unwisely accused the astronaut hero Glenn of never having to meet a payroll in private life.

In 1973, in part because labor leaders preferred Metzenbaum, Gilligan had appointed the liberal activist over a disappointed Glenn to serve out Senator Saxbe's unexpired term (Saxbe had been appointed U.S. attorney general). Gilligan insisted he and Glenn were not feuding—it was just reporters snooping in the locker room for dirty towels. But after the primary, he would get little help from the victorious and unforgiving Glenn camp. (Glenn sailed to an easy Senate victory in November, over Cleveland Mayor Ralph Perk, who famously passed up an invitation to the White House because it fell on his wife's bowling night.)

Even so, Gilligan was not lacking for confidence as the campaign entered the summer months. In essence, he waged an image campaign, stressing themes of competency and honesty in government. Yet, too often when he discussed specific issues he talked about problems that touched relatively few Ohioans—such as how his administration had improved the state's mental health and mental retardation programs. Rhodes pretty much ignored those kinds of things—the basic day-to-day responsibilities of state government. Instead, he charged that Gilligan's income tax had shortchanged Ohio's public schools and that government waste and mismanagement belied his claims of integrity and competence. His well-crafted television spots promised that a Rhodes administration would help Ohioans find jobs and get a good education but would otherwise leave them alone.

Of the Rhodes campaign, Gilligan said, "They spend money to put on television some of the best commercial advertisements telling people 'you've got to grab for everything you can get in this life.' All we've been saying the last four years is 'How about thinking a little about the elderly or the mentally retarded.' But it's like holding a candle in a wind tunnel."[17] Gradually, Rhodes crept up on Gilligan, who didn't help himself with wisecracks at the Ohio State Fair: "I shear taxpayers, not sheep," as he prepared to harvest some wool from a ewe for the TV cameras.[18]

Authors Tom Dudgeon and Dean Jauchius, two Rhodes loyalists (and full-time campaign staffers in 1974) detected working-class anger in the heartland. They later wrote that Rhodes understood "a bright thread of rage was running through most Ohioans," due in part to the burden of state income taxes and property taxes. "They were a phantom public," the authors said of financially stressed voters, "largely marginal or poor, and able to see a growing threat to their economic well-being."[19] William Russell Coil explained, "The key is not that Rhodes promised jobs. All politicians do that. Rhodes promised security. . . . Security . . . was crucial to Rhodes' conception of a working class Republican Party."[20]

Toward the end of the campaign, Gilligan and the state Democratic Party hauled out all of the material that had ever been used against Rhodes—allegations of unreported taxable income, personal use of campaign funds, parole of the aged Toledo mobster "Yonnie" Licavoli, and the Kent State shootings. They were aided by the release of a 235-page transcript of Rhodes's deposition in a $20 million civil lawsuit in U.S. District Court in Cleveland, in which Rhodes said, among other damning things, that General Sylvester Del Corso, commander of the Ohio National Guard, "wouldn't take an order" from him but had full authority and responsibility for decisions made that fateful day at the Kent State campus. "My operation was a little bit different than most governors," he said. He also said he did not "grasp" the import of Del Corso's public warning that the Guard would use "any force that is necessary even to the point of shooting."[21]

The Democrats tried to make hay out of those statements. They also tried to tar Rhodes with the tarnished image of Richard Nixon, who had resigned in disgrace earlier in the year over the Watergate scandal. "Jim Rhodes exists for the people of Ohio today on paid television commercials and mimeographed press releases," Pete O'Grady told a Democratic dinner in northwest Ohio. "That's how Richard Nixon campaigned in 1972."[22]

As the election neared, the polls narrowed and victory seemed within reach for the former Republican governor. "You can do one of three things," Rhodes said repeatedly. "Lead, follow, or get out of the way. We're going to win in November." His favorite song was "The Wabash Cannonball," but he crooned, "Back in the Saddle Again," at one Cleveland campaign stop. "The hardest thing about public life," he told a *Cleveland Press* reporter two weeks before the election, "is keeping your humbleness."[23]

But on November 5, election night, the early returns favored Gilligan, and Rhodes went to bed with his "humbleness" intact. "Helen had told Jim that day that it was the last time she was going to vote for him and he was not going to run again," former Republican state chairman Robert Bennett said of the mindset at the Rhodes household on Election Day.[24] To the dismay of close advisors, the former governor conceded shortly before 1:00 A.M. "I always try to be a good sport. The election is over," he told supporters. "Governor Gilligan has won it, and we're not going to discuss the past at all. I want to wish him well—he and his wife. . . . This is the night of calling off all hostilities."[25] His son-in-law Dick Moore had driven him home after those ill-considered remarks. On the way, Rhodes was already planning for a future out of politics. "He's talking about what he's doing the next day," Moore said. It was over. He had lost, or so he thought. The 1974 election was history.

Rhodes's long-time personal secretary Emma Scholz called Moore around 3:30 A.M. "She said, 'Dick have you got your TV on? He's won.'" Talk about a wake-up call. This was a shock. Although diehard Republican loyalists and party pros had not entirely given up—and Gilligan was wary about his projected victory—Rhodes really had thought it was over. He awakened to an apparent triumph of just over eleven thousand votes—less than one vote per precinct—and a third term. He prevailed against an incumbent Democratic governor, while across the nation other Republican candidates were buried in the anti-Watergate avalanche.

His family and close aides were jubilant. But Rhodes was not "overly excited" and took the good news in stride, Moore recalled. It was "not his style" to get too revved up after triumph, or to go into a funk after a setback.[26] Lose some, win some. "Concession is good for the soul," he said, wryly twisting another saying, when asked about his premature election night statement.[27] In fact, years later, he told a reporter he felt a little sorry for Gilligan.

A recount confirmed his election by 11,488 votes, sending a stunned Gilligan home to Hamilton County. He had failed to inspire. He had not even energized his political base. Gilligan carried heavily Democratic Cuyahoga County by a mere 87,000 votes—falling well short of the 100,000 to 150,000–vote margin Democrats believed they needed in Greater Cleveland to carry the state. Nancy Lazar Brown of East Cleveland—a twenty-three-year-old Socialist Workers' Party candidate with a surname magical in Ohio politics—drew 95,000 votes, most of which likely would have gone to Gilligan and reelected him. Gilligan's support among minority voters and organized labor fell off. Any doubts that labor had defected were erased in the mind of John T. Kady, UPI's Columbus bureau chief: when he called the Cleveland AFL-CIO office for a morning-after comment, the phone was answered, "Rhodes headquarters!"[28]

Years later, political analysts still struggled to make sense of Rhodes's improbable victory. "When Gilligan wasn't looking, his inept campaign staff literally handed the election to Rhodes, whose safe conduct through the campaign was superbly handled by a TV ad agency that saw little reason to expose the often unintelligible Rhodes in their rips at Gilligan," former *Akron Beacon Journal* reporter Abe Zaidan wrote in 2011. ("The word of the day was 'put the message in the ads and hide the candidate in the basement.'[29])

Bud Crowl was not entirely wrong about the fate of the Ohio Republican Party. Rhodes had no coattails. As a party-builder, he was at best inconsistent. Only one other Republican won statewide in a nonjudicial contest—longtime incumbent Secretary of State Ted W. Brown, who defeated state senator Tony Hall of Dayton, despite being pursued for much of the campaign by a Hall volunteer in a chicken suit. (That was supposed to embarrass Brown for his refusal to identify individual contributors to a $25-a-box chicken luncheon that raised $158,000 for the Republican's campaign.)

More importantly, young Democratic state representative Richard Celeste of Lakewood, a Yale graduate and Rhodes Scholar, upset longtime incumbent Republican John Brown in the lieutenant governor's race. Dick Celeste, the new lieutenant governor, soon emerged as the Democrats' 1978 gubernatorial candidate in waiting.

CHAPTER 8

The Third Term

DIVIDED GOVERNMENT

JAMES A. RHODES RETURNED to power in January with an Inaugural Ball held at a favored, if inelegant, venue: a drafty building at the Ohio State Fairgrounds, his home away from home every August. "He is endowed with more energy and imagination than any man I have known in my life. . . . He attacks each task like it's pure pleasure," said Roy Martin, his admiring patronage chief.[1]

But the startup in 1975 was anything but pleasurable. Rhodes, with only one lung, due to his childhood illness, caught a bad cold at the inaugural on a blustery January day. He stayed home fighting the bug for about three weeks.

Rhodes and his wife had not moved back into the Governor's Mansion in suburban Bexley, preferring their contemporary Upper Arlington home, on the other side of the county. He had made a deal with Helen—he would run for office again, but they would stay home if he triumphed. Rhodes was respectful of women—but in an old-fashioned way, at least by the standards of the 1970s. Author Coil explained: "Rhodes often joked that at home, 'The women are in charge.' The comment had a patronizing quality to it, suggesting that Rhodes allowed women authority only in their proper sphere. Rhodes, however, was quite serious. Women had been steadfast in his life whereas men had abandoned him. . . . Fellow politicians, mostly men, were fickle, opponents one day, allies the next, out of office the following week." That wasn't the case with his mother, wife, or daughters.

In 1963, when Rhodes was inaugurated for his first term, "he came home and he was all excited and he had this grin on his face and [Helen] said: 'Jim, you may be governor and the boss of this state, but in this house, I'm the boss and that's the way it's gonna stay,'" daughter Suzanne explained. "Daddy agreed with that. He said okay." Visitors to the four-bedroom wood-and-brick dwelling found that Helen was indeed in charge and Rhodes meekly followed her orders. He was no handyman and once accidentally broke a window with a hammer in a failed attempt to carry out one of his wife's commands to hang a fixture. Helen handled most of the discipline with the girls and usually drove the family Cadillac, with Rhodes slumped in a back seat. Dinner was served at 5:30 P.M. sharp, at least in the early years, and all family members were required to attend.

"Don't be in a hurry to get home," the governor often advised reporters. "The fight can't start until you get there." In truth, he loved his wife and was content in his family life, even if he did get bossed around some of the time.[2]

"The only thing Jim Rhodes loved as much as his beloved state was his own family," his rival Dick Celeste once said. "Perhaps for him, they were one and the same."[3] But for perspective, it must also be said that his home life was segregated from his public life. Helen rarely appeared at official events and spent most of the winter months in Fort Lauderdale, Florida, at a beachfront condominium on the Gault Ocean Mile, which Rhodes bought in 1976 for $144,300. Even his daughters seldom showed up for government functions.

In Columbus that first winter back in office in 1975, after Rhodes kicked his cold, he was his old, impatient self. Roy Martin wasn't wrong about his friend's energy: when the new governor returned to work in late January, it was go-go-go during the compressed workday that started early and often wound down in the late afternoon. First, Rhodes redesigned the governor's suite in the Statehouse by removing an open common area at the entrance and cutting off easy access to reporters. The Gilligan administration, which issued daily schedules for the governor and had a well-staffed press office, had spoiled the press corps. "We wanted a more orderly administration," said coauthor Lee Leonard, who covered Rhodes for United Press International and later the *Columbus Dispatch*. "They [Rhodes's staff] didn't know what he was going to do [day-to-day] and he didn't either. He was winging it."[4]

The gruff Martin was back, camped out in a cold, dark corner office. So too were John McElroy, Richard Krabach, Gordon Peltier, Robert Teater, Howard Collier, and James Duerk, the last named development director after having served as Rhodes's campaign press secretary. There was one woman in the cabinet, sixty-nine-year-old Helen Evans, at Industrial Relations. She was one of two African Americans; the other was former Ohio State All-American and Cleveland Browns standout Bill Willis, at the Ohio Youth Commission. Along with the old guard, Rhodes also hired the *Columbus Dispatch*'s respected political reporter, Chan Cochran, as his press secretary. "If we win this thing, I want you to come over with us," he had told Cochran during the race. The thirty-something reporter, who subjected Rhodes to the same tough scrutiny that Gilligan got, didn't take the off-hand job feeler seriously. But he accepted when the governor-elect repeated it after the election. Soon Rhodes also brought in as an aide a young attorney, Tom Moyer, a moderating influence on the Columbus School Board during a federal court trial that led to a desegregation order after Moyer's tenure. Many of the old guys were back, but Rhodes had the wisdom to sprinkle his staff with younger assistants—men in their thirties, like Moyer, Fred Mills, and Robert Howarth, who could relate to the maturing baby boom generation.

When a prayer-in-schools crusader named Rita Warren camped out in the Statehouse Rotunda, demanding the governor and legislature take action to permit praying in classrooms, Moyer was dispatched to defuse the situation. "We are the children of God," Warren yelled at Moyer. "We're all children of God," the young aide answered politely, as neutral onlookers nodded approvingly. Rhodes never would have confronted a shrill activist such as "Rita Rotunda," as she was nicknamed. He still avoided conflicts and distractions, even if he did roar and put on a show now and then. "He'd be giving someone a hard time, and he'd look over at you and wink," said aide William W. Wilkins.

The governor, Moyer said to a reporter, "is the first to recognize that he needs people around him who can literally slow him down."[5] Or speed him up, in some instances. He wanted to stay in touch with young folks in a hurry to make their marks—the baby boomers, with their wide ties and informal manners. Craig Zimpher, thirty when he came on as a deputy assistant for policy development, said "Rhodes had a strong desire to remain fresh, to remain young. The young people around him sort of invigorated him, refreshed him."

Rhodes was often criticized for doing little in the way of grooming successors for elective office. And few of his young staff assistants ever ran for anything after leaving his administration. But Zimpher and another youthful colleague, the lanky, dark-haired Jon Kelly, saw a more subtle style of nurturing in the governor's office. "I think he really wanted to groom a new generation of leadership [on policy]," Kelly said. "He liked to be surrounded by young people. He always wanted new ideas." Rhodes believed loyalty was owed down the ranks as well as upward, according to Zimpher: "He did not keep us tied down."[6] That is not to say the young guys had free rein. When Mills got too chatty with a reporter, Martin scolded him. "Are you running for office?" Martin barked. "I don't want to see your name in the paper again."[7]

Mills went on to serve as Ohio Superintendent of Banks; in 2012 he was named to the Ohio Constitutional Modernization Commission where he headed the Legislative and Executive Branch Committee. Kelly served on the Public Utilities Commission of Ohio; Craig Zimpher was eventually promoted to head the Ohio Industrial Commission, dealing with workers' compensation issues, and thirty years after leaving Rhodes, he returned to public service as chairman of the State Employment Relations Board.

As he settled in, Rhodes kept a close eye on the departments of development and transportation and the Office of Budget and Management. The rest of the agencies were supposed to run themselves under these broad guidelines: "Don't steal, don't drink on the job, and don't screw the help."[8] After Rhodes laid down the law, Helen Evans reportedly piped up, "Don't worry, governor, I won't."

Early in the term, Teater, who was installed at the Department of Natural Resources, showed up at the governor's office with a list of eight priority issues. "I thought I better go brief the governor on these. . . . Emma [Scholz] set up an appointment. I go down and I am sitting there, and get to about number three, he says, 'What are you doing?' I said, 'Well, I've got these things I am working on. I am making decisions on them, I wanted to be sure it was all right with you.' He said, 'Get out there and run the department. If there is something wrong, I'll let you know.' That was his management style."[9] Aide Bill Wilkins said of the agencies, "He just didn't want to see anything bad come out of there. He was all over the ones he was interested in."[10]

C. Luther Heckman, chairman of the Public Utilities Commission of Ohio (PUCO), saw the Rhodes style up close. "He knew nothing about public utility regulation, and he didn't want to [know]. He would say, 'I'm gonna tell you to do something, but if you don't think it's right, don't do it.'" Rhodes told him that he adopted his management style from one of his Democratic predecessors, Frank J. Lausche. "I appoint these guys," Rhodes confided. "I own 'em. But I don't tell 'em what to do. They're on their own."

That way, the governor had deniability if an appointee made a mistake. "He knew what he was doing," Heckman said.[11]

So Rhodes, the manager, wanted qualified people taking care of the details in his departments. But those people were not necessarily in the loop when it came to broad policy-making decisions. Even Teater, a confidant, sometimes learned of tentative plans for changes at state parks after an impromptu Rhodes pronouncement or trial balloon. "Rhodes was great at compartmentalizing," said John Mahaney, a skilled lobbyist who ran the Ohio Council of Retail Merchants. "It was like this big wall filled with pigeonholes. That way, nobody knew how to build the Atomic Bomb. He had thirty people who knew something about it, but nobody knew everything about it. Rhodes was intuitive. He had a great stomach [gut] that told him things. He was a common guy. He knew what the people liked. He had a feel for the public. Whatever else you think about the guy, his heart was in the right place."[12]

He was still an early-to-bed, early-to-rise governor, but crawling into the sack didn't mean he slept much or stopped working. Insomniac Rhodes, in pajamas, would lounge on his bed, yellow legal pads and documents spread on a blanket, working the phones into the wee hours. "He would call all over the state: factory workers, farmers, businessmen," said aide Robert Howarth.[13] "He would call you in the middle of the night and start talking in the middle of a sentence," said Wilkins. "He was the most creative guy I ever knew. He would come up with ideas you thought were crazy but turned out to be brilliant."[14] Terry Casey, a consultant who once ran the Franklin County (Columbus) Republican organization, said Rhodes telephoned his highly regarded pollster Bob Teeter in Detroit one Christmas morning just to gab about politics.[15]

Despite his informal manner and empathy for the "common guy," he always wanted to look the state's chief executive—rarely appearing tieless or even in shirtsleeves. But the somber blue suits of his first two terms were replaced by three-piece outfits with wider lapels and shades of pastel. The skinny ties and white shirts with stickpin collars from his 1960s wardrobe disappeared. "It was the mid-seventies and he . . . had the fashions of the day," said Leonard. His hair, a bluish silver, was a little longer, and his sideburns crept downward. His taste in food was still pedestrian—canned tomato soup his preference for an in-office lunch—but he glommed onto some healthy eating fads. For a while, he nearly drove his staff nuts with a cabbage-eating binge. He got on a Quaker Oats jag once and would throw a handful of dry rolled oats into his mouth, sending flakes flying through the air, the loose ones sticking to his lips. He thought they would help prevent cancer.

In Cincinnati in the summer of 1975, a jovial Rhodes hosted the annual Midwestern Governors Association conference, serving his fellow governors single-cheese, double-cheese, all manner of burgers, from . . . Wendy's. He wasn't timid about promoting his fast food investment, although he put his business interests in a blind trust, which Don Hilliker controlled.

There was one troubling sign in the Rhodes inner circle. John McElroy, his quiet, straight-talking administrative assistant, resigned a couple of months into the term with no explanation, other than that he was past retirement age and felt "saturated with minutia." In truth, McElroy left because he was losing influence. Rhodes, with pent-up energy after four years on the sidelines, was charging down the field with little patience for "if"s, "and"s, and "but"s. Rhodes's adversaries respected McElroy as a voice of reason, and the news media, appreciative of his accessibility, still valued him. Rhodes said little at the time, but the departure was a huge loss.

Moyer, who succeeded him, said McElroy left because he "didn't have enough authority, influence and didn't want to push papers. I think John could see he wasn't going to have that control over the governor that he had before," Moyer said in an interview. Rhodes's attitude was "I won this on my own," and "I've got things I want to do."[16]

Keith McNamara, a Columbus lawyer who served in the legislature during Rhodes's first two terms, said the "graybeards" who surrounded the governor—McElroy, Collier, Krabach, and others—were more than willing to tell Rhodes he was full of it when they thought his ideas wacky. The newer, younger aides, such as Moyer and Wilkins, who eventually succeeded Collier at the Office of Budget and Management, were smart and well intentioned but less likely to say no to a political legend like Governor James Allen Rhodes.[17]

The genial McElroy's departure would also make it easier for Rhodes's political foes to cast the governor as a mean-spirited partisan. For all his good humor, progressive nature, and interest in working with Democrats, he remained a polarizing figure. Rhodes was still a tough-talking, welfare-bashing, Democrat-belittling, anti-environment, Washington-hating Republican. "My way or the highway" was his unspoken credo as he settled in for his third term.

Governor Rhodes's ways would not go unchallenged, however. Working-class voters may have supported him at the polls, but labor leaders—from

Warren Smith, head of the million-member state AFL-CIO, to Ohio Education Association master lobbyist John Hall—considered him a political enemy. Rhodes often tried to go over their heads, promising factory jobs to blue-collar workers and extra contract bonuses to teachers. "All we're trying to do is create jobs," he said as an explanation for virtually every item on his agenda. "We want you to graduate with a diploma in one hand and a job in the other" was another bromide aimed at students and their parents.

At the Statehouse, the first order of legislative business was a bid for approval of three bond issues designed to unleash a wave of state-aided building projects, ranging from mass transit to housing to domed stadiums. He also sought tax abatements for businesses that agreed to expand in urban areas. At an early-morning news conference—so as to lead the front page of the afternoon *Columbus Dispatch*—Rhodes announced his $4 billion plan, which he said would create tens of thousands of jobs and make Ohio recession-proof. Financing would come from billions of dollars in bonded debt.

Rhodes never had a problem with the vision thing. "I want action and I want action now," he demanded of the legislature. "Give me the tools to fight crime, unemployment and welfare. We will make the dirt fly on construction jobs this year!"[18]

Not so fast, governor.

Before he left, wise man McElroy privately held that the bond issues were overly ambitious. So did a majority in the General Assembly, then under Democratic control in both the House and Senate. The legislature was no longer the compliant group Rhodes had manhandled when McNamara was in the Ohio House. Its new leaders thought the scheme way too extravagant and suggested a compromise, scaling it back as a means of attracting support from unions. Some estimates said the thirty-year bonds would push the state's indebtedness to $10.8 billion. One $2.5 billion bond issue was so loaded with costly goodies for cities that it was dubbed the "Christmas Tree." It was to be financed in part by a .7 percent increase in the sales tax—this from a politician who had made "No New Taxes" a campaign battle cry. The two other issues were aimed at housing and transportation needs—the latter to be partly paid off with a small boost in the state gasoline tax. Rhodes was so used to getting his way in the General Assembly that he would not compromise on any of his big tickets. So the legislature refused to approve the "recession-proof" package for consideration on the June ballot that year.

Part of the problem was that Rhodes had a powerful new opponent in House Speaker Vernal G. Riffe Jr., an insurance agent from New Boston, a dusty little town on the Ohio River. Vern Riffe was a moderate conservative, who spoke with the same Southern Ohio twang as the governor and could have just as easily been a Republican, had he been born a couple of counties over. When he first arrived in Columbus, he sported a bow tie and a flattop haircut. He drank Canadian Club, spoke of his southern Ohio neighbors affectionately as "hillbillies"—and liked Rhodes personally. But Riffe's father, Vernal Riffe Sr., was a political legend in Democrat-leaning Scioto County, where he served as county commissioner and held a number of political posts. As a consequence, Vern Jr.—or "June" as he was called in the hill country—was a loyal, partisan Democrat. The governor learned that the hard way, during the bond issues debate in the legislature.

But once Rhodes latched on to an idea, he was not easily dissuaded. After getting slapped down, he decided to bypass the legislature and take his four "eeshues" directly to the people, petitioning to put them on the statewide ballot as initiatives. No governor in memory had attempted such an audacious move, and Rhodes's troops successfully collected the required signatures. "In his battle with the legislature, he has won the battle with the people," said McGough, the Ohio Republican chairman and a close advisor.

Rhodes believed he had that kind of popular support, so he formed a group called Ohioans for Jobs and Progress and launched another campaign to persuade voters his bond issues were silver bullets for the state's employment and infrastructure needs. "Rhodes refuses to speak ill of anyone, denies any disappointment over his legislative setbacks, and proclaims, 'We're right on schedule,'" the *Dayton Daily News* reported.[19]

But again, he lost. A coalition of labor unions, education lobbies, and Democratic activists countered his $2 million campaign, arguing the issues were too costly and would incur too much debt. Lieutenant Governor Celeste joined the fray against the issues. They went down by a 4–1 count. "We gathered more signatures on petitions than we got votes in November," sighed McNamara.[20] Rhodes wasn't able to close this deal, even though his reputation as an energetic promoter was such that journalist Thomas Suddes once said he "could have sold Dale Carnegie's salesmanship course to Carnegie himself."[21]

Before the year was out, he was in another battle with the legislature—this one over "unvoted" increases in real estate taxes, a stream of revenue going to school districts and local governments. Angry, shouting property owners from northeast Ohio rallied outside the Statehouse for lower taxes, rattling the windows of the governor's office with their demonstration. Rhodes tried to freeze property taxes for two years in counties undergoing reappraisals, using the Ohio Board of Tax Appeals as his administrative instrument. But the Democratic-controlled legislature, which passed House Bill 920, its own version of tax relief, overruled him. That bill, designed to hold property taxes in check without shortchanging schools, became law without the governor's signature.

Rhodes further aggravated legislative leaders when he line-item vetoed 120 sections of the 1976–77 budget after the General Assembly approved it. "That was really where the fight started between the governor and Vern and [state senate leader] Oliver Ocasek," said Bob Howarth, then assistant to Collier in the Office of Budget and Management.[22]

The head buttings continued. The next round was an attempt by Democrats to overturn a twenty-eight-year-old law barring public-employee strikes, a priority for organized labor. Rhodes vetoed the legislation, and Republicans found enough votes to sustain him, just as they had with the budget vetoes.

But the game of hardball was being played at great cost. Rhodes's own initiatives were going nowhere, and his relationship with the Democratic majority was in tatters. Governor Jim was struggling. Democrats, emboldened by the failure of Rhodes's bond issues, resented the governor's heavy-handed tactics and reluctance to compromise. The state senate, with a 21–12 Democratic majority, had the power to override a gubernatorial veto, and Riffe's House was only one vote short of being veto-proof, with a 59–40 Democratic majority. "We intend to see, so far as we can, that the party has a role to play in enunciating policy and waving the banner of operating, if you will, a shadow government in exile," former governor Gilligan said shortly after the gubernatorial election. "There is a lot we can do, and I don't propose to withdraw in self-imposed exile, wrap myself in a toga and withdraw to a mountain some place."[23]

In the House, Riffe had chosen another tough-minded southern Ohioan, Myrl Shoemaker, to chair the all-important Finance Committee, where he kept tabs on the governor's spending. Shoemaker lived in the tiny Ross County town of Bourneville, just down the road from a burg called Knockemstiff. He wasn't going to be intimidated by a Jackson County boy. Rhodes's relations with the legislature were at a low point, and an increasingly adversarial Statehouse press corps pursued him, once cornering him in Atlanta after he slipped out of Columbus, unannounced, to attend a meeting of Wendy's International stockholders. Rhodes told the *Akron Beacon Journal* that he used personal funds to pay for the trip.

Rhodes's mercurial behavior both confounded and amused political rivals and reporters. It was still hard to keep up with him, but the governor was no longer winging it. He set the agenda and didn't let the media set the agenda—or tried not to let the media set it.

Ohio Public Radio reporter Bill Cohen sought to pin him down one September day in 1976 on a new mandatory seatbelt law.

> *Cohen:* Governor, are you in favor of the new seatbelt law?
>
> *Rhodes:* I haven't given it any thought. I thought it was the law.
>
> *Cohen:* It is. Do you favor it or not?
>
> *Rhodes:* I don't know. I put on a seatbelt every time. I'm following the law.
>
> *Cohen:* Do you think it should be the law?
>
> *Rhodes:* I don't know. I haven't asked anybody . . .
>
> *Cohen:* Some people want to repeal the seatbelt law. Do you think that's a good idea?
>
> *Rhodes:* Put it on the ballot.
>
> *Cohen:* You've told the crowd here, if you can't answer the questions get out of the business. Let me try one more time. Are you for the seatbelt law, or are you against it?
>
> *Rhodes:* . . . I'll explain it to you for the fifth time. It is the law on the books. As the governor, I have to enforce the law. If they want it changed they have to go to the secretary of state to get a ballot that complies with the state statute, get the signatures . . . and put it on the ballot.[24]

Rhodes, not wishing to pick a quarrel with automobile manufacturers or safety-conscious consumers, had shamelessly obfuscated on a simple question about a law already in the Ohio Revised Code.

At the opening of the Ohio State Fair the following summer, he wasn't able to dodge when an antiwar activist named Steve Conliff hurled a banana cream pie at him, partially splattering his face. Lingering bitterness over the Kent State shootings inspired the attack, which left the governor unharmed, if a bit sticky.

Rhodes wasn't above breaking his own rules of the road, either. In his delayed 1976 State of the State speech, he ignored the one about not picking fights with the legislature: he threw a tirade directed at Democratic lawmakers seated before him in the Ohio House of Representatives chamber. "Don't go back to your districts and say, well, I've done all I can do," he lectured them. "You've done nothing—nothing in the way of creating jobs for Ohioans."[25] Riffe and other Democratic leaders, like Shoemaker and Ocasek, were incensed. Two sides were attempting to govern in Columbus, and they were at an impasse.

The world and Ohio were changing. But Rhodes was still chasing smokestacks and repeating his mantras: "Profit is not a dirty word. . . . All social ills among able-bodied Ohioans come from the lack of a job."

Wilkins remembered the months of confrontation and finger-pointing in 1975 and 1976 as a "terrible time." "It turned out people didn't like it," he said of the feuding. "[We realized] we've got to get something done."[26] It got so bad that Ohio's governor was reduced to giving his next major speech—intended for the legislature—that September in the Rotunda of the Statehouse before an audience made of government workers, GOP lawmakers, lobbyists, and the general public. Demonstrators, protesting his planned cuts in Medicaid and welfare benefits, heckled him loudly.

It was an election year, and the presidential candidates were buzzing Ohio. But Rhodes was no longer taken seriously as a national figure in political circles outside of the state. The Kent State tragedy and his loss to Taft in the 1970 senate race reduced his stature. And he turned sixty-seven in September. That didn't mean presidential candidates ignored Rhodes or took him lightly, however—far from it. He was the governor of a major state, and the road to the White House still ran through Ohio. Rhodes liked to leave the impression he was blasé about presidential politics. And sometimes, when he had little at stake, he was. In August the *Plain Dealer* observed that at the Republican National Convention in Kansas City, "finding a golf partner was one of Gov. James A. Rhodes' biggest concerns."[27] Rhodes always liked the earthy Lyndon Baines Johnson but didn't care for Richard Nixon. After Nixon's resignation, Rhodes backed his successor, Gerald Ford of Michigan, and yet when pressed, readily admitted he had not read his own party's 1976 platform. "The Democrats said I wasn't fit to sleep with hogs. The Republicans defended me and said I was," he wisecracked about his standing in party politics.[28]

Rhodes ally Keith McNamara ran Ford's Ohio campaign, while an outsider, Massachusetts-based Dan Horgan, led the Carter team.[29] McNamara couldn't stop the tide. With Watergate still fresh in many voters' minds, a big Democratic year was in the making. Ford's pardon of Nixon hurt the GOP cause, and Rhodes saw his friend Nelson Rockefeller dumped from the ticket. Come November, Democrat Jimmy Carter narrowly carried Ohio and was elected president. Speaker Riffe picked up three more Ohio House seats in the legislative elections, giving him a 62–37 veto-proof majority. Both the House and state senate now had Democratic majorities that could override Rhodes's vetoes if the opposition party stuck together. "The people of Ohio have spoken, and I will abide by their wishes," Rhodes said in a perfunctory statement the day after the election.[30]

That was the bottom. Rhodes and his team knew something had to change. Quietly, he began to rebuild his relationships with Democratic leaders in the General Assembly. It's up to the governor, Riffe had remarked. "We went through the healing period," Howarth explained.

How did he do it? He tried to pick them off one by one.

Rhodes talked with Myrl Shoemaker about placing a new state park and lodge in his district—setting aside a collection of reclaimed farm fields in a place called Deer Creek. Subsequently, Teater met privately with Shoemaker to devise a plan. "I said, 'We'll build the lodge if you [legislators] get the money,'" Teater told Shoemaker, who was still running the Finance Committee. "We made a deal." After it became reality, a critic asked Shoemaker if his new park was a pork-barrel project. Shoemaker, who kept a dog-eared Bible on the corner of his desk, wasn't offended. "Myrl thought for a minute," Teater recalled, "and he says, 'Well, no, it wasn't pork barrel, it was top sirloin.'"[31]

Rhodes gave hope to another Riffe lieutenant, state representative Patrick Sweeney, telling him the government in Columbus might get behind a Lake Erie state park, complete with a sand beach on the lakefront in the city of Cleveland. "I love the guy," Sweeney told Statehouse reporter Bob Miller. "If the grass needs [to be] cut along the highways of my district, all I do is call. It gets done the next day."[32] One unidentified former Rhodes aide told a news service reporter, "You ask for a grain of sand and he gives you a beach."[33]

Teater said Rhodes "made politics into a great science. He didn't mean to do that, but he did that. He thought strategically. He knew when to work with the opposite party. He knew how to work with them. He befriended them, and he knew how to handle the press."[34]

Most important, Rhodes wanted to get close to Riffe. "He called me over one day," John Mahaney said. "He said, 'John-O, we've got to take over the Speaker.' And I said, 'Well that's what I would do if I were you, governor.' And the son of a bitch did it! Took over Vern. They became so close, unbelievable."[35] With Riffe, "it was a game," Wilkins said. "They co-opted each other. He would win one, and Vern would win one."[36] Riffe, of course, did not agree that he had been taken over by Rhodes or anyone else. When it came to playing politics, or poker, he played hard and shared his strategy with only a trusted few. Publicly he pointed to his father's maxim: "Son, do the right thing for your state and your country, and it will be the right thing for the party."[37]

Making new friends in the legislature was essential, but after his rocky beginning, Rhodes also needed an issue to latch onto—and 1977 would give him one, as Ohio headed into its coldest winter in decades. On January 16, temperatures dropped to twenty below in some parts of the state, and natural gas supplies ran low, panicking utilities. The previous year, Rhodes had predicted the looming natural gas crisis. Now, he would take command and manage matters as they played out.

Rhodes was in Washington attending the Carter inauguration when aides urged him to use a new law to declare an "energy emergency," as temperatures dipped well below zero. The problem was acute in the Dayton area where dwindling supplies at the Dayton Power & Light electric company persuaded PUCO chairman Heckman and Rhodes energy advisor Bob Ryan to "close Dayton." Residents were asked to don warm clothes indoors, turn down thermostats, dim lights, and limit use of electrical appliances. Public schools were told to shut down for thirty days, and retail businesses were ordered to limit hours of operation. The unprecedented action created a furor in Montgomery County. Ohio attorney general William J. Brown advised the governor that he did not have the authority to shut down a city, short of declaring a full-scale "energy crisis." Rhodes rushed back to the state, acknowledged a misunderstanding, and lifted Heckman and Ryan's "emergency" order. He asked instead for voluntary conservation measures.

Quickly, the governor called Riffe and other lawmakers from both parties to his office for weekend meetings and dispatched emergency help—food, shelter, volunteers, and supplies—to hard-hit areas. He ordered PUCO to make certain that power companies did not turn off the heat on low-income families that had fallen behind on monthly bills. It all played out as a team effort. Rhodes set up an energy crisis center with a hotline in his office suite, and he asked Carter to take all possible steps to help Ohio. The governor presided over a prayer service in the Statehouse rotunda the next weekend. Temperatures gradually moderated, and the crisis eased.

Although he visited Texas and Oklahoma scouting for natural gas supplies, Rhodes insisted all along the solution to the shortage was expanded use of coal—dirty, high-sulfur Ohio coal—to heat homes and power factories. He wanted to make it as clean-burning as natural gas and spent time promoting clean-coal technology. Coal seams could also hold gas reserves trapped in their shale, he said. Rhodes was prescient on some energy issues. He was right about the shale reserves; hydraulic fracturing of shale in Ohio, Pennsylvania, and other states produced a natural gas boomlet some three decades after Rhodes pushed for it. But he was flat-out wrong in believing that development of affordable clean-coal technology was imminent. By the second decade of the twenty-first century, a way to burn high-sulfur coal cleanly, cheaply, and efficiently on a scale broad enough to power a grid had yet to be found.[38] He was also wrong in scoffing at antipollution scrubber technology as inefficient in filtering out significant amounts of sulfur dioxide in the combustion process: the huge contraptions were costly to install at coal-fired plants, but they worked.

Later in 1977, there was more bad news. Youngstown Sheet & Tube closed its Campbell Works, idling forty-two hundred steelworkers. (Another eight hundred lost their jobs the following year at the company's Struthers plant.) It would only get worse. The seeds of decline had been planted years earlier, and time was running out on Ohio's Steel Valley. The sky would no longer turn red from the fumes pouring out of the mighty blast furnaces.

Most economists blamed the obsolescence of the aging plants and structural changes in the economy for the collapse of the steel industry. The big factories would give way to specialized steel made in smaller plants, they said. Rhodes would have none of it. He blamed the Carter administration and its Environmental Protection Agency (EPA), which he said forced the steel plants and other industries to shut down because of costly clean air regulations. Eastern states had complained that sulfur dioxide blowing their way from the tall stacks of coal-burning power plants in the Midwest was killing trees and fouling lakes. The pollution mixing with precipitation came down as acid rain.

But Democrat Brown, Ohio's attorney general during Rhodes's third and fourth terms, understood the vein the governor was tapping with his anti-EPA rhetoric. As a boy in the 1950s, "Billy Joe" Brown had sat on the roof of a relative's frame house in Steubenville in the late afternoon, peering up at the smoky sky and sniffing the acrid emissions from nearby steel plants. "It smelled good," Brown said. "It smelled like jobs."[39] Rhodes agreed, and he had a quick retort for anyone who claimed people were dying from Ohio's acid rain: "Name one."

Rhodes usually had a good sense of the hopes and fears of everyday Ohioans. He made progress with Democrats Riffe and Ocasek in the state legislature, but he didn't get anywhere with President Carter and got little help from Ohio's two U.S. senators, Democrats John Glenn and Howard Metzenbaum, the latter having defeated incumbent Senator Bob Taft Jr. in 1976.

No worry—Rhodes was looking beyond Washington for help. In Columbus, entertaining Japanese governors in the United States on a trade mission, he marched his charges to a Wendy's on High Street, a block from the Statehouse, where he purchased dozens of cheeseburgers, milkshakes, and orders of French fries. It was 10:30 A.M., but Rhodes commanded, "Eat! Eat! Eat!" and the bemused Japanese visitors complied.[40] Later, asked by reporters what they thought of their mercurial host, one of the Japanese summed him up this way: "Governor Rhodes, Governor Rhodes, go quick, go quick!"

Rhodes's long-term courtship of the Japanese would soon bear fruit, with new business and jobs for Ohio. In late 1977, Rhodes announced a spectacular "get" for the state: Honda Motors would build a motorcycle plant in a grassy meadow near Marysville in central Ohio, creating thousands of jobs. It was no surprise to Rhodes insiders. A couple of years earlier, officials at the Transportation Research Center, widely regarded as a white elephant, dating back to Rhodes's earlier stint in office, had noticed well-dressed Japanese men surveying the grounds. Roger Dreyer, director of the center—essentially a seven-and-a-half–mile oval designed as a test track in the middle of eighty-one hundred mostly flat acres—remembered his excitement when an aide called him in 1977 and exclaimed, "The Japanese are out there, wandering around." Had Rhodes done it again, Dreyer wondered—made lemonade from a lemon?[41]

The seed had been planted in Rhodes's second term. He had met Soichiro Honda during a trade mission to Japan in 1968, when Honda was mainly in the motorcycle business. The relationship grew two years later, when the two men played a round of golf during a break in a National Governors Association trek to Tokyo. "You'll sell most of your cars in America, so you should produce in America—and Ohio is the heart of America," Rhodes told his new golfing buddy. "I pointed out that Ohio was the nation's distribution center, located within 500 miles of two-thirds of the population and buying power of the U.S."[42]

When, in April 1976, Jim Duerk saw a wire service story reporting that Japanese automakers were considering building in the United States, the governor and his development chief hopped on a plane to Tokyo the next day. They met with executives of Honda, Toyota, and Nissan and decided to establish a State of Ohio trade office in Tokyo. As a potential site for a Honda plant, Rhodes suggested land in central Ohio near the Transportation Research Center. "At the start of their search for a location in the U.S., Honda's only choice was California. It had no knowledge of what Ohio was, or where it was located," said Fred Neuenschwander, development director during Rhodes first two terms. "It was through persistence that the governor and Mr. Honda became close friends. After many major discussions, both here and in Japan, Honda picked Marysville, Ohio. Of major importance in Honda's decision-making process was the accessibility of having the Ohio Transportation Research Center as a neighbor."[43]

Conveniently, a Rhodes supporter, an industrialist named Ralph Stolle, Hilliker's brother-in-law, owned most of the property adjacent to the Transportation Research Center, where Honda eventually would build its plant. Another pal, Howard Atha, head of the Worthington Oil Company, was granted oil and gas drilling rights on the site by the Research Center in 1976. The state would get royalties if gas was produced and sold.[44] Dreyer, who approved the agreement, said it was done by the book and cleared by the Ohio attorney general's office. Nothing was produced in the way of energy, and Worthington's Atha would deny Rhodes had anything to do with his deal with the Research Center. Atha eventually transferred the lease over to yet another Rhodes associate, E. C. Redman, who had been Rhodes's personal accountant. Atha made about $145,000 for drilling two test wells, both unsuccessful. Hilliker, H. Burkley Showe, and Hamilton County Republican chairman Earl T. Barnes also had the good fortune to own land near the site.

The landscape was also about to change on the political front. As 1978 approached, there was speculation that the governor might not seek reelection, though his close advisors knew better. House Minority Leader Charles Kurfess, a moderate Republican, announced he would run in the primary. Kurfess gambled, unsuccessfully, that Rhodes would retire. Lieutenant Governor Celeste was already well into organizing as the presumptive Democratic candidate. Rhodes was noncommittal in public but quietly reassembled his coalition: mainstream Republicans, conservative-leaning independents, and some bread-and-butter Democrats drawn by his emphasis on job creation.

During the Great Blizzard of 1978, Rhodes again called Democratic and Republican legislative leaders to his office. "Ohio is in trouble tonight," he said, as he set up a command post, complete with a security detail. Temperatures again dropped below zero, and activity in Ohio virtually ground to a halt under a blanket of two feet of snow, most of it falling on January 25–26. "It is a killer storm, searching for victims," Rhodes said, ordering more emergency measures to help stranded families and get the state moving again. Dozens perished.

Author Byrl R. Shoemaker, Rhodes's sympathetic biographer, said "Ohioans stranded in their homes saw on television a governor genuinely touched by their plight and doing all he could to help. . . . Critics charged that Rhodes capitalized on a crisis, even overstating its seriousness. Cynical reporters in the Statehouse Press Room fashioned fake badges, ostensibly for admission to Rhodes' perpetual press conferences. They said 'ENERGY PANIC.' The next time it snowed, one of the skeptics sniffed, 'It's a killer flurry looking for victims.'" Without doubt, Rhodes understood the political value of a striking photo opportunity or a telling sound bite. For instance, of other inclement weather, he famously repeated, "Blaming Ohio for acid rain is like blaming Florida for hurricanes."[45]

But aside from the bombast, his compassion for the people of his state was real. Reading a newspaper one morning a day or two into the blizzard, he saw a small story quoting the mayor of an ice-bound hamlet in Belmont County. "And the mayor of this little town said, 'Well, nobody will help us

In courting the Japanese auto industry, specifically Honda, Governor Rhodes took members of the Japanese Governors Association for an American lunch—at Wendy's, in which he held a large block of stock. "They want to know what we do," the governor said here, on October 22, 1975. "This is hamburger country." Rob Rhees, *Columbus Dispatch,* March 7, 2001.

because we are down here in this little town,'" recalled Tom Moyer, who was there. "I can still see him telling the trooper, or security guy, get the state plane. We're going down."

The Little Wheeling Creek had risen near Goosetown, Ohio, encasing several homes in an icy vice. "We are going to help those people," Rhodes told Moyer. Off he went, with a small entourage and some reporters in tow. "The creek had risen into this person's house, up to about right below our knees maybe, and then froze. Here's this little house—and this was just one of a number of them. He came in and he's saying, 'We are going to help you,'" Moyer said, describing one of the governor's house calls. "It was just an example of how he related to people. He really felt their pain. I would see examples of that, all through."[46]

Rhodes bombarded the White House with requests for disaster declarations and financial help with a massive snow-removal undertaking. Washington eventually agreed to pick up 75 percent of the cost of the blizzard cleanup. Rhodes even asked Carter to step in personally to help settle a mine strike called by the United Mine Workers of America. But it was March before miners went back to work.

In a time of crisis, Democrats like Riffe and Ocasek gave the governor high marks for his perseverance and hands-on leadership. "Time and time again he would reach across the divide to draw in even his harshest critics," said Moyer. "I remember Oliver [Ocasek] saying that he would be staying in his [Senate] office until the crisis was over, because 'the governor needs me.'"[47]

The snows receded; a February thaw gave way to spring and a ground-breaking for the Honda plant in central Ohio. Honda officials had not attended Rhodes's cheeseburger and Frosty brunch, but the governor offered the Japanese appetizing economic incentives to choose Ohio, including highway improvements and a rail spur. It was widely assumed that Honda also would also build automobiles in the area if the $37.5 million motorcycle plant prospered. At a grand ribbon-cutting ceremony, Rhodes brushed aside Honda's modest estimate that the motorcycle plant initially would employ fewer than one thousand Ohioans when the factory was completed. "No, no, no," Rhodes said. That just wouldn't do.

"There is extensive negotiation that takes place over a couple of days in which the Japanese send us this list, all the qualifications, if this happens and if the exchange rates are right, if, the sun shines, if, if, if, maybe in ten years we can get 2,000 jobs," Cochran said. "And Rhodes gets up at the news conference and says, 'and this move of Honda here is going to create two, five, 10,000 jobs. . . . [Shige] Yoshida's eyes were that big." Cochran spread his hands apart to describe the reaction of the future executive vice president of Honda North America. "Suddenly everyone is looking at Yoshida like, 'How did this happen?'"

Rhodes had exaggerated, stretching the information available. People vote for hope, he believed. Didn't Napoleon Bonaparte say, "A leader is a dealer in hope?" Honda's plant rose up from the plains of Union County later that year—the beginning of Honda's long, successful relationship with Ohio and its workers. Rhodes's wild guesstimate proved too conservative. By the turn of the century, the Honda work force in Ohio had peaked at nearly sixteen thousand. (By 2014, employment had slimmed to just under fourteen thousand.)[48]

In an election year, the embattled governor had delivered "Jobs and Progress." And he had the last laugh when it came to the once-ridiculed

Transportation Research Center, which eventually became a part of the Honda complex. Rhodes was on a roll. Shortly after Honda chose Ohio, Ford Motor Company, said it would build a new transmission plant in Batavia, just outside of Cincinnati. Rhodes's friends again were nearby. Barnes, Showe, Harold Flannery, and Horace Flannery (large contributors to his 1970 and 1974 campaigns) owned land near the proposed Ford factory.[49] Rhodes, of course, brushed aside reporters' questions about favoritism for his well-positioned pals. So be it, change the subject, and move on. He would endure the political flak, maybe lay low in the weed patch for a while, and then pop up and go forward again with another program. That was his pattern.

"He used to tell me, 'John-O, we all live on hope,'" lobbyist Mahaney said. "Rhodes had an instinct. All of this shit he said over and over, he believed. You can't get by with it as long as he did if you don't believe in it."[50] In good times and bad—to anyone who would listen—he bragged incessantly about his state, and by extension, himself. It came across as good-natured chauvinism. Ohio, he liked to say, had "more historical markers by accident than most states had on purpose"—whatever that meant.

"He had an ability to make Ohioans happy they were Ohioans," said McNamara, a key Republican legislator during Rhodes's second term.[51] The *Dayton Daily News* described him as part Elmer Gantry, part P. T. Barnum, and part Norman Vincent Peale.[52] Before the 1978 campaign was over, Dick Celeste would see all three personas—and he would become a "Rhodes Scholar" a second time.

CHAPTER 9

"Give It to Jim Again Since He Wants It. They Did!"

RHODES HAD WATCHED young Richard F. Celeste from over his shoulder for four years. Celeste, a Yale-educated Rhodes Scholar—a term with two meanings here—served as lieutenant governor between 1975 and 1979. His office was literally across the hall from Rhodes's corner suite. Burning with ambition, he was the oldest son in a well-known Lakewood Democratic family.

Celeste was the last person to serve as an independently elected lieutenant governor, holding no allegiance to the governor. Beginning in 1978, an amendment to the state constitution mandated that the governor and lieutenant governor be elected in tandem, so they could work as a team after the election. Celeste and Rhodes, however, had almost no contact on matters of substance. It was taken for granted almost from his 1975 swearing in that Celeste would be a candidate for governor in four years and that Rhodes, likely running for reelection, would be his opponent.

Celeste quickly got the message that there was no place in the Rhodes administration for an assistant governor. For nearly two months in 1975, he pressed for a private meeting with Rhodes to talk about an agenda for the lieutenant governor, whose only official duty was to preside over the Ohio Senate. "I called on him to offer whatever help I could since, as I put it, the people of Ohio in their wisdom elected both of us." Celeste finally got an eight-minute meeting with Rhodes that spring. He was prepared with talking points, detailing his ideas. "He listened to my rookie enthusiasm and then asked whether I played golf. 'No,' I answered, why did he ask? 'You should take it up,' he said. 'You are going to have plenty of time.'"[1]

Unlike Gilligan in 1974, Rhodes was not overconfident about his prospects for another term. Although he did not fully grasp the structural changes

gripping the economy, he knew the waves of plant shutdowns, energy short-
ages, and school closings were part of his record and limited his capacity
to roll out bold new programs as he had in the 1960s. The state's economy
was sluggish, and its cash-starved public schools desperately needed a new
financing system. "It became clear Mr. Rhodes would spend his remaining
time in office as a crisis manager," journalist Robert E. Miller wrote, assess-
ing the economic climate of the late 1970s. "Instead of spreading bricks and
mortar, like before, it would be a matter of keeping the state afloat. It would
be tough."[2] Rhodes also recognized that his young challenger had excellent
candidate skills and would run strong in vote-rich northeastern Ohio, where
Democrats easily outnumbered Republicans. Celeste's father, Frank, had been
a popular mayor in Lakewood.

With time on his hands, Celeste fulfilled the minimal responsibilities of
his office but otherwise started prepping for a 1978 campaign to capture the
office across the hall. He stayed in the public eye as one of the vocal leaders in the successful effort to defeat Rhodes's four economic issues on the
November 4, 1975, ballot. "We basically ran for governor for four years," said
Celeste advisor Gerald Austin.[3]

The 1977 off-year election went Rhodes's way. On November 8, Ohio
voters repealed an Election Day registration law that Democrats and labor
leaders had hoped would boost Democratic turnout. It was a small victory;
Rhodes had vetoed the original legislation, but the legislature overrode him.
Critics of the new law, most of them Republicans, petitioned to put it before
voters on the statewide ballot, arguing that same-day registration would
invite fraud. The governor, too, favored repeal, though he did not actively
campaign for it. The rollback was approved by a margin of more than seven
hundred thousand votes, killing so-called instant registration after its use
in one election—the one held to determine its own worthiness.

Rhodes began quietly rolling out his reelection machinery in the winter
of 1978. Soon enough, he was flying out of Columbus on the state plane
for early morning $50-a-plate breakfasts in such places as Newark, Lima,
and Zanesville. He traveled light, typically taking a press secretary and two
plainclothes highway patrolmen aboard a DC-3, dubbed *Buckeye I*. If donors
were looking for eggs Benedict, they were disappointed; even the high roll-
ers had to settle for tomato juice, toast, coffee, and a stump speech about
the governor's efforts to create jobs and the federal government's actions to
destroy them. "This is the only country in the world where 40 percent of the

legislation introduced is anti-business . . . what Congress giveth, Congress taketh away," he would say, warning against trusting in Washington. "That guy would make a hell of an auctioneer," one admirer said after a red-meat speech in Newark.[4]

After a few months of this, the official announcement of his candidacy was a mere formality. Rhodes wanted Cuyahoga County commissioner George V. Voinovich as his running mate for this first tandem-ticket election. The new system all but assured the candidates for the two top spots would campaign together, share a similar political persuasion, and identify with the same party. Voinovich had planned to run for Ohio auditor against the Democratic incumbent, Thomas Ferguson. So Cuyahoga County Republican chairman Robert Hughes, a Rhodes intimate, was tasked with feeling him out about a possible offer to join the ticket. "Rhodes wants you," Hughes told Voinovich, "but he won't call you unless he knows you're going to say yes."[5] Typical Rhodes. Never put yourself in the position of being obligated to the guy on the other side of the table, or of asking for something you're not already sure you can get.

Reporters chased rumors that Voinovich accepted the No. 2 spot on the condition that Rhodes would resign before the end of his term, meaning the lieutenant governor, by law, would become governor. Voinovich could then run in the 1982 gubernatorial election as an incumbent. Neither man explicitly denied the reports. "I generally don't answer questions with a yes or no," Rhodes told the Associated Press. Years later, Voinovich acknowledged he was aiming for the top job, but he said it was silly for anyone to think Rhodes would walk away from the governor's office before the end of his term. "I wanted to be governor. I thought I had a better chance of being elected and getting statewide exposure [by joining Rhodes's ticket]," he said in an interview. "No deals—Rhodes in no way would have given up."[6]

Voinovich did get a guarantee he would play a prominent role in the campaign, so he signed on as Rhodes's running mate. The governor welcomed his new friend from Cleveland by mispronouncing his last name, "Voin" becoming "Vawn." The Clevelander wasn't offended; he knew a big part of his job was to narrow Celeste's built-in margin in Greater Cleveland where the Voinovich name had strong voter recognition. But Rhodes also wanted to introduce his No. 2 man to downstate voters. "Vawnavitch! That's gonna do well in Cincinnati," he told him, "because they'll think you're a German."[7]

Before turning to the Celeste threat, the governor again had to deal with a dissenter inside the party. This challenger was Charles "Chuck" Kurfess, the longtime Ohio House Republican leader from Perrysburg, just south of Toledo. Kurfess naively thought that Rhodes, nearing his sixty-ninth birthday, might hang it up after a lifetime in politics. The colorful William Saxbe had taken himself out of the running in late 1976: "I quit a better job than that," he scoffed, referring to his stints as senator, U.S. attorney general, and ambassador to India.[8]

Rhodes feigned indifference. "Let 'em run! Let 'em all run!" he would shout, waving his arms, when asked about rivals like Kurfess. "We have no objections." Lobbyist John Mahaney, an informal Rhodes advisor, clarified: "When he said, 'We have no objections,' it meant the exact opposite: We have many objections. Of course he meant he had all kinds of objections."[9]

Few rallied to Kurfess's cause. Even so, when it became apparent that Rhodes would seek reelection, Kurfess stayed the course and met the incumbent head-on in the 1978 Republican primary. He named a political neophyte, Lucille G. Ford, an economist and college administrator from Ashland County, as his lieutenant governor candidate. And he scored endorsements from some young, independent GOP state lawmakers, such as Ben Rose of Lima and Saxbe's son, Rocky Saxbe of Mechanicsburg. Unable to raise significant money, however, the forty-eight-year-old Kurfess campaigned gamely but suffered from low name recognition and the lack of a defining issue. Similar to Rhodes, the likable Kurfess was a moderate Republican, and thus he ran neither to the left nor right of the incumbent governor. But he had a big problem with the party's conservative base: as House speaker he had helped former governor Gilligan create Ohio's first income tax in 1971.

In 1978, Kurfess demanded that Governor Rhodes make a full public accounting of his financial interests, including release of his income tax returns. If the governor had nothing to hide, Kurfess baited, why not release the information and let voters decide. But Rhodes said he would "comply with the ethics law of Ohio"—requiring only partial disclosure—and do no more. "What else is new?" the governor said dismissively. Kurfess said there were conflict-of-interest questions "about Rhodes's associates benefiting" from placement and location of new plants in areas where the governor's pals owned property. Rhodes didn't budge.[10]

The weekend before the primary, Kurfess claimed, "The nomination is there to be had. Now, we are close to having it in our grasp."[11] But his reach was not nearly long enough. Rhodes swamped him with 68 percent of the vote in the June primary. Rhodes had frustrated Kurfess by largely ignoring him during the campaign. But it didn't get personal, and the governor appeared in September at a debt-retirement picnic fund-raiser for Kurfess, near the banks of the Maumee. By the river, Rhodes made a rare reference to his wife, Helen, saying she advised him not to criticize Kurfess. "She told me, 'I don't want to run your campaign, but do me a favor, keep your mouth shut during the election.'"[12]

On the Democratic side, the forty-year-old Celeste had no major primary opposition. He surrounded himself with bright, young, idealistic campaign workers who saw him—a onetime Peace Corps volunteer in India—as a Kennedyesque figure. Because of their ardor and loyalty, reporters nicknamed them the "Celestials." Dick Celeste picked Franklin County commissioner Mike Dorrian—a stalwart of the old Columbus Democratic organization, nicknamed the Irish Mafia—as his running mate. Celeste's brain trust thought having Dorrian in the No. 2 spot would help the campaign in fast-growing Franklin County, a swing area.

Celeste's operation, run by his younger brother, Ted, belittled Rhodes as an old warhorse out of touch with changing times and unable to solve chronic state problems, such as funding for primary and secondary education. A number of local districts had been forced to close schools temporarily after voters refused to accept higher real estate taxes. Dozens more districts, anticipating shutdowns, asked to be audited. Ten, with levies on the November ballot, said they would have to close early for the Christmas holiday break if voters said no to property tax increases.

Celeste called for a complete overhaul of the financing system; Rhodes said he would pump more dollars into the existing equal-yield school financing formula. Neither provided details. In fact, the incumbent offered little that was new when discussing plans for an unprecedented fourth term. He ran on the standard Jim Rhodes jobs platform: tax breaks for businesses, day care centers next to trade schools, coal to meet energy needs, environmentalists as the enemies of capitalism. And his administration would help Ohio's elderly by "fighting loneliness."

The Celeste battle cry was "James Allen Rhodes—pack your bags!" First Lady Rosalynn Carter even joined in the chant at one boisterous rally in Columbus. Although Celeste did not focus on the governor's advancing age, Ted Celeste took to wearing a campaign button, depicting a "JAR" suitcase, with rumpled clothes popping out of the crease.

Rhodes, suspecting he would be out-pointed, refused to debate Celeste face-to-face. Instead, he just kept promising to create jobs, jobs, and more jobs: "All social ills among able-bodied Ohioans come from the lack of a job."[13] He blamed the Carter administration for Ohio's problems. Nothing new there. "Dull, isn't it," he said to a news-starved reporter in the closing weeks of the campaign.[14]

Rhodes saw Celeste, in his blue blazer and penny loafers, as an elite—a vestige of McGovernism and welfare-state liberalism. This was an image and ideology he was sure would not fly in Ohio. (In fact, many of Celeste's political aides were veterans of South Dakota senator George McGovern's energetic though unsuccessful 1972 presidential campaign in Ohio.) One close associate explained the governor's thinking:

> Jim Rhodes knows both intuitively and by experience that there are two kinds of liberalism in American politics. There is the New Deal version of the 1930s and 1940s, aimed at working Americans, which is based on jobs for all with government subsidies as necessary. And there is the 1960s version, the Great Society and War on Poverty, aimed at intellectual liberals and which is based on redistribution of wealth. Rhodes['s] own "Jobs and Progress" theme over the years was and is an obvious endorsement of the role of government in preventing and abating unemployment. From his substantial support of working Ohioans he also knew that the second kind of liberalism, which is often seen by working men and women as actually subsidizing and perpetuating joblessness, is not a popular political conviction in Ohio.[15]

Rhodes courted "Reagan Democrats" before the media made up the term to refer to Reagan's support among Catholics, ethnic minorities, and rank-and-file trade unionists. Voinovich, a devout Catholic who came from Democratic stock, was supposed to make deeper inroads for the ticket in ethnic communities in northern Ohio. He also made the rounds to news-paper editorial boards across Ohio, because in many cases the governor wouldn't. Voinovich said one of the editors told him, "'Jim Rhodes is a liar.' I said, with a smile on my face, 'You might be right. But would you rather have somebody who makes a thousand promises and keeps 500 of them, or a guy who makes 500 promises and keeps 250 of 'em?'"[16]

People vote for hope—that's what Rhodes believed and had always counted on in his campaigns. Get yourself elected by talking about the future, then do the best you can once you take office. A political analyst watching the campaign (but not identified in a newspaper interview) elaborated for re-porters: "Jim Rhodes says, 'You've got to give people hope.' Rhodes knows it's not what you've done, but what you are going to do."[17]

Celeste was frustrated by Rhodes's say-just-about-anything style of cam-paigning and his refusal to debate face to face. He was determined not to let his foe get away with a broken-promises strategy. "Jim Rhodes will not stand side by side with me to defend his record of broken promises, or to discuss how Ohio is to meet the challenge of keeping our schools open, or to describe how we can reform the Public Utilities Commission of Ohio," Celeste said in fundraising letter. "Rhodes is a serial promise breaker."[18] Maybe Celeste would be out-promised, but he was a fast learner. In the early 1970s, when Celeste and other cocky, young urbanites—like Patrick Sweeney of Cleveland and Art Wilkowski of Toledo—hit the Statehouse, they expected to bulldoze the legislature's old cornstalk brigade. But the city boys soon found the Vern Riffes and Myrl Shoemakers already entrenched in Columbus to be formidable politicians. Celeste and his young colleagues "studied the ways of Rhodes and Riffe and other old-school pols, particularly the southern Ohioans," Jerry Austin said. "They had never seen anything like this."[19]

By 1978, Celeste knew what he was up against. The old guys, Rhodes included, knew how to get—and use—power in Columbus. He also knew his history: it is hard for a first-time statewide candidate to win in diverse Ohio—especially in a race for governor. Celeste had run statewide once be-fore—getting elected lieutenant governor—but competing for that low-profile post was in no way comparable to a gubernatorial campaign. (Rhodes had learned how hard a first-time bid for governor could be in 1954, in his failed contest against Governor Frank Lausche.) Run once and lose honorably, then come back stronger. That had been the playbook. It was up to Celeste to beat the odds with some bold moves. The test would be to construct a plan for financing public education that would not leave the fate of school districts to the whims of an electorate deciding on school levies. When asked to raise their own property taxes to meet the needs of schools, skeptical voters too often simply said no.

Rhodes tried to draw out his opponent, asserting that Celeste was cooking up a deal that would require a doubling of the state income tax. "That's a flat-out lie," Celeste responded. "That's the voice of a desperate man trying to cling to office one more time."[20] But after widespread speculation that he would *go big* and propose some sort of tax increase to bail out public schools, Celeste failed to deliver. His tepid education plan didn't raise taxes—and neither did it come close to detailing a solution to the plague of school closings. Celeste proposed convening a panel of experts to make a thorough study of the issue, prompting Rhodes to snort: "We didn't need a committee to solve the [winter 1978] blizzard."[21]

At the City Club debate in Cleveland the weekend before Election Day, Celeste faced an empty chair (left vacant for Rhodes) and three minor party candidates. He tried to make the most of it, accusing Rhodes of a "$2 million campaign of false accusations and outright lies. . . . Dick Celeste has no intention of doubling the income tax and Jim Rhodes knows it."[22] After he won the election, Rhodes said scornfully: "Celeste debated an empty chair and the chair won."

In the end, Celeste had come up short on substance in dealing with the school crisis, but he was staggered the final weekend when Rhodes supporters flooded church parking lots with antiabortion flyers. It wasn't a big issue in the campaign. Rhodes was antiabortion, but Celeste, a father of six, would not give unqualified support to an abortion-banning constitutional amendment. Pro-life demonstrators heckled him at a Cincinnati event in October.

A Rhodes TV spot in the closing days of the contest may have convinced swing voters to stick with the man they knew best. It had been thirty-six years since his first statewide election victory as Ohio auditor. In the 1978 commercial, the governor was filmed conducting the All-Ohio Youth Choir in a rousing rendition of the Battle Hymn of the Republic—"His truth is marching on." The ad "seemed to convince the Rhodes Silent Majority 'to give it to Jim again, since he wants it!' They did!"[23]

The campaign set a spending record for an Ohio governor's race—more than $4 million combined. Rhodes spent more than $2 million (compared to $756,000 against Gilligan in 1974) much of it on TV advertising. He won by fewer than 50,000 votes, among some 3 million cast. Aided by the Voinovich's retail politics campaign skills as well as his ethnic-sounding name, Rhodes cut into Celeste's margins in heavily Democratic Cleveland and Toledo. The governor lost Cuyahoga County by only about 50,000 ballots, four years after taking a beating from Gilligan of 87,503 votes. It didn't help that on the Sunday before the election, Celeste's hometown newspaper, the *Plain Dealer,* endorsed the Rhodes-Voinovich ticket. Rhodes also captured Franklin County—Columbus and its suburbs—by 25,000 votes.

The morning after Celeste conceded, Rhodes called reporters to his Statehouse office to claim his victory. The governor surveyed the cabinet room crowded with his bleary-eyed aides and punch-drunk partisans. "Some people have been saying, 'Governor Rhodes, Governor Rhodes, pack your bags,'" he declared. "Uh, they're not here today."[24]

The indomitable Rhodes frustrated Democrats—again. Celeste almost matched him in campaign spending, but he got outsmarted and outmaneuvered at critical junctures. In October, for instance, the Rhodes campaign sent out three hundred thousand absentee ballot applications to elderly voters, a constituency he had catered to for years. Celeste, conserving dollars for the stretch run, went dark in his television advertising the week of October 15, only to see Rhodes open a media blitz that ran through election eve. (Celeste returned to the air on October 22.) Add to those strategic missteps, a disappointing Democratic turnout on Election Day. "Let's face it," Celeste said a few days after the election, "I think I ran against the toughest opponent I may ever face in my life, if I stay in politics."[25]

Other Ohio Democrats were less impressed with Rhodes's political prowess. Their party again prevailed in the other statewide contests, among them secretary of state, with Clevelander Anthony Celebrezze Jr. taking down longtime incumbent Ted W. Brown. Rhodes kept rolling along but didn't bring anyone with him on the ride. "He never did anything to encourage an heir," said George E. Condon Jr., who covered the governor's office for the *Plain Dealer.*[26] "So you had a couple of generations of potential Republican candidates who couldn't develop—the Charlie Kurfess generation." Attorney General William Brown, reelected with a higher vote total than Rhodes, didn't hide his disappointment. "We lost a governor's race to a 69-year-old man," he said.[27]

CHAPTER 10

Gathering Storm

James A. Rhodes was inaugurated for a fourth term on January 8, 1979. At sixty-nine, he was the nation's oldest governor, and at the time he was the longest serving. He believed he was still a good fit for Ohio, but a large, vocal minority was fed up with his antics and bored by his same-old style. There would be no honeymoon for a man who had boasted, blustered, bullied, and buffaloed his way into office yet again. On the last day of 1978, the *Plain Dealer,* in a political column, suggested a New Year's resolution for the reelected governor: "Let Rhodes resolve to keep his promises." What did he promise? No new or increased taxes, property tax relief for homeowners and farmers, a onetime $1,100 boost in teachers' pay spread incrementally over four years, and an end to widespread school closings. Those were the specifics, with the overlay of his never-ending push to create jobs and his advocacy for high-sulfur Ohio coal as the answer to energy shortages. "If you'd forget about them [the campaign promises], I could forget about them," he joked to reporters during his 1978 year-end Wendy's hamburger luncheon in his office.[1]

In an early January interview meant to preview his new term, Rhodes was asked what legacy he wanted to leave his beloved state. "It's not a matter of remembrance," he said, dismissively. "People are the governor. We're their expression." He was not introspective, nothing too deep here. It's simple, he said: "I love the job. I love the people. I love my work." Rhodes indeed kept it simple, telling House Speaker Riffe, "Vern, I just love being governor." Political power is a heady thing, and Rhodes "understood the use of power," said Roger Tracy, a Republican stalwart who had a long history with Rhodes both as an ally and rival.[2] The ability to run things—and hopefully make life better for the citizens of his state—fueled him.

One unhappy part of the Rhodes legacy—the fatal shootings of four Kent State University students during the antiwar demonstrations on campus—finally got some resolution on January 4, a few days before his inauguration. An out-of-court settlement—after nearly ten years of litigation and negotiation—was announced in a civil lawsuit. The dead and wounded Kent State shooting victims and their families would receive $675,000 in financial awards. Far more important was the statement of regret signed by Rhodes, National Guard command officers, and involved guardsmen.

All Rhodes would say publicly that day was, "We have no comment right now." But the carefully worded statement said a lot more. It acknowledged the students "may have believed they were right" in staging their antiwar demonstration but also said some of the guardsmen may have, "in their own minds," believed their lives were under threat. "In retrospect, the tragedy of May 4, 1970 should not have occurred. . . . Hindsight suggests that another method would have resolved the confrontation. Better ways must be found to deal with such confrontations. . . . We deeply regret those events and are profoundly saddened by the deaths of four students and the wounding of nine others which resulted."[3]

A *New York Times* editorial welcomed the overdue regrets from Rhodes and the National Guard: "At long last a note of decency supersedes the truculence with which Ohio officials responded time and again to the anger and anguish of victims' families."[4] (Years later, nearing the end of his last term, Rhodes told one of the authors of this biography that May 4, 1970, was "the most sorrowful day of my life."[5])

With some closure, at last, for the Kent State events, Rhodes began his fourth term. On Inauguration Day, he was sworn in at the restored fifty-one-year-old Ohio Theater across the street from the Statehouse; it was a curiously low-key event, more sentimental than forward-looking. "It's only in America and only in Ohio where a coal miner's son could become the chief executive," he said in his inaugural address. Improving the state's troubled education system is "our greatest challenge and highest priority as we enter the 1980s." And for Rhodes, there lay another formidable political challenge: working cooperatively with a legislature controlled by Democrats bitterly disappointed by Celeste's defeat.

"I am not perfect," Rhodes said. "The legislature is not perfect. The educational profession is not perfect. But together we can and will work for Ohio's children. . . . We do not have to bicker. We do not have to be in the name-calling industry." With that, the governor grabbed the baton and reprised his masterful campaign ad on the theater stage, leading the All-Ohio Youth Choir in a live version of the "Battle Hymn of the Republic."[6]

Off stage, not much had changed.

Rhodes named his respected executive assistant, Tom Moyer, to a vacancy on the Ohio Court of Appeals and replaced him with the equally well regarded Robert Howarth, who moved over from the Office of Budget and Management.[7] With Howarth holding down the fort, Rhodes resumed his helter-skelter schedule, leaving town and the country without advance notice to the news media, sometimes to even his own aides. In mid-March, he took off, unannounced, for Great Britain with Columbus mayor Tom Moody and developer John W. Galbreath, to hustle business prospects for Ohio. Earlier in the month, he had slipped away to Indianapolis, where he entertained GOP presidential prospects at a GOP event. Howarth soon got the message—he would be the point man in the Statehouse command center, virtually around the clock. "Bob, understand," Rhodes told him, "this is your job: when I am here, you're here. When I am not here, you're here." And then, half kidding, "Bob, your job is to keep me out of jail."[8]

Within the first few months of his term, Rhodes took several golf-weekend trips to his beachfront condominium in Fort Lauderdale. "You'll never find me," he told a reporter who threatened to track him down in south Florida. Back in Ohio, another snowy, bitterly cold winter gripped the flatlands and rolling hills. But the economy appeared relatively healthy heading into the last five months of the fiscal year. The state was sitting on a budget surplus of at least $60 million. "If the economic climate of Ohio continues to improve as it has, I think our revenue growth will be more than adequate to fund the programs we have on the books today," Budget Director William Wilkins had said the previous spring.[9] February came, and Rhodes unveiled a $17.7 billion budget for the two-year period beginning July 1, 1979. It amounted to a 22.5 percent increase in general revenue spending. Wilkins called it a "meat and potatoes budget": most of the basics would be well funded. No frills, but enough to go around.[10]

In his forty-five-minute State of the State speech to the General Assembly, Rhodes asked for a "new partnership" with the legislature. After a formal introduction by Senate President Oliver Ocasek as "His Excellency," the governor's biggest surprise was the disclosure that the anticipated budget surplus had grown to $178 million. Democratic leaders were wary. They welcomed the offer of cooperation but didn't hide their uneasiness about the economic future. "If the economy cools, then we will have locked ourselves into some very expensive programs," said Myrl Shoemaker, chairman of the House Finance-Appropriations Committee. Harry Lehman, an influential Cleveland representative, said he heard "a lot of traditional Rhodes rhetoric. He's got more ways to spend the dollar than anyone else."[11] Rhodes was no fiscal conservative, though he often tried to sound like one and often characterized Democratic foes as tax-and-spend liberals. Rhodes preferred to "spend and borrow," his critics said.

One somewhat vague promise was quietly shelved. Rhodes had wanted to put a constitutional amendment on the ballot to change the way property was classified. This was to give homes and farms a bigger tax credit, as a way of offsetting reappraisals that raised property values and real estate taxes. Business and industrial interests didn't like it, because it would have watered down their credits. In addition, it was complicated and hard to explain to voters. So it went away.

Inside the General Assembly, lawmakers had until June 30 to finalize the governor's budget, but the school-funding crisis had to be dealt with on a faster timetable. Both sides had promised to meet the challenge. Celeste needled Rhodes during the campaign: "Ohio is recognized nationally as No. 1 in only one aspect of education and that is school closings."[12]

Instead of plowing into the legislative process—introduce a bill, hold multiple hearings, etc.—Rhodes and Democratic leaders decided to work something out in private ahead of time. Negotiations would take place behind closed doors, away from the flat-domed capitol building. These education summit meetings opened in February with a breakfast at the Columbus Athletic Club, about a block from the Statehouse in downtown Columbus. There was no formal announcement, but reporters staked out the meeting, sometimes waiting in the winter wind on Broad Street for some word of progress. The two sides, along with State School Superintendent Frank Walter, met for eight sessions of an hour or two each. But much of the time was spent shooting the breeze, with the serious business relegated to the last twenty minutes or so. "Lots of 'BS' mixed with some substance," was the way one attendee described the summits. The media were all over it, as if the very future of the state was being decided. Reporters were getting precious little information for their time out in the cold, leading one annoyed journalist to ask when the summiteers were going to stop "eating the taxpayers' doughnuts" and spell out some real solutions to the funding problem.

In his budget, Rhodes had asked for $636 million in new spending for Ohio's 616 school districts. The state senate upped him, countering with a plan seeking $700 million in new money. Dollars aside, something had to be done about House Bill 920—a 1976 law that gave tax credits to offset inflationary increases in appraised property values. That amounted to freeze on property tax rates unless higher rates won approval from voters. It was killing schools, since they depended on property taxes for their main source of revenue. Of course, nobody wanted to talk publicly about raising taxes, or unfreezing them, for that matter. "The last thing the governor wanted to do was walk out of there and have to answer questions about the school problem, nor did Vern Riffe," said Howarth, who took part in the closed-door sessions. "Oliver Ocasek loved to be in the newspapers, so they would always send Oliver out to be the spokesman. The last thing the governor wanted to do was get into the intricacies of school financing."[13]

In late March, a breakthrough: it was decided public schools would get a record $784 million raise, which meant the state would pump just over $4 billion into the system in the coming two years. The money would come from other state programs, new and old. Among the first to go would be Rhodes's promise—separate from the scrapped constitutional amendment— to increase an existing 10 percent property tax rollback that kicked in when inflation swelled property values and thus also the owners' tax loads.

"If he [Rhodes] agrees to that figure, which he did, then he can't lay it on anybody," said Speaker Riffe, who knew the governor's ways as well as anyone.[14] The legislature would be "hesitant to give any further tax relief," Ocasek added. And Shoemaker said Rhodes's tax-rollback plan would be discarded within two weeks. Broken promise No. 2. It was not the most creative solution. The governor and legislative leaders had simply decided more dollars had to be found for education, even at the expense of other valued programs. But something else happened at those morning coffees, something that had been building since Rhodes asked Riffe and Ocasek for help during the brutal winters of 1977 and 1978. Something akin to bonding. "They got to know one another and really began to like one another," said Howarth. "Out of that evolved, I think, this relationship that got us through the last four years."[15]

That summer, the legislature produced an education bill that fell a little short of the $4 billion goal but still increased spending on primary and secondary education by 25 percent. Rhodes called it the greatest commitment to education in Ohio history. He wasn't around in July, when the new fiscal year began. The General Assembly deadlocked over details of a two-year, near-$18 billion state budget, but the governor was on a seventeen-day trade mission to the People's Republic of China, where he handed out balloons, promoted Ohio products, and gingerly avoided spicy Chinese food. "I know, you can shake your head but this thing [trade with China] is so enormous you can't believe it," Rhodes said in response to skepticism about the value of the venture. "I think China has undeveloped, undiscovered oil all around them."[16] Statehouse reporters who went with him said he hated the food and survived on lunchmeat, crackers, and cheese from Ohio, which he brought along in a large suitcase. During banquets, he pushed exotic meals around on his plate and nibbled on steamed rice, which he seasoned with sugar.

His taste buds didn't take to all of the fish on the banquet menus. *Youngstown Vindicator* writer Paul Schroeder recalled that at a dinner Rhodes hosted in Shanghai, Ohio's governor insisted on roast turkey instead of yet another seafood entree. The waiters met his wishes, serving turkey to every table—with the birds' heads flopping on plates. Horrified, Rhodes winced and retreated to his hotel room, where he chowed down on cheese and crackers.[17] Away from the banquet tables, he gamely took in the sights and promoted Ohio businesses and goods at every stop. At the Great Wall, he suggested the Chinese try a little capitalism to boost tourism. "If they really wanted to make some money, they'd build a tram up there and charge $5 a piece."[18]

A man in motion, he talked about opening an Ohio trade office and building office and housing complexes in Shanghai and Canton. Slow down please, Chinese officials cautioned. "In your first visit, it isn't practical to do concrete business," Peking mayor Ling Hus-jia told Ohio's hyper governor. "The problem with setting up a trade office here is lack of accommodations."[19]

Rhodes also met with Hubei Province governor Chen Pi Xian, who also held the rank of military general and was a confidant of paramount Chinese leader

When on a trade mission, Governor Rhodes, wary of foreign delicacies, packed his own supply of cheese and crackers, trail mix, and Dutch Loaf. Here, at an elaborate Chinese banquet in his honor in 1979, Rhodes helps Chen Pi Xian, governor of Hubei Province—Ohio's sister state—to some American fare. *Columbus Dispatch* file photo, March 21, 1982.

Deng Xiaopeng. (Since Hubei was a sister state to Ohio, Chen later returned the favor and traveled to Columbus, showing up at the state fair with Chinese products, including baskets of shoes. Rhodes, of course, wanted to do business, but the Chinese official put on the brakes—"Fast, too fast," he said. "General, your great virtue is patience," Rhodes replied. "My great virtue is impatience."[20])

While Rhodes remained in China, Fourth of July festivities and budget fireworks carried on without him. On his return in mid-July, he pronounced the trip a success but said he felt bad about the poverty he saw—"the small children who had no food." And back in Ohio, he suffered through no more spicy cuttlefish; Helen Rhodes fed her husband a ham and bean dinner, and he slept in his own bed in Upper Arlington.[21]

Meanwhile, his lieutenant governor was sleeping in his own bed in the Collinwood neighborhood of Cleveland several nights a week. Voinovich, then forty-two, was restless and didn't really have enough to do in Columbus. A lifelong Clevelander, he never officially moved his family down I-71. Nothing in the law or in his official portfolio prevented him from continuing his law practice, so he commuted, often leaving the state capital on Thursday afternoon and returning from Cleveland Monday night or Tuesday morning. "It's still a part-time job," he said of his $30,000-a-year state post. "I'd just like to take it low key and get the job done here. Every time I hiccup, I'm not going to put out a press release."[22]

Officially, Voinovich headed the State and Local Government Commission, a body that was supposed to coordinate programs and facilitate hand-offs between those two levels of government. He handled it without breaking a sweat, but he kept busy, also finding other things to do, and—after an unpleasant news account of his weekly commute to Cleveland—edged away from his cavalier comments about the position being part-time. "I am a full-time lieutenant governor," he said in March. "I'm putting in 55 to 60 hours a week."[23]

Rhodes, sorting out the Republican field for the 1980 presidential campaign, valued Voinovich's political skills; his quiet spadework in 1979 would lead to Rhodes's high-profile endorsement of Ronald Reagan. In the meantime, however, the governor's early favorite was former Texas governor John Connally, a onetime conservative Democrat who switched to the GOP. Rhodes wanted Voinovich to front for the Connally campaign in Ohio: that way, he could keep his distance if Connally faltered.

Voinovich wasn't ready to make such a commitment without doing the research. He traveled to Washington to check out Connally's political operation and came back unimpressed. "They had no organization and no plan," he decided. He told Rhodes bluntly that Connally could not—would not—win the Republican nomination. "I listed all the reasons why." Rhodes would have none of it. "No, no," he protested, he wanted the Texan; he went back two decades with Connally and liked him personally. He was a man's man. But Rhodes processed the information, and a couple of weeks later told Voinovich privately that he would support another former governor—Reagan. "He gave me the same reasons I had given him, and he acted like it was his idea," Voinovich said. "He would listen and he might disagree, but then he would change his mind and act like he was the one who thought of it." Connally's campaign never got off the ground. Reagan was nominated in 1980 and won the general election in a landslide. "A good leader listens," Voinovich said, "and he listened."[24]

By mid-1979, Voinovich, restless with his mundane duties, was thinking about an election in his hometown. Power brokers in Cleveland were desperate for a consensus candidate—Democrat or Republican—to run against young Mayor Dennis Kucinich, who narrowly escaped a recall. Kucinich saw his city go into default in 1978 when Cleveland banks called in their notes after he refused to sell a publicly owned municipal power company to a private electric utility. He was arguably right, but his combative, abrasive style turned off many Clevelanders.

Voinovich saw an opportunity.

In early August, he decided to run against Kucinich, leaving a job that really wasn't a good fit for a guy who liked to be in charge. In truth, Rhodes delegated little to Voinovich—even while Rhodes was gone on his China trip, his role was not expanded. "It was a political marriage," Voinovich said. "It's been a respectful relationship." Heading north for what promised to be a hard-hitting campaign, he likened himself to the man in the arena. Of his decision to run for mayor, he said, "When there were guys like Adolf Hitler and other demagogues, there were guys like George Voinovich who said, 'My career path is already set.' I didn't make it with my head, I made it with my heart."[25] Voinovich was always an aggressive campaigner, and he easily vanquished Kucinich. But he stayed on as lieutenant governor during the mayoral campaign, leading Rhodes to suggest that Voinovich retain the lieutenant governor title even after moving into City Hall. "Governor, I can't do that, it's unconstitutional," Voinovich told his old boss.[26]

On November 7, 1979, Rhodes put out a one-paragraph press release, announcing he would "take no action with respect to the vacancy in the office of Lieutenant Governor . . . since the Ohio Constitution makes no provision for filling a vacancy in this office."[27] As had been made clear to Dick Celeste in 1975, Rhodes didn't think he needed an assistant governor.

While Voinovich concentrated on Cleveland, the one-man show in Columbus had its own campaign going—an unrelenting blame game directed at Jimmy Carter's Environmental Protection Agency (EPA). The state's volatile economy was one step forward—five hundred new jobs at an XM1 tank plant in Lima—then one big step back: fourteen hundred steelworker jobs wiped out in Mahoning County when Jones & Laughlin announced the shuttering of its Brier Hill and Campbell works.

Ohio experienced a modest upsurge in oil and gas production. Some three thousand wells were completed in 1979—the best year since the Morrow County Boom peaked in 1964—with most of them bringing in both gas and oil.[28] It wasn't enough to make a difference in the overall economy. Only Washington County, along the Ohio River, had activity approaching a boomlet. For Rhodes, the economic malaise could be traced to a nondescript office building near the Potomac River: the headquarters of the federal EPA. His scapegoat for the declining manufacturing base was not the apparent structural changes in the economy, but environmental regulation. He claimed cleanup orders from Washington forced companies to shut down plants because they could not afford to carry out costly compliance mandates. His solution was to burn more Ohio coal, providing jobs for miners and cheap fuel for factories. Ohio EPA director James McAvoy—a wisecracking Irish American who head-faked the media by disclosing that he *had been* a member of the Sierra Club—was the point man for Rhodes's attack. Soon McAvoy was a drinking buddy of lobbyist Neil Tostenson, who represented coal mine owners.

Rhodes laid out his case that summer in a Columbus speech to the Ohio Brotherhood of Teamsters, a union that at the time often favored Republicans. He opened by denouncing a trucking industry deregulation proposal promoted by "your enemies in Congress." That group included Senator Howard Metzenbaum, a Democrat and possible Rhodes target in 1982, when the senator faced reelection. But trucking deregulation was just a warm-up. Rhodes wanted to vent about the environmental movement and how it was—to his mind—destroying jobs to save snail darters and the like. "I am talking about the extreme professional environmentalists who are the hard core of the overzealous lobbying groups in Washington," he told the union. "These are the people who are the cause of our present problems. They have stopped us from burning coal in many parts of our nation, greatly increasing our dependence on oil. We have a small, noisy minority in America who are against growth, against progress, and who don't particularly care about having our nation accept the responsibility of world leadership. The professional environmentalists are wrong. We can burn coal without sacrificing the goals of clean air and water."[29]

A "small, noisy minority"? Rhodes didn't specifically name the federal EPA or anyone else. He didn't have to, but he was belittling one of the most dynamic political movements of the second half of the twentieth century—which had broad support among the public. He didn't understand the environmental movement—the public health issues, the desire to protect special places from human intrusion, the wilderness areas, the concerns about motor-vehicle pollution. In his way of thinking, a beautiful publicly owned place should have golf courses, tennis courts, and swimming pools. And cleaning up rivers to make the waterways suitable for swimming and fishing was a fine idea, as long as you had a job and money to buy a rod and reel.

In private, top aide Howarth argued against Rhodes's strident tone. "I never understood the governor's policy on the environment. I mean we disagreed on that," Howarth said in a 2004 interview. "He just could not get rid of the disdain he had for environmental protection. I think it came from his background when he saw the mines, and the money people were making from the coal mines." Rhodes liked to say that people and their jobs were "more important than trees." When Howarth pointed out the interconnectedness of the natural world and human existence, it didn't register: "'People are more important than trees,' and he would stop there."[30]

Bob Teater, the state's director of Natural Resources, said Rhodes once badgered him for a month to allow a large contributor to build a private marina in southwestern Ohio at Caesar Creek State Park, which—like all state parks—was closed to private development. "I just said, 'We can't do that. It is public water. We are going to leave it to public use.'" Rhodes persisted for several months on behalf of the unnamed supporter, at one point even demanding, "Why aren't you building that marina?" Teater, a political moderate who genuinely cared about Ohio's unspoiled natural places, refused to give ground. After a big blowup one day, he got a phone call from the governor's office. "Well, here we go," he thought as he picked up the receiver, "my last day on the job." Instead, a jovial Rhodes came on the line, acting as if their argument had simply been a show, presumably to let the disappointed marina builder know Rhodes had tried his best. "The governor said, 'You know, I have never asked you to do anything wrong, or anything that would be illegal or improper. And I am not going to now, so I wanted you to know that.'"[31] Perhaps. Or maybe Rhodes finally understood he was going too far and pulled back because he sensed trouble ahead.

Publicly he was unrelenting in his hostility to environmental regulation. With its governor's bombast and record for noncompliance—or begrudging compliance—the midwestern state with the dirty, coal-burning power plants was becoming notorious in the environmental community. That summer, Ohio was the only state without a federally approved sulfur dioxide plan. Twenty-two of its counties were not on board with federal standards. In addition, state government was challenging—or lagging behind on—clean water requirements and automobile exhaust standards for carbon monoxide and nitrogen oxide. Congressman John F. Seiberling, Democrat, of Akron, put it well: "Ohio's economic growth is not going to be helped by its reputation as the dirtiest state in the nation. We're not going to overturn the Clean Air Act, so why can't we just get on with this thing."[32]

From the tall stacks at Ohio's coal-fired power plants, sulfur dioxide emissions blew eastward and rained down sulfuric and nitric acids on lakes and forests in the Northeast. In 1974, Yale ecologist F. Herbert Bormann reported that rainfall with lowered pH was restraining forest growth and causing fishkills.[33] Acid rain leached calcium from the soil, starving plants, and also dissolved minerals laden with aluminum, harming plant life. (By 2012, there were signs that federal clean air laws were working, with acid rain reduced by as much as 40 percent in New York, New Hampshire, Vermont, and Maine. A U.S. Geological Survey study reported, "The deforestation of northeastern U.S. soils from acidic deposition has finally bottomed out," said West Virginia University biogeochemist Brenden McNeil.[34]

Despite the acid-rain threat, McAvoy stated that utilities should not be forced to install expensive scrubbers, which removed sulfur dioxide from emissions during the combustion process. Prodded by the Rhodes administration, the U.S. EPA gave waivers to two Cleveland Electric Illuminating plants, allowing the utilities to temporarily continue burning untreated coal.[35] Rhodes claimed scrubbers worked properly only 30 to 40 percent of time. Yet Columbus & Southern Ohio Electric, which used the devices, reported that they functioned as much as 60 percent of operating time and would work completely efficiently within two years.

Without question, Rhodes was deeply interested in clean coal technology, including the next generation of stack scrubbers. But he didn't connect the dots. Why couldn't the development and manufacturing of state-of-the-art pollution abatement equipment, by itself, emerge as a viable industry in Ohio? In the 1982 Democratic gubernatorial primary, one candidate, Jerry Springer (yes, the future TV talk-show host), based his entire economic plan for the state on a future that embraced coal: mining it, powering factories with it, and developing technology to make it clean and safe. It never happened. But in Ohio and other coal-rich states, utilities were installing equipment they hoped would satisfy the EPA. The scrubbers scrubbed—limiting sulfur dioxide emissions—and forty years later research showed effective pollution controls encouraged more hiring and investment: "Pollution abatement technologies often create demand for skilled labor and financial investment. Studies have found that when regulators required power plants to install scrubbers in their smokestacks, it created incentives for innovation that lowered the costs of operating the anti-pollution equipment."[36]

As a new decade approached, Rhodes was focused on the short-term cost of compliance for power companies, their investors, and their ratepayers. He thought the energy crisis was a farce. And he was worried about the shrinking coal industry in eastern and southeastern Ohio. The Ohio Mining and Reclamation Association—Tostenson's group—said forty-two hundred coal miners lost their jobs as orders for high-sulfur Ohio coal dried up, with utilities shopping for cleaner out-of-state coal. John McGuire, administrator for the U.S. EPA's midwestern region, maintained that only 910 of the eliminated jobs could be attributed directly to sulfur dioxide regulations; of course, even 900 lost jobs is a lot of lost paychecks. By late 1979, most of the deep mines in Ohio were closed and coal production was down 6.5 percent from 1977 levels.

In a *Columbus Dispatch* op-ed, Rhodes wrote, "The professional environmentalists gave no thought to the consequences of their action, and the result is that today we have placed our future in the hands of [oil-producing] Arab nations, who can bring our economy to a standstill at will."[37] He kept pressing for waivers on cleanup orders or extensions of deadlines imposed by the command-and-control dictates of the 1970 Clean Air Act. Ohio would stand up to the "needless nitpicking . . . of federal EPA bureaucrats who believe their way is the only way."[38] He complained about "feather-brained bureaucrats" in Washington, "out to put coal miners out of work."[39] McAvoy, ramping up the rhetoric, went so far as to declare war on the EPA, because the agency insisted Ohio power plants had to be outfitted with pollution-control scrubbers by mid-October or face fines of $10,000 a day. Ohio Edison and Columbus & Southern—two large, coal-burning utilities—were eventually granted extensions to comply with the sulfur dioxide regulations.

In November 1979, Rhodes took his show to Austin, Texas, where he regaled the attendees of Republican Governors Association's annual conference with his "Save America, Burn Coal" plan. Predictably, his fellow governors warmly received the idea of stepping up coal use to reduce foreign oil imports, and they passed a meaningless resolution supporting Rhodes. Cutting foreign imports by 50 percent in the foreseeable future may be an ambitious goal, Rhodes conceded, "but that's what the public wants to hear." After all, people vote for hope.[40] The EPA fought back. "They're calling the Ohio River Valley the Golden Triangle for energy," the EPA's Chicago Region spokesman Frank Corrado said, "but coal-burning is one of the dirtiest forms of energy there is. We want to make people think about the choices that are involved."[41]

Just after Thanksgiving, Youngstown was sacked. U.S. Steel said it would close its Ohio Works there, idling up to thirty-five hundred hardhats. Jones & Laughlin followed with its announcement of layoffs at its Brier Hill and Campbell works. The company cited obsolescence at its factories and competition from foreign steel imports. "Economic Pearl Harbor" for the Mahoning Valley, screamed a *Youngstown Vindicator* headline.[42] Rhodes put the blame squarely on the government in Washington: "The 4,900 affected steelworkers in Youngstown are the victims of a federal bureaucracy which lacks the spine and the determination to do what is best not only for steelworkers, but for every citizen of our nation."[43]

Thus began a not-so-merry holiday season in northern Ohio, a region facing a huge structural shift in an industrial economy that had kept lunch buckets full and cities thriving for nearly half a century. It is not known whether Rhodes saw the *Toledo Blade*'s Christmas Day issue, with its AP story about Youngstown's plight. But he was a voracious newspaper reader. Jones & Laughlin would shutter its Brier Hill Works before the New Year. The newspaper quoted a soon-to-be laid-off Brier Hill steelworker telling his family that he would not be able to afford a generous Christmas celebration in the future. "This is it. This is the last big Christmas," M. L. Johnson said. The story did not mention the EPA.[44]

Jim Rhodes, in full uniform, gets ready to fling one down the field. Rhodes played quarter-back and halfback at Springfield High School and was a high-scoring guard in basketball. He had "mercurial moves and great balance," said those who saw him play. Photo courtesy of Suzanne and Richard Moore.

A middle-aged Jim Rhodes shakes hands with the hero of World War II—General Dwight D. Eisenhower. Photo by Ronald E. Thielman, furnished by Suzanne and Richard Moore.

(Top) Jim and Helen Rhodes pose in their Easter finery with their three daughters and some furry friends. Photo courtesy of Suzanne and Richard Moore.

(Right) The Rhodes family members pose on the front porch of their home (circa 1960). Photo courtesy of Suzanne and Richard Moore.

Governor Rhodes helps Richard Stultz, eight, of Columbus, land the first fish caught at the 1968 Ohio State Fair. Fishing was free for children at the pond provided by the Ohio Department of Natural Resources. *Columbus Dispatch* file photo, August 22, 1968.

(top) Rhodes with Richard Nixon and other luminaries at a Republican campaign event. To Nixon's right is his wife, Pat. To her right is William B. Saxbe, who was a U.S. senator and U.S. attorney general appointed by Nixon. Photo courtesy of Suzanne and Richard Moore.

(Right) Rhodes at the Case Western Reserve Medical School complex in 1969. Conscious of his southern Ohio roots, Rhodes worked extra hard to sell himself in the northern part of the state. He lavished attention—and when he could, state-funded projects—on vote-rich Cleveland. James A. Hatch, *Plain Dealer,* September 17, 1969.

Governor Rhodes, nearing the end of his second term, in January 1971, enters the chamber of the Ohio House of Representatives to deliver his last (for the time being) speech to the General Assembly. At the governor's right rear is Representative William G. Batchelder, a Medina Republican who was still serving in the House, as Speaker, in 2013, forty-three years later! *Columbus Citizen-Journal,* January 5, 1971.

This cartoon of Governor Jim Rhodes touting jobs for Ohio and twisting someone else's arm to do it sprang from the creative brain and artistic talent of coauthor Rick Zimmerman. It was published in the *Plain Dealer* on December 29, 1968, as part of a series titled "How the Legislature Really Works." Much of Zimmerman's satirical artistic work ended up on the bulletin board in the Statehouse Press Room. Leonard Collection, Ohio History Center, Columbus.

HERE'S HOW—Gov. James A. Rhodes, to get things done in the General Assembly, uses both "carrots" and "sticks" (or arm-twisting, as the case may be). While spreading the gospel to the people of Ohio, Rhodes also works to win the legislator over to his viewpoint, gently or otherwise.   Plain Dealer cartoon (Richard Zimmerman)

Governor Rhodes poses with Flippo the Clown, a Columbus TV personality, on December 1, 1977.

Jim Rhodes is all smiles on December 13, 1974, a month after upsetting Democratic Governor John J. Gilligan to claim a third term as governor following a four-year hiatus in private business. Rhodes won reelection four years later and served a total of sixteen years—at one time a national record. Ken Chamberlain Jr., *Columbus Dispatch*, January 1, 2001.

Jim and Helen Rhodes in the governor's office. Photo courtesy of Suzanne and Richard Moore.

(Top) Jim Rhodes at one time was a major stockholder in Wendy's and a good friend of founder Dave Thomas. This *Dayton Journal Herald* cartoon spoofs the governor's association with the hamburger king and his penchant for keeping state expenses low. Used by permission of Bob Englehart.

(Right) This cartoon, drawn after the 1978 gubernatorial campaign, combines Governor Jim Rhodes's affinity for the Ohio State Fair and its animal judging with the media's cynical view that the governor was fully capable of promoting his own candidacy at the expense of truth. Cartoon by Taylor Jones, *Charleston (West Virginia) Gazette.*

OHIO GOVERNOR JAMES RHODES 11-27-78

Governor or not, Rhodes was not afraid to go barefoot as he did when growing up in southern Ohio. Here, he is assisted by a trooper with the Ohio Highway Patrol. Photo courtesy of Suzanne and Richard Moore.

Governor Rhodes angles for some bluegill and crappies with his grandson, Jimmy John Jacob, six, at an ice fishing expedition at Alum Creek Reservoir, north of Columbus. As a boy, Rhodes fished, hunted, and trapped. He never forgot those skills and loved to share them with youngsters. Red Trabue, *Columbus Dispatch*, February 9, 1979.

Jim Rhodes and his future lieutenant governor are in full campaign mode for George Voinovich in 1978. Published in *The Plain Dealer,* September 17, 1978. Photograph by Ray Matjasic, furnished by George Voinovich.

Rhodes and Bob Hope confer at a Republican gathering, while future governor George Voinovich, directly behind the entertainer, looks on. Photo by Gene Hersh, furnished by George Voinovich.

Rhodes, in his last term as governor, has microphone-worthy words for someone at a luncheon in Cleveland, while political allies huddle; Ohio Senate president Paul Gillmor and Cleveland mayor George Voinovich, to his right. The politicking took place at Hofbrau House, a landmark German restaurant on the city's East Side. David I. Andersen, *Plain Dealer*, April 24, 1981.

With Rhodes at a Republican Party function, from left: President George H. W. Bush; Woody Hayes, the legendary Ohio State football coach; and Michael Colley, chairman of the Ohio Republican Party. Neal C. Lauron, *Columbus Dispatch,* July 27, 2004.

In a special Governors Day ceremony at the Ohio Historical Center, former governor James A. Rhodes appeared with Governor George V. Voinovich, far left, and former Democratic governors Richard F. Celeste and John J. Gilligan, far right. Though once combative, here they share a laugh.

Rhodes, out of public life, pictured with two of his daughters—from left, Saundra Jacob and Suzanne Moore—at his Upper Arlington home on New Year's Day in 1989. Jacob died in 1999. Chris Stephens, *Plain Dealer,* January 1, 1989.

Before long, Ohio's governor made the newspaper account his own. "Come with me to Youngstown this Christmas," he would say, "and stand in a steel-worker's kitchen and listen to that mother tell her children, 'There will be no Christmas this year. The federal EPA has taken away your father's job!'" Rhodes said he only wished he could bring a hardened EPA bureaucrat to the poor woman's kitchen to witness the pitiful scene. Reporters called it the "No Christmas in Youngstown" speech.[45] He was on a crusade. His enemies were the "callous, faceless bureaucrats" of the EPA. And so it went. Rhodes and Carter's EPA fought to a standoff. But as an election year approached, the governor took heart at the distinct possibility that a more sympathetic Republican administration might succeed the pro-environment Democratic president.

Of immediate concern was the declining state of the national economy, which would drag Ohio down with it. Just after Thanksgiving, Rhodes predicted the onset of a severe recession—an economic panic, he called it. In a speech to the Ohio Farm Bureau Federation, he said, "Unless we get some common sense in this country, the '30s will look like a strawberry picnic. . . . The federal EPA has gone so far that now you need a license to kill a cockroach in your own home." Betraying a weak grasp of international economic systems, Rhodes claimed the U.S. "is the only country in the world that is trying to dry up free enterprise."[46]

A recession was already under way, according to the U.S. Commerce Department. In Ohio, automobile and appliance sales were falling off and tax revenues had dropped $25 million below July estimates. The state was having cash-flow issues. And that November, Standard & Poor's and Moody's lowered Ohio's bond rating, meaning the state might have to pay higher interest rates to attract bond buyers. Similar to most large government organizations, Ohio relied on bond sales to investment houses to finance capital construction projects. Myrl Shoemaker's caution about Rhodes's "meat and potatoes" budget now seemed a premonition: "If the economy cools, then we will have locked ourselves into some very expensive programs."

As the holidays approached, the General Assembly voted to extend unemployment benefits an extra thirteen weeks for those idled by plant shutdowns. As an alternative, a jobless factory worker could choose a year of free retraining at a state-funded institution. State senator Harry Meshel, a Youngstown Democrat, said the bill would help hard-hit families "eat for another 13 weeks" and avoid welfare. "We're not at this point certainly, blaming the [steel] industry or anybody else," he said.[47] No time for finger-pointing—a $100 million gap between income and the state's obligations loomed.

Another crisis, another test—perhaps another broken promise—was ahead. Rhodes was seventy and about to enter his fourteenth year as Ohio's governor. It would be his most challenging.

CHAPTER 11

Recession!

HELEN RHODES HAD NO DOUBTS about her hyperactive husband's energy level or his resolve. In an impromptu exchange with reporters after Rhodes returned from China, she said he "can't sit still." He won't retire after his term as governor ends in 1982, she said. "He has his fingers in several things."[1]

Rhodes, in fact, did not stand by and wait for a free-market miracle as the economy worsened; he was engaged. But what he didn't have his fingers in was the debate over the "new economy," fundamental shifts in the job market that would take hold in the last two decades of the twentieth century. At universities and think tanks, economists were talking about structural changes they believed would alter Ohio's industrial base and point toward the emerging communications, service and health care sectors, alternative energy, and smaller, specialized manufacturing plants.

"That lexicon was foreign to his experience," said Bill Wilkins, who by 1980 was heading the Department of Administrative Services for Rhodes.[2] Manufacturing jobs peaked nationally at 19.6 million in 1979, but heavily unionized states like Ohio, Michigan, and Illinois were already being written off as the Rust Belt.[3] Employers looked to cheaper labor and warmer climes in Georgia, South Carolina, and Texas—the Sunbelt. With its northern cities shrinking, Ohio was losing population, jobs, and also clout on Capitol Hill. Its congressional delegation slipped from twenty-one to nineteen after the 1980 census showed only modest growth in the state.[4]

"After the Carter economy and when things got better for Ohio economically, I don't think the governor appreciated that there was an evolution from smokestacks to high tech—and I don't think many people did," said Rhodes's executive assistant Robert Howarth. "I don't think we were talking about high tech. However, he did know that the key to Ohio's economic future and success was the work force and the young people being trained."[5] Howarth's predecessor, Tom Moyer, had a similar take. "He certainly was not a Third Frontier person in the last term. For him, big manufacturing, that is where his heart was. He understood it. He thought, too, it created so many jobs."[6]

Nor was Rhodes a booster of a service economy. "We can't all sit around and cut each other's hair," he was fond of saying when the topic came up. Rhodes's critics believed his best years were behind him "In his last two terms, his administration didn't have a handle on what was going on," said State Representative Robert Netzley, a western Ohio Republican to the political right of Rhodes. "Things just seemed to run out of control."[7] Senate Leader Ocasek said Rhodes clung to a philosophy, which I have been slower to adopt: "what's good for industry is good for Ohio."[8]

Inflation roared across the country in February 1980 at an 18.2 percent compounded annual rate.[9] In April, the United States' industrial production dropped by nearly 2 percent—the steepest slide since early 1975. General Motors reacted to slumping sales by furloughing more than four hundred at Cleveland area factories; Ford Motor Company pressed the United Auto Workers for concessions to keep a stamping plant in operation in suburban Cleveland. Housing starts also fell—and the worst was yet to come. By midyear, 366,000 Ohioans were out of work.[10] Facing a $266 million budget gap, Rhodes ordered a hiring freeze and a 3 percent across-the-board cut in government spending; it took effect in July, along with a 5 percent boost in the cost of liquor sold at state-run stores, where prices were already high. The legislatively approved price hike—essentially a sin tax—was supposed to yield nearly $21 million in the course of a year. It was nicknamed "booze for buildings," because the money went for loans to private firms to help modernize plants and equipment and avert factory shutdowns. The governor also signed a bill doubling the motor vehicle registration fee. But he and the legislature were only nibbling at the edges of a growing problem.

"We are victims of a depressed economy," Ocasek said, trying to stimulate debate on the need for a broad tax increase. "I don't think we can go on and on being 50th [in per-capita tax effort]. Ohio is not guilty of being a tax-and-spend state. We stretch a dollar farther than anyone." In the Ohio House, Myrl Shoemaker said it was clear that Rhodes's budget for the two-year period between July

1979 and July 1981 had proven too optimistic. Inflation was high, but the national economy was sagging—"stagflation" was the word being used. "It [Rhodes's revenue projection] meant we had to have a heated economy and inflation had to stay high too," Shoemaker said. "We're charged with responsibility, and you just can't let everything go to pot." The governor's budget director, William Keip, didn't disagree. "I guess we were too optimistic," he said, with the benefit of hindsight. "We have delayed the problem and [barring a turnaround in the national economy] we'll have to deal responsibly with it in the next biennium, absolutely."[11] Even that assessment—that the fees, freezes, and cuts had "delayed the problem"—would turn out to be too rosy.

In November, disappointing state tax revenues forced Rhodes to reduce spending by another 3 percent, but a projected deficit of nearly $500 million was still staring him in the face. Something had to be done. Republicans won a narrow majority in the Ohio Senate on Election Day, and Democratic speaker Riffe's numbers dwindled in the House. But Rhodes decided to turn to the lame-duck legislature for immediate action: he asked to appear before a joint session of the General Assembly. On December 15, 1980, a somber Rhodes entered the historic Ohio House of Representatives chamber and strode to the rostrum, positioning himself in front of the Lincoln Chair—the spot where President-elect Abraham Lincoln addressed the Ohio legislature on February 13, 1861.[12] Vern Riffe and Oliver Ocasek, unsmiling, stood behind him, applauding politely.

Rhodes stared at his text and began reading slowly and deliberately: "Ohio is the victim of the economic blizzard that is rampaging across the country—blowing fear and despair into the homes of millions of our citizens. This economic blizzard is taking its toll in human misery in every part of our state." He rarely deviated from his prepared remarks, yet by the time he was finished everyone on the floor and in the gallery felt they had just heard the most emotional speech James Allen Rhodes had ever delivered. Though the governor methodically plowed through the speech, he spoke as though the weight of the state were on his shoulders. His forcefulness in a time of crisis—the intensity of his purpose—conveyed authenticity where a blustery, gesticulating performance would have rung false. "Who could have predicted that today we would be facing 20 percent interest rates, 13 percent inflation, and 9 percent unemployment in Ohio?" he asked. "There are 350,000 children on welfare in Ohio; they are helpless and defenseless."

Rhodes spread the blame around—"no political party escapes responsibility"—but placed most of it in Washington's lap. "The velocity of this blizzard will not be abated," he said, "until the federal government gets rid of OPEC oil, gets rid of the overkill of government regulations on business and industry, and Congress passes a law that mandates the federal EPA to pay half of the costs of their findings and actions."

As for predicting the future, Rhodes had indeed warned the year before of a looming economic panic, but his administration didn't act decisively to buttress the state against the coming hard times. Eighteen months into the fiscal biennium, the spending plan that he proposed had a $496 million hole in it. "The budget I am discussing today was passed by this General Assembly [in 1979], and I signed it," he owned up.

The crisis was real—the problem would grow by $80 million in another month without immediate action. Spending cuts alone wouldn't do it. Put another campaign promise aside, higher taxes would be part of the solution. Rhodes said he would trim the budget by another $101 million, but he also told the lawmakers he wanted $395 million in revenue to close the gap. He recommended temporarily higher taxes on corporate income, beer and wine, cigarettes, and power company gross receipts. The taxes would all expire on July 1, 1981, the close of the fiscal period.

Now, midway through his speech, Rhodes laid it on thick, reprising and updating his no-Christmas-in-Youngstown anecdote with a hypothetical Ohio family hit by the "economic blizzard" and seeing its breadwinner jobless. "It falls on the courageous wife to line up the children and tell them, there will be no Christmas this year, your daddy does not have a job. This man has lost so much. Let's not take away the support for his children—and support for all the children of Ohio."

He closed, uncharacteristically, with a self-penned prayer that he said would serve as his Christmas proclamation. It came perilously close to going over the top. "Heavenly Father . . . Ohio, this blessed land, faces a crisis of grave proportions. . . . Guide us through these trying deliberations. . . . Help us to remember always that our children are your children. . . . Help us as you always have. Bring light where there is darkness. Bring hope where there is despair."[13] Amen, brother. Rhodes had made his point emphatically, and then prayerfully. The response that day in the House chamber was subdued, but within forty-eight hours, the governor got his deficit package, higher taxes and all. And the children of Ohio were sheltered—at least temporarily—from the blizzard.

When he assigned responsibility for the recession, Rhodes did not mention the man in the White House. Neither did he mention President Carter's successor, President-elect Ronald Reagan. Maybe he didn't want to box in Reagan, who would inherit many of the Carter administration's problems and policies.

Rhodes worked hard for Reagan and had high hopes for his presidency. But his path to becoming Reagan's "favorite governor" (in the view of Rhodes's devotees) was long and winding. John Connally, whose candidacy faltered early in the primary campaign, was Rhodes's first choice. The governor also gave George H. W. Bush a hearing, before endorsing Reagan in April 1980. His one-on-one meeting with Bush earlier that year has become the stuff of political folklore. Bush, a Connecticut Yankee who once asked a counterman for a "splash of coffee," was not Jim Rhodes's kind of man.

Bush recounted a breakfast with Rhodes in his 1988 autobiography, *Looking Forward*. Ohio's governor, Bush wrote approvingly, had made a "mockery of the standard Democratic charge that the Republicans are the elitist 'country club' party." In truth, Rhodes was a longtime member of Scioto Country Club in suburban Columbus and lived within walking distance of its fairways. "So there I was with Jim Rhodes one morning, drinking orange juice and outlining my presidential campaign and program for America—my 'vision for the future.' I went down the list: foreign policy, national defense, the economy," Bush wrote. Rhodes wasn't impressed. "Cut the crap, George," he interjected, "because if you're serious about running for president, you might as well get a few things straight. What you're talking about is dandy, but I want to show you what people vote for, what they really want to know." He then pulled a thick, frayed leather wallet from his pocket and slammed it on the table. "That's it right there, my friend," he said. "Jobs. Who can put money in people's pockets—you or the other guy. That's what it's all about George—jobs, jobs, jobs."[14]

Others gave saltier accounts.

"God damn it George! This is all people care about. [Rhodes fingers his wallet]. Who's putting money in it, and who is taking money out of it." That's how Republican activist Keith McNamara, a friend to both Bush and Rhodes, heard it.[15]

Writing in the *Hartford Courant,* political reporter John McDonald said Bush, similar to many other GOP hopefuls before him, journeyed to Columbus as a pilgrim, "hoping to learn at the feet of the master, the legendary James A. Rhodes." And Bush got schooled: "The secret to political success in Ohio can be boiled down to one good four-letter word: jobs. Politicians who forget that word do so at their own peril in Ohio."[16] Rhodes liked Bush but found him persnickety. Ohioans, he said, would have a hard time relating to a guy who bothered to get out of the shower just to urinate—only he didn't say "urinate." So Bush didn't get Rhodes's backing, and the month before the Reagan endorsement, Ohio's governor was still playing up his neutrality in the Republican primary race.[17]

On March 10, in a statement that he would not be a delegate at the Republican National Convention, Rhodes said he regarded all of the candidates "still active in Ohio" as personal friends and didn't want to do anything that could divide the party. "I will support any of them enthusiastically in November," he said. "We must come out of the convention in Detroit [in July] unified, and determined to win."[18] But as the weather warmed and Reagan's lead over Bush grew, the old master had second thoughts. Rhodes and his closest political advisors—Republican leaders like Cleveland's Bob Hughes and Cincinnati's Earl Barnes—had feared Reagan was too extreme in his conservative beliefs to win a general election. Rhodes had lined up Ohio party officials and donors for Ford in 1976, leaving Reagan out in the cold. But now Reagan was running an aggressive anti-Washington campaign that was to Rhodes's liking. And the former California governor was no friend to environmental regulation. Rhodes was already a member of the Republican National Committee, the GOP's organizational arm. Was he promised a prominent role in Reagan's Ohio campaign in exchange for his support? That seems likely, but no such explicit agreement was disclosed.

Without forewarning, Rhodes called the media and party regulars to the Governor's Mansion on a Sunday in late April in the midst of one of Reagan's campaign swings through the state. Reagan would be at the executive mansion on what turned out to be a near-perfect spring day—and it wasn't for a routine courtesy visit. Rhodes didn't live in the gray brick Tudor revival home in suburban Bexley, but he used it occasionally for special events. And this was special. A month after announcing he would stay neutral, he formally

At a Sunday news conference at the Governor's Mansion, Rhodes endorses Ronald Reagan for the Republican nomination for president. He often waited in intraparty battles until he was sure of backing a winner, which is partly the source of Reagan's mirth here. "Timing is everything" was a Rhodes mantra. Mike Munden, *Columbus Dispatch,* April 21, 1980.

endorsed Ronald Reagan. It was all in the timing, he said when surprised reporters asked what had prompted his reversal. "I think Saturday was too early and Monday was too late."[19]

Rhodes charged into the campaign. The weekend before the June 3 Ohio primary, he introduced Reagan at a large outdoor rally at Fountain Square in downtown Cincinnati. "Ronald Reagan is the man to lead America in these critical, depression times caused by the present administration," Rhodes said. "Deep in the heart of America, there's a gnawing feeling we are no longer the strongest nation in the world."[20]

Then, as would be true in following decades, the road to the White House ran through Ohio. President Carter and his challenger, Senator Ted Kennedy, also campaigned aggressively for the votes of Ohio Democrats. On June 3, Reagan won the Republican primary and Carter bested Kennedy, guaranteeing the Reagan-Carter match up in November. Rhodes would be with Reagan all the way to the finish line. "Nixon turned him down, Ford ignored him, and as a result he went fishing," Barnes, the Republican state chairman, explained. Richard Nixon carried Ohio, but Gerald Ford lost the state narrowly to Carter. This time Rhodes would be listened to—this time he would have real influence. Reagan had decided to pay attention to an incumbent governor. At a private August 27 meeting with Reagan and three other Great Lakes states' governors—William Milliken of Michigan, Dick Thornburgh of Pennsylvania, and Jim Thompson of Illinois—in downtown Columbus, Rhodes vented. In recent appearances, Reagan had been off message, with controversial remarks about China, Taiwan, and evolution. He was not hitting the jobs issue hard enough. Midwestern voters were worried about the lousy economy, Rhodes said—not a two-China policy or the missing link. "Jim Rhodes gave him the riot act," a GOP source said.[21] "They laid down the law," said Rhodes press secretary Chan Cochran. "They said 'Enough of this bullshit. It is about the economy.' If you go back and check, you will find the campaign turned on a dime. . . . In two campaigns, before Clinton ever came on the scene, Jim Rhodes was saying, 'It's the economy, stupid.'"[22]

Soon Reagan was talking about a "depression" in the land—not a *recession*—and he was blaming Mother Nature for the air pollution that others attributed to auto exhausts and factory smokestacks. Addressing the International Brotherhood of Teamsters that summer in Columbus, Reagan spoke of a "Carter depression," created and molded by a president "insensitive to the problems of working people." The word "depression" was not in the text of the speech handed out in advance to reporters; it was inserted at the insistence of Rhodes, who traveled in a limousine with Reagan from the Columbus airport.

Unemployment in Ohio was 10.2 percent in July, with 536,000 out of work. Nationally it was just under 8 percent, painful but not at depression levels—but close enough, as far as Rhodes was concerned. He set the stage for Reagan's inflammatory remarks in his introduction: "There's no relief from the misery they've [the unemployed] been forced to endure under heartless, callous economic policies of the current administration."[23]

The presidential nominee's Rhodesian one-liners—"Trees cause more pollution than automobiles" (the direct quotation is attributed to Reagan in 1981, after he was elected)—caused a minor stir. At one campaign stop in the West, a heckler appeared costumed as a tree, bearing a sign that read, "Stop me before I kill again." Rhodes had insisted the haze over the Blue Ridge Mountains was a form of pollution coming from natural causes. Some of it does. "They didn't name those [mountains] for the Blues Brothers," he once wisecracked, drawing bewildered laughter.[24]

Scientists say in warm weather trees and plants give off volatile organic compounds, terpenes and isoprenes, which do, in a small way, contribute to air pollution and human discomfort. But trees also soak up carbon dioxide, a greenhouse gas. And the impact of the compounds they emit is minor compared to the fumes pouring out of smokestacks and tailpipes.[25]

Cochran said that at Rhodes's insistence, he wrote a trees-and-pollution news release that he believed would never be used, because it was so over the top. He put it on Rhodes's desk and left for a vacation in California. "Three days later, I tune in the evening news and my release is coming out of Ronald Reagan's mouth, word-for-word." The press secretary was flabbergasted. If the governor's aides were concerned about the decibel level of his anti-environment rants, Rhodes was unrelenting. "I'm telling you, we've got to take care of the people," Rhodes told them. "I don't care about the trees. It's the people that are important."[26]

By October, Rhodes's cabinet office at the Statehouse was a political war room, with aides scurrying about and the governor barking orders. Rhodes didn't actually run or manage the Reagan campaign, as some of his fans claimed, but he had "across-the-board involvement," said Ohio-Pennsylvania coordinator Frank Donatelli. He was usually at Reagan's side during his frequent trips to Ohio.[27]

Late in the month, Rhodes smelled victory. He told voters Reagan would triumph "because people like you want to build and construct and cultivate the best in America, instead of trying to tear it down."[28] Carter never had a chance in Ohio. The Iranian hostage crisis left voters nationally questioning the impotence of his foreign policy, but in Ohio the crumbling industrial economy alone was probably enough to do him in. Reagan and running mate George Bush carried the state by 454,131 votes. The president-elect phoned Rhodes with the good news on election night. Afterward, a satisfied Rhodes put his feet up on the desk in his office and savored the triumph. "People voted for hope against fear," he said. "They hope things will get better with Reagan. And there was some fear of people working that they'd lose their jobs and things would get worse."[29]

But things didn't get better.

President Reagan soon had ownership of Carter's recession. No help was coming from Washington. Rhodes tried to take it all in stride. "In the way I operate, I don't have the ups and downs," he told an interviewer. "When you have a duty to perform, you perform."[30] In February, he offered an austere budget that he said could get the state through the next two years without raising taxes. Even the temporary tax increases enacted over the holidays would be allowed to sunset on July 1 as promised, he said.

It was another promise he would be unable to keep.

That winter, Ironton, a city on the Ohio River, and six other Ohio cities declared fiscal emergencies under a late 1979 municipal assistance law—the "Cleveland bill" enacted to save the lakefront city from default. Ohio auditor Thomas Ferguson said Ironton was running a deficit of at least $708,000. In the Mahoning Valley, nine thousand steel-related jobs had been lost since 1977.

In his February State of the State address, the governor tried to paper over his no-new-taxes vow by saying the legislature should put the question on the November ballot. He proposed raising the state gasoline tax a penny, to eight cents per gallon; the extra penny was to help back a bond issue that would finance highway construction and other infrastructure projects. The stimulus, he said, would create twelve thousand jobs a year. "Ohio is a wounded state. Our people are suffering." Rhodes read methodically from a prepared text. "Together we must make job development programs the hallmark of the legislative session." He wasn't interrupted a single time by applause.[31] His two-year, $21 billion continuation budget was bare bones, not meat and potatoes. It cut some programs—including $1.6 million for the Ohio Rail Transportation Authority—but allowed the temporary taxes imposed in December 1980 to expire on schedule in July.

Rhodes kept returning to the energy issue, convinced that stepped-up production of domestic coal and natural gas was one of the keys to a turnaround. That summer in Atlantic City, at the National Governors Association annual conference, he picked a fight with California governor Jerry Brown, no shrinking violet when it came to political confrontation. Rhodes took umbrage over criticism of President Reagan's unpopular Interior Secretary James Watt, who seemed to see his role in reverse, similar to Rhodes's Ohio EPA chief James McAvoy. Rather than advocate for conservation in administration circles, he led the charge against regulation and for more potentially harmful exploration of untapped mineral resources. In a federal lawsuit, the State of California had succeeded in blocking Watts-supported drilling in small tracts off the Santa Barbara coastline.

"I'm tired of bleeding hearts promoting OPEC [foreign] oil," Rhodes told his fellow governors. "We cannot afford to have people residing in $2 million and $3 million mansions along the Pacific Coast dictating economic conditions for industrial states. I am for the Secretary of the Interior to drill any place in these United States and not be dictated to by the Arabs of this country. . . . I'm all for those people who are doing great work in saving whales and tadpoles in California. I am for Secretary Watt. I think he should drill any place he can: on the Atlantic Ocean, the Ohio River, Lake Erie." Rhodes didn't have to name names: Jerry Brown was the tiresome bleeding heart. The hostility from Ohio's governor seemed to surprise and amuse Brown. Despite pestering from reporters, he chose not to engage. "He just doesn't understand. He has not taken the time to find out what is going on," Brown said of Rhodes. "I am sorry about that. I have the greatest respect for him. I didn't take it personally. He's got a good sense of humor."[32]

Other governors fretted about dramatic reductions in federal aid to states under Reagan, but Rhodes stayed on message. The energy issue was *his* talking point, and his baiting of Brown continued into a second day: "There are many governors here from states with 5%, 6% or 7% unemployment that are concerned about everything from the whales, to the northern California coastline, to the snail darter, to acid rain, to clams in the Ohio River." Clams in the Ohio River—acres and acres of clams?

When he wasn't talking about shellfish or fidgeting in stuffy policy meetings, Rhodes toured the famed Atlantic City boardwalk with family members in tow. He enjoyed junk food and the carnival atmosphere. But he skipped the gambling casinos and a speech by Vice President George Bush and returned to Columbus a day early. His outbursts left Governor Brown to contemplate the nature of marine life in flyover country and how his bombastic adversary had gotten himself elected four times in one of the nation's most politically important states.[33]

Back in Columbus, Plan A—Rhodes's gas tax increase—was scrapped as state revenues lagged behind expectations. In its place, Rhodes gave tacit approval to a 3.3-cent boost in the gasoline tax, marking the first such increase since the early 1960s. Still, the economy sagged and welfare caseloads grew.

Rhodes wouldn't talk specifics, but he knew what was coming: more taxes, more program cuts. Under the Ohio Constitution, the state budget must be in balance at the close of a fiscal biennium. "When the chips are down, it all falls back on me," he said. "They want me to take the gun. I have no objections."[34]

At the June 30 close of the fiscal year, the Republican-controlled Senate and Democratic House deadlocked on a new two-year budget, forcing lawmakers to adopt an interim budget just to keep government from going off the rails. Then, a second stopgap plan. And finally, in mid-November, a $20.8 billion budget for Ohio that included $1.3 billion in new taxes. Rhodes, who throughout his career had inveighed against higher tax increases, signed the bill into law.

But even before leaves began falling that autumn, there was trouble anew as state coffers opened a $1.3 million gap between revenue and receipts. As Ocasek had pointed out, Ohio ranked fiftieth in the nation in state and local tax burden per $1,000 of personal income. Some of Rhodes's conservative allies thought that was a good thing, but the governor went before a joint session of the legislature on September 8, asking for another $1.3 billion in taxes and specifying that the levies would be temporary. In his ten-minute speech, he asserted, "Ohio's economic problems are temporary, and any tax increases should also be temporary."[35]

The temporary plan didn't fly. Rhodes had picked up the gun and cocked it but then left it on the table, sighed one lawmaker. Conservatives immediately sported lapel buttons that simply said, "No." Human service advocates lobbied Statehouse corridors wearing badges declaring, "Thanks governor, but it's just not enough." State representative Ken Rocco of Parma, one of Riffe's lieutenants, said Rhodes shouldn't escape political liability for the budget mess. "It's like saying everybody else is responsible, but him. That somebody else has been chief executive for 16 years."[36]

Rhodes's vaunted political instincts had failed him. Sensing a leadership vacuum, Riffe jumped in with his own $1.8 billion tax package, similar to Rhodes's but larger and permanent. The time for temporary fixes was over. Riffe, mulling over a possible 1982 campaign for governor, remembered his father's advice: "Son, a leader's got to lead." He was fifty-five and at a crossroads in his political career. "I am assuming my responsibility as Speaker of the House," he said. "Now, what's going to happen to my political future, that's up to the people. . . . This is a bold step." Rhodes stayed on the sidelines. "You are pushing peanuts," he told reporters who tried to put daylight between Rhodes and Riffe on the looming tax hike.[37]

As the tax battle came to a crescendo in the House and Senate chambers two floors above his corner office, Rhodes decided to let it play out and kept his mouth shut. "Truthfully, I do not know what is going on [in the legislature]," he said.[38] Riffe's package was eventually scaled back by about $500 million, but the people of Ohio would get a higher sales tax, broadened to cover cigarettes, repairs, and installations. Also, items like car washes and fountain soft drinks were subjected to new taxes. Gas taxes went up. And corporations, insurance companies, and public utilities would pay more. Aid to Families with Dependent Children (AFDC)—welfare—was frozen until July 1, 1982. Taxes on beer and wine rose—again. Senate Finance chairman Stanley Aronoff of Cincinnati said it was the largest tax increase in Ohio history. Rhodes said little. The few winners included public schools, awarded $750 million in increased spending, and state-supported colleges and universities, getting an extra $268 million.

The parties were split, with some liberal Democrats joining conservative Republicans in opposition. "It clogs the nostrils of decency," said one foe, state senator Harry Meshel of Youngstown. "It appears we've taxed everything except flatulence and indigestion."[39] More clogging was ahead.

Away from the tax wars, Rhodes contemplated a literal life-and-death issue: Ohio's new capital punishment law. No one had been executed in the state since March 15, 1963, the second month of his first term as governor; during his first eight years in office, he commuted eight death sentences. The Ohio law was carefully written to overcome constitutional objections raised by a 1978 U.S. Supreme Court decision. Nationally, the high court had ruled the death penalty unconstitutional, then reinstated it under certain conditions. Senate Bill 1, sponsored by Richard Finan, a Cincinnati Republican, passed the General Assembly in early July, over the objections of death penalty opponents. Rhodes signed it into law on July 17, 1981, in Dayton. He didn't oppose capital punishment, but neither did he take the responsibility lightly. "Certainly," he said when asked if he would again consider commutations. "We'll be fair, we'll look at everything. I am as compassionate as I've ever been."[40]

Compassionate and unburdened by ego. That was how Rhodes wanted to be depicted. His humanity shone through in times of tragedy and mourning— public and private milestones, the political and personal. When his old rival

Mike DiSalle died unexpectedly in Italy in September, Rhodes called him "a noble political opponent"—opponent, not enemy—and a "great governor." DiSalle "established a great reputation as a young mayor of Toledo," Rhodes said, "and enhanced this even further by becoming . . . an excellent representative of the people of Ohio."[41]

And there are many examples of Rhodes's concern for the living, young and old. John Byrne was a student at Upper Arlington High School when he and a partner worked on the yard at Rhodes's suburban home, pulling up mulch and replanting flowers on a rainy spring day. As the downpour persisted, Rhodes emerged from the front door and asked the two young men how they were doing and if they could finish the work. About a half hour later, a fellow from the nearby Scioto Country Club pulled up in a golf cart and measured both boys for expensive golfers' rain suits. The gray outfits, paid for by Rhodes, arrived within the hour, and the job got done. "You worked hard for him, and he worked hard for you," Byrne said. "You got the sense he was a people person."[42]

Rhodes was a "people person," but he was hardly without ego. Absent a healthy sense of self, the coal miner's son never would have succeeded in politics. So he spent much of 1981 sounding like a soon-to-be candidate for the U.S. Senate. His closest political advisors seemed convinced he would challenge Howard Metzenbaum, who was up for reelection in 1982. "I think [a Senate race] is in cement," Republican state chairman Earl Barnes said.[43] When Barnes asked Rhodes why he would even want to go to Washington, the governor replied, half joking, "Burning Tree, Earl, Burning Tree"—a reference to an exclusive golf club in suburban Maryland. Bob Hughes, the Cuyahoga County Republican chairman—and a cheerleader for Rhodes and his political interests—confidently told reporters, "If he's breathing, he's running."

As the holidays approached, Rhodes again entertained reporters with a hamburger luncheon in his cabinet room. He was biding his time on the Senate decision, but he didn't discourage the speculation. "The unknown people try to get in early to gain some notoriety. I have until March 25, 1982 [the candidate filing deadline], to make up my mind. . . . I have never had any trouble raising money. . . . Everything is based on ego. It's what people think. I don't have an ego. I have been [mentioned] in the paper as the new ambassador to China . . . no golf course, so that would eliminate me immediately."[44]

But the cronies and pundits making a case for a Rhodes candidacy should have listened more closely to Helen Rhodes in her rare public comments in

1979. "I hope he's had enough [of public life] now," she had said. "I know I have. I did several years ago."[45] In his heart, Rhodes knew Washington wasn't for him. The inability to control his schedule, keeping his independence in a city dominated by Reagan conservatives, and facing scrutiny from a national press corps unaccustomed to his malaprops and unique brand of southern Ohio humor all weighed against a Senate campaign. The brainy Metzenbaum would be a formidable foe with a pile of money for a campaign in a midterm election that looked promising for Democrats. And besides, who ever heard of a seventy-three-year-old freshman?

Rhodes buried the idea just after the New Year broke. He said he had lost the yearning to walk "the glory road" to the nation's capital and would remain in Columbus after his term as governor ended.[46] He also shut down another rumor mill: he would not seek his old office by running for state auditor against Democrat Thomas Ferguson, a highly partisan adversary. The media and even some of his closest advisors had missed the story. Aside from whatever misgivings Rhodes had about remaking his political career at an advanced age, he had kept communication lines open with Metzenbaum and even spoke with him on the phone occasionally. He knew the aggressive Clevelander, "Senator No," would be tough to bring down.

In hindsight, it's hard to imagine the governor campaigning for the Senate in 1982 as his revenue-strapped state struggled under the weight of the stubborn national recession. In recessionary times, manufacturing states like Ohio experience slower recoveries. And so in January of his last year as governor, Rhodes turned to an old ally, Howard Collier, to help him close yet another gap in the state's two-year budget. Mr. Fix-it headed back to Columbus from Toledo, where he served as chief administrator at the Medical College of Ohio at Toledo (later the University of Toledo Medical School).

Collier, the usually jolly, white-haired Santa Claus was, shocked by what he found in the state's books. The man, who smoked Winston cigarettes and had a voice that sounded like a ventriloquist trying to speak while drinking a glass of water, said the state faced the worst financial crisis since the Great Depression. If the economy remained stagnant, Ohio's budget could be nearly $1 billion in the hole by July 1983. So Rhodes ordered a series of deep spending reductions but refused to cut welfare benefits. Still the gap grew, and Rhodes and the legislature went back and forth into June with competing deficit reduction proposals. Conservatives resisted the looming tax increases even when coupled with substantial spending slowdowns.

Eventually, a bipartisan package of $411 million in spending cuts and $591 million in new taxes—including increases for businesses and utilities—emerged. The tax piece also called for a 25 percent surcharge on personal income taxes and an additional hike for wealthy Ohioans. Because the surcharge was imposed at twice the 25 percent rate, to pick up revenue from the first year of the biennium (July 1981 through June 1982), it amounted to an effective 50 percent rate.[47]

It was the fourth major tax increase in two years for a governor who made "no new taxes" a virtual battle cry in most of his statewide campaigns. "Nobody likes taxes," he said, "especially elected officials in both the Democratic and Republican parties." But without the higher taxes, "we in effect would have had to close the state of Ohio down and force county and city governments to raise taxes."[48] A Democratic governor could have made the same argument in the same place. This wasn't the way Rhodes wanted to go out. He had made it through ten years without signing a major tax increase and had won reelection promising to hold the line on taxes. That record was now in shambles. "He had all these ideas—and he had this genius flowing all the time—but we had such a bad economy he couldn't do anything," Bob Howarth said of the troubled last term. "It wasn't at all that the governor didn't have 1,000 ideas about how to get another Honda here, or how to help the small [businesses] and this and that."

It wouldn't be a smooth exit. Howarth had a misunderstanding with the Ohio Historical Society and ordered Rhodes's official papers and documents hauled to a dump about week before he left office. A mix-up on the pickup date led the assistant to believe the historical society was passing on the papers, after museum workers failed to show up at the governor's office at the scheduled time. "I wish I had called the historical society back," Howarth said, years later. "I sent a couple of guys out there to the dump to see if they could possibly find our files. They called me and said, 'There are acres and acres of trash here.'" Conspiracy theorists, including Statehouse reporters, had a field day, certain the governor had buried evidence of his misdeeds.[49]

Rhodes "was frustrated the whole four years," Howarth said, "because he hadn't gotten done what he wanted to do. The economy was such that he spent his time managing the budget instead of innovative things like he did in the 1960s. He had to take a bad situation and do the best he could. . . . But I think he was frustrated when he left because of that."[50]

Rhodes kept his good humor through most of it and betrayed little emotion as his term wound down. "He had a rascally twinkle in his eye and a smile perpetually playing at the corners of his mouth, at least when he wasn't wearing his stern, official governor's face." said reporter Mary Anne Sharkey, who covered the Statehouse for the *Dayton Journal Herald* and the *Plain Dealer*.[51] It was the same thing Bill Wilkins had noticed: a look in the eye that said, *Don't sweat the small stuff*.[52]

Former Toledo mayor Jack Ford, whose dad had known Rhodes in high school, was among the state's Democrats who came to appreciate his connection with ordinary people. "He was a guy who had a supernatural empathy with the so-called little guy and who would go out of his way to make sure that's where he lined up," Ford said in 2005. "He was just as at ease in board rooms as he was on street corners."[53]

Was Rhodes then a populist? Not at all argues Robert K. Schmitz, who lobbied the legislature on behalf of Ohio savings and loan institutions during Rhodes's third and fourth terms. A "populist puts his finger in the air to see which way the wind is blowing"—poring over polls to determine where voters stand on issues. Rhodes already "knew what people were thinking," Schmitz said. "He did not have to go ask them. . . . Jim Rhodes was one of the great political minds in Ohio because he thought like the people. . . . It was innate. You can't teach it."[54]

Plain Dealer reporter Joseph D. Rice said Rhodes easily warmed up to Cleveland City Council president George Forbes—a notorious tough guy and, like Ford, an African American Democrat—by treating him as an individual, not as a member of a political class. That was Rhodes's special charm, Rice said: "his ability to relate to people as individuals."[55]

Rhodes's concern for the poor was genuine, but he was always conflicted over the welfare system and government's role in providing a social safety net. He routinely railed against the welfare bureaucracy. He argued that former Ohio State football star Archie Griffin could do more good in the inner city than a raft of welfare workers. "He was a poor person [as a youth]," said lobbyist John Mahaney, one of Rhodes's closest political confidants. "Rhodes deeply cared about people."[56] Yet he rarely advocated for higher AFDC or General Relief benefits, even though he was reluctant to cut public assistance. He said he believed most folks would prefer to work and earn their keep if they had the opportunity. "The people in the inner city want more than a handout. There is no dignity in a handout. They want jobs."[57]

That remained his focus throughout his sixteen years at the helm.

His tenure came to an end on January 10, 1983: a cold, rainy day. In truth, he was already a "former governor," since his successor, Dick Celeste, had been sworn in at an unannounced private ceremony two days earlier. The wary Celeste forces wanted to prevent any last-minute mischief by the departing governor and his team. Rhodes appeared unfazed as his beloved All Ohio State Fair Band played patriotic tunes on the Statehouse steps. What was he thinking about? "To get out of the cold," he told a newsman who had hoped he might wax nostalgic.

After Celeste's inaugural speech, Rhodes buttoned up his raincoat and walked to his new business office—James A. Rhodes & Associates—about a block north of the Capitol. There he held court—though it was a smaller court than he had been accustomed to. When a reporter told him Auditor Tom Ferguson still held a grudge, Rhodes replied, "Go back over there and tell him [Ferguson] that I like him."

"You can't get too emotional," he said. "This day has been coming. We've all known it. I'm going to have [more] momentous occasions in my life."[58] He was not introspective and perhaps thought he would eventually return to public life in some capacity. It was Rhodes's way to avoid highs and lows—no jubilation, no tears. "He was always looking ahead. I don't think he ever looked back. He never looked back. He never second-guessed himself," said Wilkins.[59]

His admirers saw him as progressive, a visionary resilient and intuitive—with "a great stomach that told him things," as Mahaney put it. That's what kept him ticking through a career in public life spanning five decades. "You have to understand how I live," he once said to an interviewer. "I don't worry about things. I'm not an excitable person."[60]

CHAPTER 12

How Does He Get Away
with That Stuff?

Jim Rhodes shrugged off the notion of legacies and insisted that Ohioans would forget about him soon after he left office. "We are not in a state of ego," he liked to say.

That was a show. He was not an introspective man; that much is true. But he had a healthy ego and wanted to be remembered. So in early 1982—his last year as governor—he commissioned a statue, *of himself,* to be sculpted and dedicated before he left office. A Capital University fine arts professor named Gary Ross got the assignment; some $70,000 to fund the project would be raised from private sources. By summer, the sculpting was well under way and Rhodes was intensely interested in the progress. He even posed. The governor, just over about six feet tall, had put on a little weight and wanted the artist to slim him down in the statue. The edifice was modeled after a 1960s photo of Rhodes that aides found behind a desk in executive assistant Roy Martin's office. "He was not without ego. . . . The statue went from Governor Rhodes in the '80s to Governor Rhodes in the '60s," Bob Howarth said. "We'd go out there [to Ross's studio] in the summer. We'd go out every week to see how it was coming along."[1]

It got done before the snow flew. On December 5, the larger-than-life statue (the likeness was six feet, six inches) was revealed on the northeast quadrant of the Statehouse grounds, the legislature having given permission. But the ceremony didn't come off without a little last-minute mischief from one of Rhodes's sharpest critics: Democratic auditor Tom Ferguson.

Ferguson—or someone from his office—got up early that rainy Sunday morning and put a large sign in the fifth-floor window of the high-rise that housed the state auditor's office, facing the green where the Rhodes's statue was to be unveiled. The sign, in big red letters, read: "Remember Kent State." The auditor, who always suspected Rhodes covered up the full extent of his involvement in the Kent State shootings, was seething over a half-baked Rhodes proposal to merge Kent and the University of Akron into one mega-university. "He can't obliterate history that way," Ferguson said.[2]

The sign came down before the dedication, and the event went ahead without a hitch, complete with dignitaries from both parties and members of the public. "I am now waiting for the skies to open and part, and for the sunshine to come down so we can canonize you," said state senator Harry Meshel, a frequent Rhodes critic but all smiles on this day.[3] When the governor's seven grandchildren pulled the cord, removing the drape (about half the covering had already slipped away), the two hundred onlookers saw a somber likeness of Rhodes, in stride, carrying a briefcase and looking straight ahead. The looking-ahead part was in character, but as governor, Rhodes almost never carried a satchel; that duty was left to one of his faithful Ohio Highway Patrol security men. Hard-to-please critics said the statue looked more like a door-to-door salesman than a populist politician. *Akron Beacon Journal* columnist Abe Zaidan called it a "tribute in bronze to his brass."[4]

But there it was on the lawn of Rhodes's beloved Statehouse—and there it remained until 1991, when it was moved across Broad Street and placed in front of the Rhodes Tower, a forty-one-story state office building, so named by the Ohio Building Authority members he had appointed. Rhodes was conscious enough of the controversy of having a building named after him that he was far away—in China—when the silver letters went up on the front of the edifice.[5]

Rhodes was a man of few words when reporters tried to coax sentimentality out of him or anticipated at least a little emotion. "I know," he said bluntly when a reporter told him he had surpassed the length of service record for postcolonial governors in all of the United States. "You're going to work someplace and I happen to be governor."[6]

False modesty? Or was he genuinely unimpressed with honors? "Nothing," he said after the unveiling of his Columbus statue when someone asked what he wanted to be remembered for. "Ten years from now they'll look at that statue and say, 'When was he governor?'"[7] Of course, there are dozens of statues, buildings, and memorials honoring Rhodes. They are scattered about the state of Ohio: among them are a tower at Cleveland State University, a basketball arena in Akron, an institution of higher learning in Lima—the James A. Rhodes State College—and at least two other statues. In Toledo, a seven-and-a-half foot colossus, a taller twin to the Columbus monument, was dedicated in 2005 outside of a state office building downtown.

Toledo was the scene of political one-upmanship befitting a Keystone Cops comedy playing out in slow motion over two decades. Backers of Rhodes and his Democratic adversary, Toledoan Michael V. DiSalle, named and renamed the twenty-two-story One Government Center three times, slapping one of the ex-governor's plaques over the other, almost as if Rhodes and DiSalle were wrestling to see who would come out on top. Rhodes got the honor first in 1983, right after he left office. But on June 18, 1986, the Ohio Building Authority, under the direction of Democratic governor Richard F. Celeste, changed the name of the building to honor the former Toledo mayor, DiSalle. Rhodes's name had been etched into the stone. No problem. Workers put a plaque over it. Fast-forward to November 9, 2001, when Republican Bob Taft was governor, and a bronze plaque was screwed on top of DiSalle's granite marker, changing the name back to Rhodes.[8] However, the Ohio Building Authority got Rhodes's years of service as governor wrong: it went by the dates of election instead of inauguration, and the plaque had to be redone. The *Blade,* always in Rhodes's corner, had a field day, calling it a "sorry mistake" and a "public embarrassment." It scolded: "It's not rocket science or even political science."[9] In the end, the building kept DiSalle's name, but the plaza and fountain at One Government Center are named for Rhodes. Fittingly, Rhodes's obituary in the *Blade* even included this sentence: "Critics, even some of his supporters, observed that his psychological bent to have his name chiseled in stone, amounted to an 'edifice complex.'"[10]

"There was a personal admiration of him that you would not see today," University of Akron political science professor John Green said at the time of the Toledo statue's unveiling. "When Rhodes and his opponents duked it out, they fought fiercely. But when the election was over and the day was won, they kind of befriended each other."[11] In fact, one of Rhodes's bromides was "Never get so angry with someone that you can't have breakfast with him the next morning."

As then-Toledo mayor Jack Ford, a Democrat, said of Rhodes, he "was the first to look out for a Toledo or a Nelsonville or a Springfield," and he left footprints all over the state.

But his heart was always in the hills of southern Ohio.

The Jackson County Historical Society and the Ohio Association of Commodores, which Rhodes established in the 1960s to raise money for small Statehouse projects, received its own copy of the bronze, briefcase-carrying statue of Rhodes. It was dedicated in an attractive plaza next to the Jackson County Courthouse on May 2, 2013, with the surviving Rhodes family, including grandchildren and great-grandchildren, present.[12]

Fifteen benefactors are listed on a large bronze plaque—these include former aides Bob Howarth and Jon F. Kelly; Jewell Evans, the widow of restaurateur Bob Evans; their son Steve Evans and his wife, Becky; and Marguerite Hughes, widow of Rhodes's political sidekick Bob Hughes. The statue is surrounded by a low brick wall bearing small bronze plaques with Rhodes's achievements as governor and many of the sayings for which he was famous.

* * * * *

Rhodes always seemed to *out-Buckeye* his political adversaries. It was his patriot game. He was a homebody, while his well-traveled rivals—the DiSalles, Gilligans, and Celestes, for instance—sought out elite universities like Georgetown, Notre Dame, and Yale. Dick Celeste ventured to Oxford, England, as a Rhodes (no relation) Scholar. And Jack Gilligan vacationed in Michigan.

Rhodes spent a big chunk of his formative years in Indiana and attended classes at Ohio State University for only a few months. And he frequently vacationed in Florida, at his Fort Lauderdale condo on the Millionaire's Row. Regardless, "he loved Ohio and he loved campaigning," said former Ohio Republican chairman Bob Bennett.[13]

But when reporters needled Rhodes about his frequent trips to Florida, he got testy and started bragging about how often he patronized Ohio attractions. When he got on these rants, some of what he said made no sense. Most times, reporters cleaned up the language and approximated Rhodes's intent; after all, whether you agreed with a governor's statements or not, they should not be made to appear as nonsense.

In this case, a reporter transcribed Rhodes's exact words. Lee Leonard wrote this account for United Press International in 1980. Rhodes boasted about Ohio's state park lodges—which, in fairness, he had a major role in

building—and ridiculed lodges in other states as "tool sheds." He insisted
he had visited not only every ski lodge in Ohio but "every ski":

> I am the only governor in the history of the state of Ohio that has visited
> every museum, every cultural center, every state fair and everything we
> have, attractions, in the state of Ohio, including the Giant and the Monster
> [theme park rides]. . . . I'm the only governor that has visited every ski
> lodge . . . and every ski, and snowmobiles. . . . I visit every place in the
> state of Ohio where there's action . . . what we have in the way of parks
> and recreation and lodges . . . When you go to any other state, or the sur-
> rounding states or the Tetons, or any of the national lodges or anything
> like that—they're all tool sheds! We're the only place that they have an
> indoor swimming pool outdoors. We have more activity in some of our
> lodges than they have in Yellowstone National Park. . . . We have the finest
> lodges in America. We have more recreation per square mile than any
> other state. So what we get is an abundance of people. Our trouble is, in
> the southern part of the state, people from Kentucky coming into our
> lodges, they like to see how a good one looks like.[14]

The national press corps couldn't fathom how Ohio reporters could put up
with Rhodes, do their jobs properly, or interpret his lingo, given monologues
like this one. It wasn't uncommon to hear somebody in the traveling press
corps say to an Ohio reporter, "Is this guy for real?" Or "How do you cover
this guy?" Or "Hasn't anybody written an exposé?"

The national reporters didn't get it. They didn't realize that Ohio reporters
wrote about Rhodes's antics all the time—and the people of Ohio kept on
electing him. Though exasperating, Rhodes was fun to cover and a challenge, too. The traveling press would see him at a presidential campaign
event, upstaging his own candidate; or at a governors' conference, spending
as little time as possible sitting in his assigned seat; and at news conferences,
spewing forth nonanswers and non sequiturs in response to their questions.
And they would scratch their heads; he seemed a buffoon. Jules Witcover,
the syndicated columnist, called him "the Casey Stengel of politics."

At a regional or national governors' conference, if Rhodes was the host,
he would be out in the street in a baseball cap in front of the hotel, directing
traffic as the limousines of his fellow governors pulled up. As for the business

sessions, he got bored. In 1978, Rhodes attended, sort of, the Midwestern Governors Association conference in Lexington, Kentucky. He ducked in and out, using as his excuses a strike by public employees in Cleveland and meetings with his environmental advisors in Columbus.[15] Governor Arthur A. Link of North Dakota, the conference chairman, was trying desperately to get a quorum so the governors could vote on policy statements—something Rhodes had about as much use for as a wet bag of trash. He had skipped the first two days of the meeting. A news story described his appearance: "Two hours after the phone call [from Link, pleading for him to come] Rhodes breezed into the conference room and took his place in the soft, black chair that had been empty two days. Dr. Ellen Fifer, chairman of the conference's Health Care Task Force, was in the middle of a report to the governors." She asked them to complete a lifestyle profile, involving thirty-six questions about their habits, including exercise, nutrition, and safety. Exercise for Rhodes would have been golf, not jogging. "When I see one of them [joggers], I want to go to sleep," he once famously remarked.[16] The story continued: "While the other governors completed the form, Rhodes gazed at it with a bemused expression and peered about the room to see who was there.[17] When it appeared he was about to be asked to start writing, he jumped up and took a walk into the hall with aides. 'I didn't want to answer the one about housework,' Rhodes explained [to reporters.] 'I would have put down no to most of them anyway.'" Constructively, Rhodes did meet for about twenty minutes with Kentucky governor Julian Carroll, to see what could be done about a closed bridge over the Ohio River between the two states. Then he said he had to go back to Columbus.

Reginald Stuart, a reporter for the *New York Times,* probably summed up the feelings of the national press after dealing with the Ohio governor. He said Rhodes was "a governor for all seasons. He's got all the answers," Stuart said, flapping his thumb and fingers together like a duck quacking.[18]

*　*　*　*　*

Rhodes may have come across as a blustery know-it-all to some, but he was well read and had a particular interest in American history—especially the nation's first ladies. So his interest in Jacqueline Kennedy Onassis should have surprised no one. Fine, but who is that silver-haired man at the newsstand buying a—what?—*Hustler* magazine? "We are walking out of the Neil House [an aging hotel across the street from the governor's office] and Rhodes just—zip—darts into the newsstand," recalled Press Secretary Chan Cochran. "He comes out—no brown bag—it was in a yellow cover." Word that the governor of Ohio had bought a pornographic magazine soon rippled through the Statehouse. In a tizzy, Rhodes's personal assistant Emma Scholz caught up with Cochran and demanded to know what was going on. The press secretary feared imminent disaster. "But you have to understand, I was only the *assistant* press secretary. Rhodes was his own press secretary." In that role, Rhodes called a news conference for the next morning to explain the purchase.

Morning came, and Rhodes arrived in the Statehouse underground parking garage with a car full of files in boxes—four long storage cases. Aides hauled them up to his office, where the governor awaited the onslaught of newsies. "Everybody showed up and boy were they loaded for bear, they were going to have a good time that day," Cochran said. First reporter's question: "Why did you buy *Hustler* magazine? He says, 'For my collection.' What collection? 'Right here.' And Rhodes pointed to the files at his feet. 'It's all about first ladies of the United States. They are the most maligned group in American history.' He starts in on Dolley Madison being hounded out of the White House, Mary Todd Lincoln tried, and so on."[19]

And *Hustler?* The sleazy magazine had provided another chapter by publishing clandestine photos of Jacqueline Onassis sunbathing topless on a Greek island. That was Rhodes's only interest in it. After about forty-five minutes of this, Hugh McDiarmid, the *Dayton Journal Herald*'s esteemed Statehouse columnist, had had enough. He led an exodus of frustrated reporters out of the governor's office.

Rhodes knew some first ladies on a first-name basis. He wrote to Nancy Reagan on April 6, 1981—a little over two months after her husband's inauguration—urging her to buy White House china from Sterling China in Wellsville, Ohio. It was widely reported that she was in the market to replace the executive mansion's formal tableware. Rhodes wrote, "Dear Nancy, A product of American ingenuity and good old-fashioned hard work, the makers of Sterling China have developed a reputation for the excellent workmanship and enduring beauty of the product."[20] There is no record of Mrs. Reagan's response, but she went elsewhere for the taxpayers' china.

Rhodes was respectful of Pat Nixon, but he wasn't impressed with her husband, President Richard Nixon—even before the Watergate scandal forced him out of office. When the former president accepted an invitation to speak at a fund-raising dinner for Ohio Senate Republicans in Columbus on February 18, 1981, Rhodes skipped the event. He didn't cite any official duties as an excuse: "I have to be home to pay the paperboy."[21] Rhodes didn't spend a lot of time building up the Republican Party. Those who would follow were left on their own.

Rhodes's knowledge of history is typified in a story told by Gene D'Angelo, a longtime friend and executive at WBNS-TV in Columbus.[22] During his second term, Rhodes was leading an Ohio contingent to the National Governors' Conference in New Orleans. When they got to the Crescent City, they went to their hotel, but the rooms weren't ready. Rhodes directed aide Jim Duerk to get a bus. When the bus arrived, the Ohio party climbed aboard, and Rhodes started telling the driver where to turn and which way to go. They wound up at a park commemorating the Battle of New Orleans—an American victory over the British redcoats. Rhodes jumped down and led the group at a brisk pace through the park, pointing out markers, monuments, and other items of interest. At one point, he dove under a bush and crawled around looking for a marker until he found it.

Somebody asked, "Governor, how many times have you been here?" He responded, "I've never been here." He knew it from his reading. His favorite was Andrew Jackson. The War of 1812 was special to him. He said, "We took out a mortgage in 1776 and burned it in 1812."[23]

* * * * *

Rhodes was peculiar when it came to food. He was obsessive, even though most of his preferences and faddish compulsions fell into a category people would later call "comfort food." It is unlikely that he sampled any blackened redfish during his time in New Orleans. He didn't drink coffee or much alcohol, and he didn't smoke cigarettes, though he enjoyed gnawing on unlit cigars.

He usually ate lunch in his office, opting for canned tomato soup and packaged deli meats. Dutch Loaf was a favorite. He was prone to eating binges—fixating on something he liked and had heard was healthy. Tom Moyer remembered the governor's "eating kicks"—cabbage and grapefruit, along with a ready supply of lunchmeat. "He would decide 'Something is really good for me.' Got on a grapefruit jag. He'd bring in grapefruits. He would cut things up.

He tried to peel them. 'Here Tom have some grapefruit.' My stomach began to churn. [I] had a staff member get me some soda crackers and milk."[24]

Rhodes also enjoyed cooking and sharing food. He sliced apples, passed around limburger cheese, and popped popcorn. "He could live on popcorn," said Paul Gillmor, who often traveled with Rhodes on state business.[25]

George E. Condon Jr., a longtime White House reporter, knew Rhodes as a boy in Cleveland through his father, newspaperman George E. Condon Sr. As a grownup, he covered the governor's third term at the Statehouse. But it was an incident from his boyhood involving State Auditor Rhodes that stuck with him—perhaps because of its good-humored strangeness. Condon, who was then eleven, recalled a "man standing at my front door barking out orders while juggling two bags of groceries and the largest pots and pans I had ever seen." Rhodes claimed that he made the best vegetable beef soup in the state—and he was there to prove it. "What followed that day was a few hours of frantic culinary activity in our kitchen, with potatoes and beans and chunks of beef flying every which way until so much soup was produced we had to store the leftover in the winter-chilled garage for more than a week before it was gone."[26]

During his fourth term, Rhodes accepted a dinner invitation at the Shaker Heights home of reporter Joe Rice. He brought along two state highway patrolmen, and they joined in the meal. Rice's wife, Janet, did the cooking: a beef roast and spaghetti and meatballs. Rhodes preferred the pasta and reached across the table to spear an extra meatball. Afterward, Rice said, his unassuming guest "went into the kitchen and started doing dishes."[27]

So he cooked and washed dishes, but the governor never played bartender. Drinking was another matter. He thought no good could come from boozing, yet he was not one for total abstinence. On rare occasions, after a long day on the road he would order a beer—usually a Michelob—while enjoying the company of reporters or political associates like Gillmor, the senate president during part of Rhodes's fourth term. Lobbyist John Mahaney, one of his political pals, said the governor "would open a can of beer, take one swig, then put it down and never touch it again."[28] "He didn't care if you drank," said Bill Wilkins. But "he saw so many people that got in trouble" because of alcohol.[29] By the same token, his friend Roger Dreyer told of being at a social event when Rhodes nodded dismissively toward a group of lobbyists, yukking it up at the other side of the room. "You see those lobbyists over there, lots of money," he said. "Did you ever look at this? Some of them are drunks."[30] Despite this sanctimony, Rhodes loved the comedian Foster Brooks—who made his name playing a drunk—and he delighted in the company of the flamboyant Florida governor Claude Kirk, who was fond of drink.

He laughed a lot and regaled reporters with stories about Governor Kirk or Bob Hope. But even his closest aides seldom saw him in emotional distress. He was not a touchy-feely guy. When former Columbus mayor Dana "Buck" Rinehart hugged him at a dinner in his honor, Rhodes squirmed and pulled back. "Buck," he said, "you need to learn that Republican men don't hug each other."[31]

But in the privacy of the governor's inner chamber, Moyer saw sadness and emotion—he saw it in the drained look of the man who sat in his office suite after the Kent State tragedy. And he saw it after a surprise birthday party for the governor in the early 1970s; Emma Scholz was in charge that day, and she directed Moyer to keep Rhodes out of the cabinet room while the cake, decorations, and gifts were being taken care of. When it was time, Moyer turned to Rhodes, saying "Oh, Governor there is someone in the cabinet room I want you to meet, and he came, and they [staff] sang Happy Birthday to him, and he was like shocked, very humble and actually had tears in his eyes. And he went back in his office and I asked, uh . . . 'That was really a nice event to do,' and he said, 'Yeah.'" Nothing more. Now, the young aide feared something was wrong, so he went back to Scholz for insight. "She said, 'Well, he has a very difficult time with events like that for him, because his parents, his mother was so poor that she could never provide him with a birthday party. He didn't get presents.'"[32]

Rhodes was a compulsive take-charge guy who happily went about fixing things that weren't broken. "He would reorganize meetings that didn't need to be reorganized," said Bob Teater, "so cabinet members had to have back-up plans to get ready for Plan B."[33] The governor often thought he had better ways of handling social events. Roger Dreyer remembered Rhodes at a steak-fry put on by oil company executives in western Ohio. Rhodes didn't like the way the tables and chairs were set up, so he began shouting out directions to staff people, insisting the room be rearranged. Soon furniture was being pushed about to meet the governor's specifications. No one asked for his help, but "he got up and took over the meeting."[34]

Thomas Green, a former lobbyist for Columbia Gas of Ohio, served for a time as a Rhodes campaign aide. On a trip back to Columbus late one afternoon after a campaign sortie, Green was in the back seat along with Rhodes's patronage chief, Roy Martin. Chuck Shipley, a former highway patrolman and permanent Rhodes loyalist, was at the wheel. The governor, sitting next to Shipley, "wanted to go to a guy's funeral but he couldn't remember his name or what funeral home," said Green. "He kept trying to make us remember the name and the funeral home. We finally determined that the funeral home was Schoedinger, but there are a number of those in the Columbus area. Finally Rhodes said 'Upper Arlington.'

"Roy was in the back saying, 'We're not goin' to a funeral home. We're goin' home.' But Shipley was driving and he was going to do what the governor said. So we stop at the funeral home and Rhodes bounds out of the car and lopes in. Martin says to me, 'Go with him! Go with him!' So I go in and by the time I get in there, Rhodes is at the casket, looking at this guy.

"I go up to the casket and we're standing there looking down. I turn my head toward Rhodes and whisper out of the side of my mouth, 'It's the wrong guy.'

"He says, 'I know.'

"So he turns and goes over to the widow and says what a fine guy this fellow was and 'He was a good friend of mine.' The widow says, 'I didn't know my husband knew you.' Rhodes said 'yes' and she said, 'My husband hated you.' The husband was a Democrat and a labor union guy.

"Rhodes wouldn't give up. 'Aww, that was just talk,' he said. 'We played golf a few times.' The son said, 'My father didn't play golf.'

"Rhodes knew he'd been caught. He said, 'I'm sorry for your loss,' and then he said to me, 'Let's get out of here and don't tell Roy it was the wrong guy.' Then he made me write a letter to the widow expressing his sorrow for the death."[35]

* * * * *

Jim Rhodes had the reputation for being able to make things happen—and fast—when he wanted to. This may be the best example of his political power. Ed Michael Jr., owner of Michael's ice cream parlor in Jackson, tells of a group of local businessmen coming to his father's house and saying: "You know the governor. Jeno Paulucci wants to build a factory that would hire two thousand people, but he needs to have the runway extended at the Jackson County Airport so he can land his plane." Paulucci, who also founded Michelina's and Chun King, wanted to make Jeno's Pizza Rolls in Jackson. At the time, Ed Michael Sr. ran the ice cream shop where Rhodes, as a boy, had his first job roasting peanuts. As Ed Jr. told it, "Dad called Rhodes and he got them to extend the runway. They had the ceremony (at the airport) and Rhodes was there. Afterwards, he said, 'Eddie, is there anything else you need?'

"'Yeah, they're gonna tear down the Greyhound bus station and people here won't be able to travel anywhere.'

"We drove from the airport back to Michael's and in the fifteen or twenty minutes it took, there was a guy on the phone from the PUCO [Public Utilities Commission of Ohio] and he said, 'Mr. Michael, we assure you that the bus station will stay in Jackson.' That was the greatest display of political power I've ever seen."[36]

Jim Rhodes learned how to push the political levers on the way up. When he was state auditor, he and Roy Martin, who later controlled the patronage out of the governor's office, would do the good-cop, bad-cop routine on a hapless local bureaucrat.[37] If the auditor's office examination found a minor problem, Rhodes would have Martin call the official and say, "Come to Columbus next Monday." That would give the fellow time to sweat all weekend. When he arrived in Columbus, Martin would sternly lay out all the bad stuff in the audit. After a bit, Rhodes would breeze into the room and soft-pedal the findings. "We'll take care of it," he'd say. Whew! "Ohhh, thank you governor!" He had another political ally for life.

When Rhodes was governor in the 1960s, state aid to private and parochial schools was new, and not welcome in some rural areas. And the Ohio legislature was dominated by the "Cornstalk Brigade," as conservative lawmakers from rural areas were called. But Rhodes didn't see why all schoolchildren shouldn't be helped. "A textbook is a textbook," he told the Catholic bishops. "They [parochial schools] should have 'em."

But votes were scarce in the Ohio House of Representatives for a spending bill that included aid to nonpublic schools. One by one, Rhodes called the recalcitrant lawmakers into his office. John Mahaney, the longtime lobbyist for the Ohio Council of Retail Merchants, recalls his powers of persuasion: "Vertus Kruse told Rhodes he couldn't vote for it because of his district and Rhodes called him in and showed him a glass with about an inch of water in it. 'You see this?' the governor asked. 'If you don't vote for this bill, that lake you want will have about this much water in it, because I'll have it drained.'"

Another Republican legislator entered the governor's office vowing to oppose Parochiaid. "Rhodes held his thumb and forefinger about an inch apart and asked, 'What's this?' The legislator replied, 'a thumb and finger.' 'No,' said the governor. 'This is how much blacktop that's gonna be put on Route 104 if you don't vote for that bill.'

"Lloyd George Kerns [a veteran rural lawmaker and owner of a quarter-horse farm] saw the parade of his colleagues coming out of the governor's office with their tails between their legs. He was puffing out his chest and loudly proclaiming, 'I'm going down there and just tell him no.' Rhodes called him in, and about fifteen minutes later he came out with his arm crooked behind his back and said, 'I just got educated. I'm gonna vote for it.'"[38]

Onetime Columbus mayor Buck Rinehart, who received more than his share of advice from James A. Rhodes, took a small but bold step on a development issue after getting a peek at one compartment of the amazing toolbox from which Rhodes drew his political weapons.

"In the spring of 1989, there was great anticipation over the opening of City Center Mall (in Downtown Columbus). It was a huge, huge deal. All the business leaders in the community were lined up for it. They were focused. We had the funding. It was going to open in August. But the business community was concerned because right across High Street was a strip bar called the 40 Carats. I called Rhodes and said, 'Governor, I'm under a lot of pressure from the business community to make 40 Carats go away.' He said, 'You haven't used your code enforcement people. Tell 'em to blanket this place. How do you think the Israelites got over to Canaan?'

"But 40 Carats was clean as a whistle. They couldn't get anything on 'em. At the end of July, on a Sunday morning about 3:00 A.M., I get a call that the 40 Carats is on fire. I go down there, and it's burning up. So I order it torn down as a threat to the health, safety, and welfare of the public, and Loewendick [construction company] comes in and bulldozes it. At 6:00 A.M., Rhodes is on the phone: 'Who the hell put the torch to the 40 Carats? That was a brilliant idea [to order it torn down]. I should have thought of that myself. You take credit for it. It's something good that will benefit the people.'"[39]

Rhodes wasn't shy about taking credit—and he loved to promise things. Sometimes he couldn't deliver. If he was speaking to a crowd, especially in a rural area, and it was pointed out that one of his vows was yet to be fulfilled, he would look directly at the person, point his finger and say, "You got it!" Then he would ask one of his underlings to put the wheels in motion.

During the 1978 campaign, when he was defending his record against Democrat Dick Celeste, Rhodes was in Mansfield to announce the expansion of facilities at the Mansfield branch campus of Ohio State University. He had a written text but "he never paid any attention to those [prepared] speeches," said Tom Green, a campaign aide at the time. Rhodes promptly misspoke and announced the expansion of facilities at Ohio State's *Marion* branch campus—some forty miles south of Mansfield.

"Governor, you're in Mansfield," one of his campaign assistants pointed out. "You just announced it [the project] would be in Marion." Rhodes retorted, "Well, that's where it'll be." By now, Rhodes and his aides were in the car departing the scene. Kent McGough, the Republican state chairman, urged the governor to turn back, admit his mistake and apologize. "No," the governor responded. "We'll get these people a building, too." And he did.[40]

* * * * *

Jim Rhodes was a country boy at heart and he loved the Ohio State Fair. He loved all fairs—the carnival atmosphere, the kids having fun. He loved that a day at the fair brought families together. When he became governor, he vowed to make the Ohio State Fair the largest in the country, and he succeeded. Attendance swelled to 3 million, topping Texas's fair, although there were suspicions that fair workers, lemon shakes, and corn dogs were tallied as part of the daily attendance. The governor kept the price of admission as low as possible and at one point included all-day amusement ride passes as part of the admission fee.

Rhodes would cut the ribbon to open the fair at 6:00 A.M. Later governors, whom Rhodes no doubt regarded as slugabeds, pushed the time back to a more civilized 10:00 A.M., or even the afternoon. For two weeks or more (during the peak years, when the fair lasted seventeen days), Rhodes moved his office and a few staffers into a mobile home on the fairgrounds to conduct the state's business. Then he would periodically whiz around the dusty grounds in a golf cart, stopping to greet fair-goers, encouraging 4-Hers, and shooting baskets or playing games of chance with kids. He told reporters this is what he would have wished for as a kid.

Rhodes was the first governor to sleep in the barn with the 4-H kids and their sheep and pigs. For the cameras, he'd bed down amid the straw on a cot, but before dawn he'd be up, shouting at his young charges to "Get up!" and handing them brooms and pitchforks to get busy. A Junior Fair Endowment Scholarship was established in his name, and he presided over the Sale of Champions, in which young 4-Hers made thousands of dollars as their prize animals were auctioned off to big meat retailers.

Steve Evans, son of the restaurateur Bob Evans, tells this story. "At the fair, Rhodes was king. One year in the 1970s, Bob Evans went to the administration office. Big Bear and Kroger and all the other big markets were there. They were going to have the bidding on the grand champion lamb, hog, and steer. Rhodes fixed it so the bidding would not go below a certain figure. He said, 'Listen, guys, this is college money for these kids. They've worked hard.' They [the store execs] always did what the governor asked. And they got the publicity in return for bidding up those animals."[41]

To help boost attendance, Rhodes got top-flight entertainment for the nightly concerts at the grandstand. Bob Hope appeared a record fifteen times, but Rhodes also got the Oak Ridge Boys, his favorite, plus the Jackson Five, Pat Boone, Kenny Rogers, and Mac Davis. As a concession to the 1970s, he brought in the Beach Boys and Kool and the Gang. Free tickets were in demand for the VIP section and available through the governor's office for certain privileged characters.

After he left office, Rhodes continued to patronize the fair, and not for the publicity. He just loved it and delighted in showing it to others. Reporters covering the opening of the 1991 fair will not forget Rhodes, in his golf cart, directing the new governor, Clevelander George Voinovich, where to go and what to do, waving his arms and whistling as if Voinovich were a small dog: "Fweet-fweet-fweet! Georgie! Georgie! Over here!"

Rhodes was genuinely touched in 1983 when his successor and former bitter rival, Democrat Dick Celeste, sent him passes for the entire run of the fair for himself and his wife. "I consider it an honor that you would recognize me in this way," he wrote to Celeste, adding that he was sending Fair Manager Jack Foust $154 to cover the cost.[42]

* * * * *

In and out of public office, Jim Rhodes had big ideas and big dreams. He read the *Wall Street Journal* and was in tune with what the business community wanted and what might work. For example, he read about the Spruce Goose, a huge transport plane belonging to billionaire Howard Hughes. It gave him the idea of using the Husky, a large cargo plane, to ferry trucks from Cleveland to Los Angeles.[43] That hasn't worked out so far.

"He'd say, 'I wonder why nobody thought of doing this or doing that,'" his daughter Suzanne Moore said. "We were riding downtown one day, and he said, 'Wouldn't it be great if there was an underground walkway between City Hall and the Statehouse? That way, the people who wanted to go from one to the other wouldn't have to go outside.'"[44]

Perhaps Rhodes's wildest idea of all was building a bridge over Lake Erie from Ohio to Ontario, so Ohio's industrial and commercial haulers wouldn't have to go all the way to Detroit or Buffalo to get to Canada. When he proposed the bridge in 1965, it was greeted by hoots of derision. The *Toledo Blade* called the idea "harebrained."[45] The Ohio Historical Society voted Rhodes's announcement of his plan "the ninth most embarrassing moment of Ohio history."[46] The cost of the bridge was pegged at less than a billion dollars—cheap by today's standards. But the proposal was dropped.

In July 1970, when he was getting ready to leave office after his first two terms, Rhodes revived the bridge idea, appointing a special commission to study it. By then there was a whole new cadre of Statehouse reporters ready to dissolve into side-splitting laughter and ridicule the proposal. F. P. Neuenschwander, then the director of development, said there was an eight-hour time lag in the delivery of Ohio products to Canada because trucks had to go around the lake. A bridge would save $60 to $80 for each trip to or from Canada, he said. In 1967, the firm Howard, Needles, Tammen & Bergendorff had conducted a feasibility study, which showed a variety of options. The longest route was eighty-three miles, between Cleveland and Port Stanley, Ontario. Other possibilities were from Painesville, Ohio, to Port Stanley; Ashtabula to Port Rowan, Ontario; and Erie, Pennsylvania, to Port Dover, Ontario.[47] The study also said a four-lane toll facility between Cleveland and Point Pelee could be built with a $69 million subsidy, and tolls would repay the subsidy by 1993. Other options included a toll-free bridge between Sandusky and Point Pelee, or Cleveland and Point Pelee, or Cleveland and Erie Beach.

The "little kid" never left Jim Rhodes. He loved to interact with boys and girls at county fairs and the Ohio State Fair. Here, with his wife, Helen, he plays ring toss at a fair as youngsters watch. Columbus *Dispatch* file photo, January 25, 1994.

The bridge was to be 50 feet above the water with 150-foot-tall suspension spans in the shipping lanes. It was to have turnarounds with refuge areas, for use during Erie's notoriously sudden lake storms, deck lighting across the entire span, and an electronically operated storm warning system.[48] An artist's conception of the bridge was rendered, sending the Statehouse press corps into further gales of laughter.

Financing would be split among Ohio, Ontario, and the U.S. and Canadian governments. Estimated costs ranged from $235 million for a two-lane bridge between Sandusky and Point Pelee to $786 million for a four-lane bridge between Cleveland and Erie Beach. Tolls were to be $6 for cars and $25 for trucks between Sandusky and Point Pelee, or $10 for cars and $25 for trucks between Cleveland and Erie Beach. Sandusky to Point Pelee afforded the lowest cost per mile; it was only thirty miles and would include eight miles of existing roadway on Kelleys Island and Pelee Island. The study estimated that an average of 18,100 vehicles a day would use the bridge. Rhodes said the bridge would create 5,400 to 24,500 jobs a year during the five-year construction period and put $200 million to $1 billion into the local economy during those years.

"One of these days, it's going to be constructed," Rhodes said.[49] "It won't be today, or tomorrow or even next year. But I believe this will happen much sooner than people think." He said he expected opposition from the Toronto area because of a possible shift in industrial development. "There will be people against this proposal for various reasons, some serious and some just to be against," he said. "A few years ago, people never thought a man would walk on the moon, and they laughed at the idea of an interstate highway system."

Rhodes predicted it would create 150,000 new jobs and make the Ohio-Ontario region the "greatest industrial complex on the North American continent, and one of the most productive regions in all the world."[50] Of course, nothing happened. Rhodes left office and became engaged in his own projects. And during his third and fourth terms as governor he never brought up the idea.

But the concept wasn't dead.

In 2010, more than forty years after Jim Rhodes proposed the idea, Richard Rogovin, a Columbus lawyer with a bridge-building company, sought advice on a similar project from the Ohio State University College of Civil and Environmental Engineering.[51] He proposed a forty-five-mile bridge running along a geological shelf in the lake to provide a more direct route for commercial and industrial traffic to Ohio's largest international trading partner. So far, there is no bridge, nor a plan to build it, but sometimes Jim Rhodes's big ideas take a long time to bear fruit.

* * * * *

In the late 1990s, when Rhodes was pretty much confined to his home, a delegation trying to raise money for a youth campground in southern Ohio got an audience with him. One member was Ben Rose, a Lima attorney who had served in the Ohio House of Representatives and had run for state auditor. "They brought in this fund-raiser from Durham, North Carolina. He had been a fund-raiser for Duke. He wore a tweed jacket and a bow tie. We warned him that he'd be lucky if he got to talk about what he wanted to for 5 percent of the time. Rhodes had had a stroke. He gave the guy 50 percent of the time.

"He knew we were talking about having the camp in Pike County. So he told stories about a former governor named Jumpy White, because he jumped on another presidential candidate's bandwagon at the Republican National Convention. He told stories about bootlegging, where the sheriff arrested the liquor agents at the county line and the court backed him up. He told about how he had founded the Knothole Gang for boys and girls who wanted to go to baseball games. Then he waved his hand and said, 'Follow me.' He was in his wheelchair and he directed us into the sunroom, where he had his bed set up. 'Lie down on this bed!' he commanded the tweedy fund-raiser from Duke. It was a vibrating bed that Rhodes said he had developed. 'One hour on this bed is worth five hours of your life,' he told his visitors. 'We're gonna sell these beds all over the country.'" After his sales pitch for the bed, Rhodes was glad to contribute to the youth camp. "There is nothing more important than helping young kids," he said. (Friends and family said later there was no indication that Rhodes invented or marketed the vibrating bed.)[52]

* * * * *

Rhodes always patronized the same barber, and one day he told the man that he and a small group of Ohioans were going to Italy on a visit that would include an audience with the pope in Rome.[53] After the trip, the next time he got a haircut, the barber asked, "How was your trip? Did you see the pope?"

"We sure did."

"What did he say?"

"He said, 'Where the hell did you get that haircut?'"

* * * * *

Late in his fourth term, Rhodes attended the dedication of the Owens-Illinois building on the Toledo riverfront, a project that had developed on his watch. Toledoan Jim Ruvolo, chairman of the Ohio Democratic Party, was there on the banks of the Maumee. He recalled:

"He didn't want to come because he had a golfing date, but they got him to come. So he flew in in a helicopter and had on plaid golf slacks and a sport coat that didn't match. He went up to the mic and started crowing about how many jobs this was going to create for everybody and their children and grandchildren.

"When he was leaving, this young, naïve TV reporter ran up to him and breathlessly asked him, 'Governor, how many jobs is this going to create?' He takes his hand and touches her shoulder and says, 'As many as we need, young lady.' Then he was off, leaving her mystified. She looked over at me. I just smiled and shrugged."[54]

* * * * *

Rhodes went to one National Governors Association Conference that was held on the U.S. *Independence,* off the coast of the Virgin Islands. Of his accommodations, he recalled: "They asked me which room I wanted. I said, 'Where's Rocky [New York governor Nelson Rockefeller]?'

'He's in 101.'

'I want 101A.'

'Why?'

'Because if that ship sinks, I know they're gonna come after him. They're gonna have the Marines, the Navy and Air Force out there.'"[55]

During an energy shortage in subfreezing temperatures, Rhodes ordered the Public Utilities Commission of Ohio to make sure utilities kept the heat turned on for poor people and worried about receiving payment later. A reporter asked, "What if they don't pay their bills all winter? Aren't you inviting them not to pay their bills?" And Rhodes retorted, "They might want air conditioning."

One liners, aphorisms, truisms, axioms, or just plain nutty sayings—these all came out of the mouth of James A. Rhodes, many more than once.[56]

* * * * *

"The only two jobs where you start on top are digging a hole and governor."

* * * * *

"Never build anything underground because you don't get the credit for it."[57]

* * * * *

"When I talk about this, I ain't E. F. Hutton. Nobody listens."

* * * * *

"The best way to get rich is to use other people's money."

* * * * *

"Woody Hayes once introduced me as the biggest athletic supporter in the state of Ohio."

* * * * *

"The Democrats used to say I wasn't fit to sleep with the hogs. The Republicans defended me and said I was."

* * * * *

During a discussion of driver education: "We had driver education in Jackson before anybody else, but the horse died."[58]

* * * * *

"One of the secrets of life is to get as many people obligated to you as possible. Do as many kindly things as possible, and then when you want something from them, they'll respond."[59]

* * * * *

"Nothing gets done until somebody does something."

* * * * *

"I come from the hills of Ohio. I was 22 years old before I knew that a bust was a sculpture of an individual."[60]

* * * * *

At the 1988 Republican National Convention: "Platforms are something you run from, not on."[61]

* * * * *

"The people have spoken and I will abide by their decision."[62]

CHAPTER 13

The Last Roundup

JIM RHODES was not halfway through his fourth term as governor before speculation started over what he would do next. Rhodes encouraged it, taking immense delight in tantalizing reporters, lobbyists, and political junkies wondering about his future. His future, of course, included the likelihood of running for public office again. But what activity would he pursue if he didn't? And there would indeed be activity. Inactivity was foreign to James A. Rhodes. "Activity" could well have been his middle name.

Rhodes helped Ronald Reagan carry Ohio in the 1980 presidential election by giving him pointed advice, which Reagan actually took. The Californian made a television commercial in front of the rusted-out hulk of an abandoned Youngstown steel factory and blamed President Carter's policies for its demise.

The calendar had barely flipped to 1981 when Rhodes's political juices were set to boiling. The flamethrower was liberal Democrat Senator Howard Metzenbaum, who was quoted in a news story as blaming the Rhodes administration for "foot-dragging, incompetence and downright negligence" in blocking $60 million in federal heating assistance to the poor. The governor summoned an aide to the office at 6:00 A.M. to construct a blistering press release, blaming Metzenbaum for the energy crisis and all of America's other woes. "His is a record of waste and inefficiency to gain the favor of special interest groups," Rhodes was quoted, in a torrent of righteous indignation. "No one has caused more misery for the senior citizens, the poor and the unemployed of Ohio than Senator Metzenbaum."[1] Many thought the outburst signaled the start of Rhodes's 1982 Senate campaign, even though a Republican pollster had found that the governor's negatives had caught up with his positives among voters. But it was just Rhodes being Rhodes. He had thick skin, but every once in a while someone would penetrate it and set him off, as Metzenbaum did here.

After stringing everyone along for a year, the governor said he didn't want to go to Washington. And it was the right call. He wouldn't have been a good fit in a group of one hundred talkers and procrastinators. Jim Rhodes was a doer, and the governorship was the right fit for him. On January 6, 1982, he issued a release saying his "sole reason" for shunning the Senate race was "I owe it to my family to remain in Ohio." Still, there was chatter that he would stay in the loop by seeking and winning one of the lesser statewide offices until he could run for governor again. Maybe auditor—his old "catbird seat"—would be his landing place, or perhaps treasurer, or even secretary of state.

Although Rhodes had fun conducting the guessing game, his impeccable political sixth sense kept him out of the 1982 election. It was all he could do to keep the state financially afloat during his last two years as governor, and Reagan was having his own troubles in Washington. It was not a good time for Republicans; they were trounced that November. Democrats captured every statewide executive office in Ohio.

During preliminary sparring in both parties for the 1982 gubernatorial nominations, Rhodes showed his utter mastery of the political game in a way that defied convention. This one fell into his hands by sheer happenstance. Chief Justice Frank Celebrezze of the Ohio Supreme Court threw his hat into the ring, challenging his fellow Cuyahoga County Democrat Dick Celeste. His declaration of candidacy had been expected, and Rhodes was ready to appoint a Republican to succeed him as a justice on the court—a woman at that. Celebrezze was required by law to leave the court to run for governor, so he sent his resignation letter to the governor's office. Rhodes formally accepted it.

But before the day was over, Celebrezze changed his mind. He quickly sent Rhodes a letter pulling back his resignation. What a chance for the governor to do mischief! By refusing this second letter, he could force Celebrezze to live with his mistake and throw the Democrats into turmoil. Instead, he accepted the withdrawal, allowing Celebrezze to remain chief justice. "I did the proper thing," Rhodes said.[2] But his action was true to his credo that you try to obligate others: now Celebrezze owed him a gigantic favor.

Once Rhodes had dropped the idea of running for the U.S. Senate or any notion that he might seek to return as state auditor, talk turned to how he would occupy himself in the four years between 1982 and 1986 when, presumably, he would seek a fifth term as governor. Before the '86 campaign, there was plenty of time for Rhodes to go back into private business, and speculation centered on what he would sell, aside from himself. Early guesses focused on some sort of groundbreaking technology, such as a new type of super battery—the kind that would power electric cars in the twenty-first century. That idea possibly stemmed from a little-publicized adventure during the early 1970s international oil embargo.

During 1973's days of long lines at the gasoline stations, Rhodes and his good friend Len Immke, a prosperous Columbus Buick dealer, found out about a man in Springfield (some say Dayton) who was working in a garage out behind his house. The fellow had a car that he claimed would get eighty miles to the gallon. Rhodes's eyes lit up at the thought: as Immke recalled, he said "We can sell this idea to GM or Ford for a billion dollars! We need to go down and see this thing." So they went to the guy's house and found he was in his garage with the windows covered over with paper "like it was *Back to the Future*."

"Inside was this old car, an AMC Gremlin or something like that. He was a tinkerer, and he had outfitted this car with a regular engine and a smaller fuel-efficient engine. He had the crude, crude basics of what we now call a hybrid," recalled David Lavelle, Immke's nephew. But after a full day of testing the vehicle at Immke's dealership, duplicating the road resistance and figuring the gasoline mileage, it didn't measure up. Rhodes, Immke, and Dave Thomas, the founder of Wendy's, sank a considerable amount of money into the project and told the mechanic to keep working on it. But before their dreams could be realized, the oil embargo broke, and gas prices went back down. "I think it just died a slow death," Lavelle said of the project.[3]

At any rate, Rhodes's mystery product became known as "The Widget" among Statehouse reporters, who questioned him at every turn, trying to find out what this amazing governor would think of next and what he would do in his "out" years. One day at a reporters' free-for-all in the governor's cabinet room, Rhodes allowed that he would go into private business in something like industrial and land development. He revealed that he was already working as an unpaid consultant to help get an unspecified product off the ground.[4]

That was all they needed. The reporters were like dogs in heat, and Rhodes, eyes twinkling, teased them along. He said it would be an "American invention" that would hopefully be manufactured in Ohio, preferably near Columbus. "This is something that could revolutionize industry in Ohio," said the governor, adding that he would invest "millions" of dollars from his personal wealth.

"Is it bigger than a breadbox?" asked one reporter.

Another grabbed her earlobe. "Sounds like . . ." she said.

"Everybody will want one," Rhodes countered in his best Ron Popeil, TV salesman's voice, driving the curious pressies crazy.

This could have been the super battery or the car that would get eighty miles to the gallon. But the mystery was solved when Rhodes hired an engineering firm to develop a system of filters and airlocks that when installed in a building would make the air more than 99 percent pure. The governor envisioned an entire domed community breathing this super pure air while sleeping, shopping, working, and playing golf. It was aimed not only at fragile senior citizens but the public at large; Rhodes was obsessed with attacks on the body, especially by cancer, the disease that had claimed his mother. (Grandson Ric Moore said years later that his grandfather "wasn't sure it was the air that was making people sick. It was also the food."[5] That explains Rhodes's regular adherence to a diet of grains, vegetable soup, and fruit.)

The air filtering idea slipped into the background when the old firehorse heard the "call to post" for the 1986 gubernatorial campaign, and answered it—the first out of the gate, to no one's surprise. While working on his clean-air project, Rhodes had kept his hand in the political game. He watched, with some degree of satisfaction, as his successor, Democrat Dick Celeste, struggled with missteps, scandals, and raising taxes. The former governor watched in silence, heeding his own advice to let one's adversaries do themselves in. This was a time to remain out of the spotlight.

Even though Rhodes had presided, however reluctantly, over the largest tax increase in Ohio history, Celeste had to make that "temporary" 50 percent income tax increase permanent and then add to it by another 40 percent to balance the budget, as required by state law. Thus was born the "90 percent tax increase" that Celeste got tagged with. In truth, Statehouse news reporters, in their unceasing efforts to outsmart Rhodes and get back at him for his elusiveness, deliberately had described Rhodes's original tax increase in the worst possible terms. The actual rate increase was 25 percent—but to balance the budget, the withholding rate was doubled so the state could realize the gain in one year instead of two and reporters legitimately called it a 50 percent increase. Celeste had to live with that number when he and the Democratic legislature raised the tax again in early 1983 to balance the budget—and he paid the price. He tried in vain to recoup, producing figures showing his part of the increase actually was only 27 percent, but the damage was done. He was blamed for the entire increase. Republicans won back the state senate the following year by promising to reduce the tax rate, and they did, with Celeste signing the bill.

As the 1984 presidential campaign took shape, Rhodes, like a bear emerging from hibernation, began to assert himself. Walter Mondale, the vice president under the erstwhile Democratic president Jimmy Carter, was nominated to run against President Reagan. But Mondale was weak in Ohio; it took Celeste weeks to endorse him over Colorado senator Gary Hart. And then Hart defeated Mondale in the Ohio primary.

Campaigning for Reagan in Cincinnati one day, Rhodes—to the horror of GOP handlers—discarded his assigned talking points and began to cast doubts on Mondale's health, referring to a medical report indicating the former vice president might have a weak heart.[6] Rhodes wasn't going to let the Democrats have a free ride after attacking Reagan for his advanced age. (Reagan had a more effective and good-humored retort, instead stressing Mondale's "youth and inexperience.")

But on another campaign trip for Reagan, things didn't go so well for Rhodes. Reagan and top state Republicans took a train trip through western Ohio, always fertile ground for the GOP. The train was to stop in Lima in Allen County, a Republican bastion that always put on enthusiastic rallies for its candidates. On the way, Rhodes sought an audience with Reagan, to give him advice. Reagan's handlers may have rebuffed him. "They either kicked Rhodes off the train [in Lima] or he got frustrated and left," recalled Ben Rose, a former Republican state representative from Lima. "So the train left and there was Rhodes on the platform with the wind blowing all this campaign debris, flyers and trash around. Here was a guy who once was the most powerful man in Ohio and he's all by himself on the railroad platform. They finally got somebody to drive him to the next stop in Bellefontaine." Rhodes took this slight in stride, never complained, and continued to stump for Reagan with vigor.

Rose recalled a Reagan rally in Jackson in southeastern Ohio where Rhodes showed he still had the touch on the campaign stump: "Rhodes was in front of a storefront Republican headquarters in Jackson and the people are all sitting there in their folding chairs watching this gifted actor."[7]

"Everything you got here in the last four years has come from Ronald Reagan," said Rhodes, before homing in on his favorite topic: family. "Got four things in Jackson County—readin', writin', 'rithmetic and Route 23," he said, remembering his own youth and the road north. Rhodes was rolling.

Couldn't wait to get that suitcase for Route 23 [to Columbus and bigger things]. When you do not have jobs, you break up families.

Young people must leave home to get a job. When they leave home to get a job, you break up homes. They all come back home the first year for the ten holidays. Ten years later they come back for two—Christmas and Easter. Another five years, they just don't have time to come back to Jackson County. When you break up homes and the sons and the daughters have got to leave here to get a job, don't tell me that's easy. The cord from the mother to the child is 25,988 miles long. That's around the world. And when that child cannot get a job, the mother suffers more.[8]

By now, Rose recalled, "the audience is held spellbound . . . [and] Rhodes is waving his arms and yelling, 'The only way we're gonna keep your kids here is with JOBS! We gotta have jobs so they don't leave and you can see your grandkids!' Tears are streaming down the faces of these people."[9] No wonder some people thought he could win a fifth term: on this day at least, the magic was still there.

In September, at the Ohio Republican Convention, Rhodes upstaged Vice President George H. W. Bush with a rip-roaring speech assailing Mondale. He said Mondale and former president Carter turned their backs on Youngstown when excessive federal regulations forced the closure of the Jones & Laughlin steel works in 1979, "and now he has the nerve to ruthlessly travel over Ohio and try to say that President Reagan is the culprit." He continued, "Here we have a lifelong knee-jerk liberal who will tax, tax, tax, spend, spend, spend, and regulate, regulate, and regulate the steel industry. Walter Mondale is not qualified to be president of these United States."[10]

The crowd loved it. "Rhodes is back," said one reporter. Not to disappoint, Bob Hughes, the Cuyahoga County GOP chairman and Rhodes's best political ally, egged the reporters on. "He's got his dark suit on," Hughes stage-whispered with his Cheshire cat grin. "That means he's running." Rhodes brushed aside the speculation. "Somebody's got to take after 'em," he said. But it was almost a given that Rhodes would also "take after" Celeste in 1986, and the aging political master did nothing in 1984 to discourage that idea.

The discouraging came from some of the folks Rhodes trusted most—his closest friends and advisors. "We don't hear the bugle's call," said Robert Teater, a longtime confidant and former director of natural resources in the Rhodes administration.[11] Roger Dreyer, executive director of the Ohio Petroleum Marketers Association and a Rhodes loyalist, also said there was no groundswell for a fifth Rhodes term. "His message got worn out," Dreyer said. "He went a bridge too far—there wasn't any doubt about that. He ran a bridge too far."[12]

Backstairs at the Statehouse, top Republicans were trying to get Ohio Senate president Paul Gillmor, a forty-five-year-old moderate, to be the party's standard-bearer. Gillmor was one of the few Republican leaders left in the government after the 1982 blowout. He was a consensus builder and had a solid legislative record. But getting him to commit was like pushing a barge through wet sand. Gillmor, from Port Clinton, in northwestern Ohio, felt a responsibility to the Senate, and he liked legislating.

"Paul wasn't all that keen on running for governor in 1986," his widow, Karen, recalled years later. "He was a legislator and not an administrator." Nevertheless, some Senate Republican staffers eventually talked him into it, she said. "The feeling was that as the highest Republican elected official with the pristine ethics record that he had, that he would be the best one to go against Dick Celeste."[13] And Gillmor wanted very much to see Celeste ousted from the governor's office.

In January 1985 at Reagan's inauguration celebration, Gillmor hosted a breakfast. "Everybody thought Celeste was weak," recalled Robert Bennett, then vice chairman of the Cuyahoga County GOP. "Rhodes was going around buttonholing people and playing up to them. I said [to Gillmor] 'Paul, you need to get out there early because Jim Rhodes wants to run.'" Bennett's boss was Bob Hughes, the chief cheerleader for Rhodes. "Nobody knows Paul Gillmor," Bennett recalls Hughes as saying. "They know Jim Rhodes. He's been there twenty times."

But Bennett was getting other signals from the Cleveland business community. Rhodes always did well in Cleveland for a Republican, but this time his foe would be Celeste, whose family was from the Cleveland suburb of Lakewood. When he was elected in 1982, folks there said, "At last, a governor from Cleveland!" Bennett said, "I was getting feedback from the [Cleveland area] financial community: 'Jim's had four terms. That's enough.' They wanted to move in a different direction."[14] Bennett would go on to become one of Ohio's greatest Republican chairmen in the 1990s and 2000s, surpassing Hughes as a GOP guru.

Rhodes was thick with the big-county Republican chairmen, notably Hughes. Ohio Republican chairman Michael Colley of Columbus also thought Rhodes would be a strong candidate on the 1986 ticket. But Bennett says he lost ground with big-company CEOs in 1982, when he had to raise taxes. Moreover, he recalls, some of the corporate titans Rhodes had cozied up to earlier had retired or left because of business consolidations. Also, the CEOs weren't coming to Columbus anymore; they turned government lobbying duties over to government relations professionals.[15] The rules of the game had changed, to Rhodes's detriment.

Celeste had picked up baggage as his first term passed the halfway mark. He had to raise taxes early, and several cabinet appointees betrayed him with scandal. Then, in March 1985, disaster struck. Seventy state-chartered savings and loan associations had to be closed to avoid a run by depositors after the exposure of imprudent investment gimmicks at one of the thrifts. The associations in question happened to be owned by Marvin Warner, a Cincinnati financier and a political benefactor of the governor. Celeste righted the ship, but it took more than three months and even longer before the depositors were made whole. Coincidentally, the risky investments of Home State Savings Bank were first noticed in 1982, by the savings and loan chief in the Rhodes administration's Commerce Department, but the governor ordered no follow-up.[16] Nevertheless, it was an issue waiting to be exploited. And Jim Rhodes was the man to do it.

"Rhodes saw this 'maybe' window," said Terry Casey, a Republican political consultant, then the executive director of the Franklin County GOP. "Celeste had doubled the income tax and had a lot of negatives himself. So maybe [Rhodes] could win. He knew it was an uphill roll of the dice, but it was something to do. Rhodes knew the only way he could win was to get people to throw out Dick Celeste."[17]

Rhodes started his primary campaign with direct aim at the governor: "During Home State, Celeste did the work of two men—Laurel and Hardy," referring to slapstick comedians perhaps too ancient for many voters to appreciate. "We made the tough decisions," Celeste retorted, and these decisions led to recovery.[18]

Meanwhile, another Republican state senator from north-central Ohio thought he had enough political capital to enter the primary fray. Paul Pfeifer, who had served more than a dozen years in the legislature and helped bring back the Ohio death penalty for convicted murderers, had run for the U.S. Senate in 1982 as a default candidate and got clobbered by Democrat Metzenbaum. But in 1984, he had sought to remain a player by heading a citizens' committee of Ohio business titans raising money for President Reagan's reelection campaign.[19]

Pfeifer believed he would benefit from the Ohio maxim that you have to run statewide once and lose before you can win; he ignored the reality that nothing says you *will* win on the second try. So Pfeifer, Gillmor, and Richard Finan—another Republican state senator from suburban Cincinnati—traversed the state, speaking at Lincoln Day dinners and other Republican events and getting feedback suggesting an alternative to Rhodes was necessary.[20] Cleveland mayor George Voinovich had been high on the list, but he wasn't interested and let everyone know it early in 1985. Rhodes paid them no attention and went about ripping Celeste for raising taxes.

Concerned that some Republican chieftains wanted to shove Rhodes aside, Bob Hughes wrote a letter to six hundred of them in late October 1985, recommending against endorsements at the county or state level in any Republican primary contests. He sent the missive despite the fact that the normal practice was *not* to endorse in GOP primaries. "It smacks of elitism and bossism and discourages good candidates," Hughes wrote. Had he thought Rhodes would lock up the endorsements, he wouldn't have written the letter.[21]

On November 9, 1985, Rhodes held his campaign kickoff with a $100-a-person luncheon at Scioto Downs, a harness horse racetrack two miles south of the Columbus city limits. It was a typical low-budget party: Rhodes once said, "Give 'em about 50 cents worth of food and save the rest for a TV blitz," according to former Republican State chairman Kent McGough.[22] In officially announcing his candidacy, Rhodes promised to get rid of the tangible personal property tax on business. He also called for the establishment of an independent think tank of education and business leaders, to combine their talents and ideas for spurring the economy.[23]

In December 1985, Pfeifer announced his candidacy. He had at least one thing in his favor. As chairman of the Ohio Senate Judiciary Committee, he led a series of hearings into well-documented allegations that the Celeste administration was steering state contracts to campaign donors and requiring the correct political blood type (Democrat) for state jobs. The hearings took on a soap-opera atmosphere, and Democrats howled loudly that Pfeifer was grandstanding to advance his political career.

To announce the start of his campaign, the senator and a small band of his supporters took a step-ladder out onto the northeast quadrant of the Statehouse grounds, where a twelve-foot-tall (including the base) bronze statue of Rhodes had been placed. Pfeifer climbed onto the ladder and opined that when you have your own statue on the Statehouse lawn, you're a legend and it's time to retire.

"Somebody needed to step up there and do something," Pfeifer said years later. "I knew 'Jim Rhodes one more time' was not gonna do it. Gillmor was hemming and hawing. He should have been out there raising money and lining up support. I held back a long time. I should have been out there, too. I was just not certain that I wanted to be governor. It's a job where one of fifty thousand employees can screw up and ruin your life."[24] Rhodes had no such fear, however. Some of his employees had screwed up. He dealt with it by calling in the Highway Patrol to investigate and when the report came out he would claim credit for catching the crooks. Then he'd move on.

In his early outings, Pfeifer spared neither Rhodes nor Celeste. But Gillmor, who had yet to formally declare his intentions, took it easy on Rhodes while highlighting his own legislative record of passing an income tax reduction and putting more money into schools than Celeste had. The three planks of his platform, enumerated at a Franklin County Republican Party meeting, were going to be honesty and ethics in government, fiscal common sense, and a climate fostering economic development. "We kept every one of our promises," said the Senate GOP leader, implying that Celeste hadn't.[25]

Finally, in late January, Gillmor formally announced with the theme "Leadership You Can Trust—For a Change," playing on the lack of trust in Celeste but also the public's yen for a change away from Rhodes. Gillmor had taken coaching from a high-powered New York consulting firm to help him lower his squeaky speaking voice to project more authority, and to coordinate his awkward hand gestures with his verbal rhetoric. He again cited his record of legislative accomplishments and said Celeste had broken campaign promises and run an inept and crooked administration.[26]

For his running mate, Gillmor chose fellow senator Charles Horn of Dayton. The colorless Horn added no fire to the campaign, but he had extensive local government experience as a former mayor, city councilman, and county commissioner. He also passed Gillmor's benchmark for honesty by conceding that Pfeifer had asked him to run with him, and he had turned him down.[27] Pfeifer chose Vicki Pegg, the Montgomery County recorder, as his running mate—another bow toward local government.

Rhodes, in early December 1985, also had tapped local government, reluctantly choosing Hamilton County Commissioner Bob Taft as his running mate. Taft's father, Robert Taft Jr., had beaten Rhodes in a bitter Republican primary for the U.S. Senate nomination in 1970, and Rhodes still was smarting.

"Taft was Rhodes' last choice for lieutenant governor," said Bob Bennett. "Rhodes was in trouble with the Cincinnati business community. The county [GOP] chairs all said Taft was the strongest, but nobody was gonna tell Jim Rhodes that. Finally I went up to him [at a meeting of the GOP leaders] and said 'Bob Taft is the only one who's gonna help you.' He came up out of his chair, leaned over and looked me right in the face. 'You've always been a Taft man!' he said." Rhodes's elephantine memory reminded him that fifteen years earlier, Bennett had worked for the elder Taft's campaign. But Rhodes deferred to the wisdom of the county party heads.[28] "Out of this will come new leadership for the state of Ohio," he pronounced.[29]

Taft had pluses. Though not the most dynamic campaigner, he was young (forty-three), bright, and experienced in government finance. He had worked in the state of Illinois budget office and served on the Finance Committee in the Ohio House of Representatives. He was assigned to hammer Celeste for raising taxes, because having Rhodes do it was hypocritical. Further, of course, Taft had an impressive political pedigree. His great-grandfather, William Howard Taft, was president of the United States and chief justice of the United States. His grandfather, Robert A. Taft, was "Mr. Republican" and a U.S. senator who had been a top contender for the GOP nomination for president in 1948 and 1952. And his father had been a senator.

By April, both Rhodes and Celeste were airing television spots as if the general election campaign were in full swing. "We want to be ready and running when the primary's over," explained Jim Duerk, Rhodes's longtime business associate and campaign coordinator.[30] Since 1985, through his campaign committee, Celeste had been running monthly thirty-minute televised town meetings in which he fielded questions from a selected audience. By spring, he had his son Stephen talking with him on TV about the positive things the administration had done. Rhodes, though, was less charitable, airing newspaper headlines about Celeste administration scandals, paired with testimonials about his own vigor for the job of governor. One frequently aired TV spot had a faux newscaster giving "Statehouse Updates" chronicling the misadventures of the Celeste administration.

Rhodes was stung when his friend Dave Thomas contributed $10,000 to Gillmor's campaign and continued to raise money for the senator. "It is time for a change and I think most of us realize it," Thomas wrote in a letter sent to two thousand key Republican contributors and business leaders. "Jim Rhodes did an outstanding job as governor, but, quite frankly, his last term was far from his best. Paul Gillmor can beat Celeste and Jim Rhodes can't."[31]

When Gillmor released a poll in mid-April showing he was only five percentage points behind Rhodes, the latter quickly called a news conference and said if elected, he would speed up a 5 percent tax cut, to be enacted by the legislature, and accelerate business tax breaks.[32] But Rhodes's backers also used surveys to sway the public mood. One poll had Rhodes so far ahead that, in some people's opinions, it was hard for Gillmor and Pfeifer to raise money for their campaigns. "[Bob] Hughes put out this phony Cleveland State poll that showed Rhodes running away with it, and he froze all the money," said Pfeifer.[33] "Gillmor couldn't raise any money. I couldn't raise any money." Years later, though, Karen Gillmor said that finances were not an issue. "We had a lot of fund-raisers," she recalled. "Money wasn't a problem. The lobbyists respected Paul. He had an open door and he got things done. Paul could have written the check himself."[34]

Rhodes picked his spots. He would show up and glad-hand at Republican-oriented events but would disappear when it came time for the candidates to speak on the issues. He also attended only the party functions where he knew he would win the endorsement. If there was doubt, he wasn't there.[35]

Gillmor, taking a page from Pfeifer's book and going a step further, had a television commercial produced in which the mouth of Rhodes's statue became animated and actually spoke: "I know that Jim Rhodes isn't up to another four years as governor."[36] Said the voiceover, "When you have a statue of yourself on the Statehouse lawn, you've been in office long enough."[37] Another Gillmor ad had an older man walking down the Statehouse corridor, past the portraits of former governors, with a similar commentary.

Pfeifer tested Rhodes's popularity in Cincinnati by appearing before the Hamilton County Republican Executive Committee and asking for its endorsement. Gillmor was there, too, having hinted of a conspiracy on the committee's part to endorse Rhodes. Evidently, Taft was helping the cause in Cincinnati. "It was on the sixth floor of this ratty building above a Frisch's [restaurant] and it was hot as hell," Pfeifer recalled. "Marcos was about to fall in the Philippines. I said, 'The problem with Jim Rhodes is that he's like Ferdinand Marcos. He's got complete control of the palace guard but nobody else.' There was loud booing, and I just turned and got out of there. Gillmor said to me, 'Thanks a lot.'"[38]

Instead of spreading out to cover more territory, Rhodes and Taft frequently traveled together, either to display the younger guy on the ticket or for the younger guy to correct verbal gaffes. At a breakfast fund-raiser in Steubenville, Rhodes told area Republicans they should be proud of Youngstown State University and its baseball team. Taft reminded Rhodes they were in Steubenville and that he meant the University of Steubenville.[39]

One place Rhodes wasn't going was to the editorial board of the *Akron Beacon Journal,* which he hated, according to Taft. He arranged for Taft to go, but, Taft said, "At the last minute he decided to go with me. All he wanted to talk about was the 99 percent clean air [invention]. Rhodes was, above all, a salesman." "I don't think I realized how diminished his political operation was," Taft recalled, years later. "Not that he was senile. I think he was definitely past his prime in terms of his energy and his connections with the people. The campaign organization was lacking. Roy Martin was gone. He [Martin] had a lot to do with getting stuff done. Their idea of a campaign was to come in in the morning, look at the newspapers and see what was there, and then go do something and put out press releases. Whoever came in with a good idea, that was their campaign."[40]

All three Republicans promised to get rid of the motor vehicle registration system in which "deputies" appointed by the administration collected not only the registration fees but a surcharge funneled into the political fund of the party in power. Ironically, Celeste was the one who did away with the political surcharges after he got reelected.

On primary election night, Bob Hughes monitored the absentee ballot returns, the first ones counted, in Cuyahoga County. "My dad had the ability to look at the absentee tally when it came in and tell who was going to win," said Hughes's son Jonathan. "He'd say, 'This guy's out, this guy's okay.' When it came to the 1986 primary for governor, he looked at the totals [for Cuyahoga County], and he didn't say anything that I recall. That meant it wasn't good."[41] Rhodes needed a decisive win in Cuyahoga County if he was going to run strong against Celeste. Bob Hughes was prescient. Rhodes won the primary by seventy thousand votes, attracting 48.2 percent of the vote, but he only narrowly carried Cuyahoga County, where the voter turnout was unusually low. That spelled trouble for the fall. The final statewide count in the primary was Rhodes, 352,261; Gillmor, 281,737; Pfeifer, 96,948. Horn helped Gillmor carry the Dayton area, and Gillmor won Toledo's Lucas County.[42]

The day after the primary, Rhodes said corruption in the Celeste administration would be the major issue in the general election campaign. "He's got the money to do anything he wants to do except buy honesty and integrity," Rhodes said. Later in the year, the former governor would recant that exception.[43] The postmortems began. "It appeared that many Republicans wanted Rhodes so they could get their old jobs back," said Karen Gillmor.[44] She said Paul Gillmor and Paul Pfeifer split the vote in northwestern Ohio, home base to both. Others agreed, saying if Pfeifer had dropped out, Gillmor would have won the primary. "One-on-one, if Gillmor had opened up his wallet, he could have won that primary," said Terry Casey, then executive director of the Franklin County Republican Party.[45]

Some people thought Rhodes put Pfeifer up to staying in the race as a spoiler. But Pfeifer said afterward that if Gillmor had asked him to exit the contest, he would have. "I later asked Paul [Gillmor] if he had asked Pfeifer to get out of the race," said lobbyist Tom Green, who used to sail and power-boat with Gillmor on Lake Erie. "He kind of squirmed and said, 'I never did. He wouldn't have gotten out.' He should have talked to him. *We* should have talked to him."[46]

Some faulted Gillmor for declining to spend some of his personal fortune from the family-owned Old Fort Bank and other financial holdings. "Paul Gillmor could have beaten Jim Rhodes, but he decided not to put his own personal money into the campaign," said Neil Clark, the chief operating officer of the Senate at the time. "He could have put $300,000 into the campaign, but he wouldn't do it. It kind of shocked us all."[47]

The grumbling among some Republicans continued into the fall. At a Rhodes fund-raising event in Washington, Heather Gradison, the politically active wife of Cincinnati congressman Willis Gradison, waited in an informal receiving line to greet Rhodes. When she got her chance, she didn't hold back. Unsmiling, she told him in a low but firm voice that now that he had gotten what he wanted—another bid for governor—he had better deliver and bring down Celeste. Rhodes said little. He got the message: You were not our first choice; you damned well better win.[48] "I meant it," said Gradison, who was chairman of the Interstate Commerce Commission at the time. In an interview years after the incident, she said many Ohio Republicans thought "the wrong guy won the primary" in 1986.[49]

The leaked poll showing that Rhodes would get 55 to 60 percent of the primary vote could have depressed the Gillmor turnout. But the Senate leader, always loyal and gracious, refused to characterize it as deliberately false, adding he would support Rhodes in the general election. "That wasn't my poll," Rhodes said. "I think the poll was a little bit off. My only, only job in this is to win."[50]

When it was certain that Rhodes was the Republican nominee, some Democrats rubbed their hands together with glee. Not Celeste. He paid no attention to the post-primary remark uttered by Mark Shields, once a Democratic operative and consultant but by then a TV political analyst and columnist: "The Ohio Republican party has just nominated the one guy that Dick Celeste can beat."[51] Recalled Celeste, "Everybody wrote me off. So I had to work hard. I never took that race for granted. I spent a fair amount of time reaching out to Republicans and independents."[52]

James Ruvolo, the Democratic state chairman, had a plan. "The whole idea for the 1986 campaign was to get Dick out of town," he said. "We had to build Dick up. Some things had happened, and he was getting some bad press. It was hard to get him on TV in Cleveland, Cincinnati, and Toledo. They don't cover anything [that happens] in Columbus. The other thing we did was to contrast his energy with the lack of energy that Rhodes had. We were emphasizing the age difference without saying it."[53] So Ruvolo planned a lot of bus trips with the entire Democratic statewide ticket, which included experienced campaigners—the same candidates who had swept the state in 1982.

"This was a contrast election," said Curt Steiner, a Republican consultant who had been an advisor to Gillmor's campaign.[54] "Celeste's task was to say, 'Remember Jim Rhodes [as governor] and how that went.' That's how they started their commercials." And the most recent memories of Jim Rhodes as governor involved raising taxes. "The good old days of build, build, build were not there anymore," agreed Taft.[55] "He had done all that. I think a lot of his last term was on autopilot."

About the third week in June, Bob Bennett in Cleveland received a telephone call from Alex Arshinkov, the GOP chairman in neighboring Summit County. Arshinkov, a perennial Rhodes booster, was horrified when his own polling showed how far behind Rhodes was. "He's practically coming through the phone: 'Rhodes is getting 26 percent of the vote! He's dead!'" related Bennett.[56] "Alex dropped his money for Rhodes and put it all on Roy Ray"—a state senate candidate from Akron in a tight race. Even with prospects dimming, however, Vice President Bush kept a commitment and came to Columbus to boost Rhodes by speaking at a $150-a-person fund-raiser.

In mid-July, there was another spark of hope: a pair of Franklin County grand jury indictments resulting from the Pfeifer hearings that cited Celeste patronage appointees Pam Conrad and Larry McCartney for fund-raising violations. An incensed Ruvolo quickly produced an eighty-three-page sheaf of clippings and documents, titled "Jim Rhodes: 25 Years of Witch-Hunting: An Annotated Historical Guide of Modern Political Witch-Hunts by the Grand Old Party of Ohio."[57] He released the packet to the media at a sun-drenched news conference on the lawn of the Governor's Residence.

"History shows Republican prosecutors and investigators scurry around trumping up charges and feeding them to the news media to generate election-time 'news'—even if they have to leak the stuff from so-called secret grand jury proceedings," Ruvolo wrote in his introduction. "Scare headlines scream the allegations about Democrats. Republicans puff themselves up with pompous gas about 'corruption' in Democratic offices. But then history teaches us about a second incredible coincidence: Once the election is over, nothing ever comes of the charges. The pattern is clear. Rhodes runs. His GOP crony investigators target Democrats. Headlines scream. Some Democrats win; some lose. But, later, those election-year charges fade like a 1950 Rhodes for Governor bumper sticker." Rhodes responded to the allegations: "I have never campaigned by grand jury in my life. I've never been involved with a grand jury except for the one Mike DiSalle called on me."[58]

On offense, a big part of the Democrats' strategy was to lure Rhodes into debating. The ineloquent Rhodes had been burned by participating in debates, and he knew he didn't come off well on television. "We wanted to get him into a debate," Celeste recalled. "So we ran these commercials with a backdrop of the Ohio State Fair, saying 'C'mon, Jim, get into the ring.' We were hoping to throw him off his game. I think he appreciated seeing a lot of his own tactics work, even if it was against him."[59] The only response they got, until Rhodes ultimately accepted a one-on-one faceoff in Dayton, was Rhodes's facetious invitation for Celeste to debate him at Democrat Marvin Warner's farm in Clermont County, suburban Cincinnati.[60]

Rhodes had a strange partner during his campaign: Tom Van Meter, an Ashland Republican who had been in the Ohio Senate for ten years, until his unsuccessful 1982 bid for governor. The brash Van Meter helped Rhodes in several ways. He got a fifty-five-page paperback book published, titled *Richard's Poor Almanac,* which chronicled Celeste's misadventures, and he helped fund some antigay messages that were supposed to help Rhodes. That spring, Van Meter had also tried to get back into the Senate, where his own Republican leaders had declined to appoint him to a vacancy because he was too strident. He narrowly lost the primary to Dick Schafrath, the former Cleveland Browns and Ohio State tackle whom Senate GOP leaders backed.

An outspoken conservative as a state senator, Van Meter had blasted Governor Rhodes on occasion over policy differences, though they became fast friends in their respective campaigns. Some thought Van Meter was trying to ingratiate himself with party leaders for a possible future governor run. But Bob Taft thought Rhodes was banking on Van Meter to help rally conservatives. "The religious right was becoming a factor," Taft said. "It started with Reagan. Rhodes discovered this and he thought it was going to speed him to victory. He saw it as a new political opportunity. In his gut, he knew there was something there pulling people into the party. It was electorally significant."[61]

Actually, Rhodes had tried to promote the idea of attacking gay rights when Dana "Buck" Rinehart was running for mayor of Columbus in 1983.[62] He trotted it out again because Celeste clearly supported the gay-rights agenda, even though a majority of the public did not. Van Meter was the courier between Rhodes and Citizens for Decency and Health, a Cincinnati organization with an antigay agenda. "We had done an HIV education issue campaign in the gay bars," Celeste recalled. "[Citizens for Decency and Health] distributed a flyer, printed on both sides and folded up, to rural areas along the interstate."[63]

In August, Rhodes promised a tax deduction for working mothers to cover their child care costs.[64] He turned seventy-seven the following month. Even the seniors seemed to desert him. "Young people sleep longer," he told a statewide group of Republican women in Columbus. "And more often." He said if he got tired he could turn things over to Taft. Reporters asked about his plan for a senior citizens program. "We'll have that next week," he said.[65]

Rhodes and Celeste continued to spar. "His answer to every problem is to appoint a committee," Rhodes said, referring to the disappointing 1978 Celeste school-funding proposal. "He wants to be in charge of everything and responsible for nothing," Celeste said, referring to his foe's governing style.[66] The candidates clashed most ferociously over the environment. Celeste was a clean-air, clean-water guy who wanted high regulatory standards. Rhodes *always* favored jobs in a playoff of employment versus environment: "Government regulations are the greatest detriment to the working people of this country," he said. "I never saw an environmentalist in Youngstown. If you have to choose between the EPA and people working, you have to stay with the worker."[67] Celeste maintained that careful environmental regulation would not hamper business.

An Ohio Poll out of Cincinnati had Celeste leading by the astronomical (and unbelievable) margin of 42 percentage points in August. Other surveys showed him up by 20 points. In mid-September, Celeste warned his team, with a mixed metaphor: "Jim Rhodes is a very good late-inning ballplayer. Rhodes is always toughest in the last quarter."[68] Later that month, Rhodes spent $250,000 on a TV commercial, aired in Cleveland, Columbus, and Cincinnati, touting the university expansions, new medical schools, and upgraded state parks that had taken shape during his years as governor.[69] George Voinovich and Columbus mayor Rinehart helped with the narration.

Countermanding the plan to make Taft the antitax spokesman, Rhodes kept hammering Celeste for increasing the personal income tax; he challenged him to prove there had been a $528 million deficit that had to be closed to balance the budget. Rhodes promised that if elected, he'd reduce the income tax by 5 percent. At the same time, he proposed increasing and spotlighting the growing of potatoes as an agricultural crop to complement the "great" fast-food restaurants and grocery stores in Ohio. "We don't have to go to Idaho and Maine and Oregon and these places," he said. "We have it here. Our soil is the finest in the world."[70]

In early October, Rhodes had his personal accountant, E. C. Redman, release his federal income tax returns, along with the accountant's professional recap of them. It was an attempt to bait Celeste into releasing his returns. The Rhodeses' returns for 1981–85 showed a five-year taxable income of $3.64 million and a long-term capital gain of $7.15 million, much of it from the sale of motels he and his business partners had acquired in Orlando and Chicago.[71] Gerald Austin, Celeste's campaign manager, was not impressed with the disclosure. "Tell us who the clients are over the last four years," he said. "Who pays James A. Rhodes & Associates? Dick Celeste has earned his living as governor of Ohio."[72]

The Republican campaign was disjointed and seemed to sag. Rhodes was dispirited by Helen's declining health. In late October, he suspended his campaign to be with his wife after she was admitted to the Cleveland Clinic with a "serious vascular condition" in her legs.[73] Helen, who had diabetes, was there for about two weeks as doctors replaced diseased arteries that had caused her pain and limited her ability to walk.[74] Her husband visited frequently and slept in a chair in the room on at least one occasion. He was often accompanied by a friend and close political ally, Clevelander Bob Hughes.

Almost wistfully, Rhodes returned to his roots to campaign in southern Ohio. The hilly region's small voter base was already his strongest part of the state. Rhodes took his rented $300,000 bus back to Jackson County and on to Gallipolis and Rio Grande. He had dinner with his good friend Bob Evans at the restaurant "down on the farm," making sure to feed traveling reporters sausages.[75] Crowds were small, but Rhodes seemed relaxed and happy just to be near "home."

"Jim knows it's over. He's just out there having fun," said Tom Dudgeon, a lobbyist who advised Rhodes and wrote for him sometimes. Reporters, however, didn't treat it like it was over, and they didn't want it to be over. The scrap between these two heavyweights was good copy, and they wanted it to continue as long as possible. Jim Duerk agreed that Rhodes was having fun. "He loves it," said the former governor's sidekick. "I think he's having more fun than he had in the summer. Some guys twenty points behind might say, 'Aw, the hell with it.' He always sees something on the horizon that might be poppin.'"[76]

On a campaign bus in late October, Rhodes laid out a spread—"We've got Dutch Loaf, crackers and maybe ham"—and told the working press what to expect in the way of news that day. "We'll give it to you early so you can get rid of it and take a nap. . . . Don't tell the boss."[77]

Rhodes was disappointed that the Celeste scandals didn't resonate with the voters. "Maybe the day's past when anybody cares about corruption," he said. "Maybe this is the way they want Ohio to be run. I don't know. But I never came up under that. I came up under the old system that you were honest and you had to be honest in public life, for acceptability. I just think that he has a lot of explaining to do, and every time he gets in a good one [scandal], he's in India or Japan or some other place, and everybody accepts that. If that's the lifestyle, you can't do anything about it." Rhodes stayed on the attack, criticizing the Celeste administration for mishandling the AIDS issue and for "pushing pornography." He said he would fire "homosexual sympathizers" in the Ohio Department of Health if he were elected.[78]

The highly anticipated Sunday, November 2, debate in Dayton was the only joint appearance of the campaign. Rhodes agreed to it only as a last resort to try to turn the tide in his favor. As the candidates faced each other, Celeste discussed his record—a balanced budget, higher employment, strong school funding, and an end to fast-growing utility and health care costs. Rhodes continued to dwell on Celeste's "scandals"—badgering state employees for campaign donations and bartering state contracts for contributions.

Rhodes pushed the antigay themes and then, because Celeste's wife, Dagmar, was Austrian, hinted the pair were Nazi sympathizers. He was drawing an oblique conclusion based on the then-recent allegations that Kurt Waldheim, the Austrian secretary general of the United Nations, had Nazi affiliations.[79] "Pathetic," Celeste practically spat to reporters when asked after the debate to comment on Rhodes's performance. "Jim Rhodes is preoccupied with a *National Enquirer*–style campaign."[80] Some years later, a more mellow and forgiving Celeste said, "He was kind of losing it. He brought up the Austrian conspiracy in reference to my wife. He brought up the Nazis. He brought up the gay issue."[81]

Rhodes may have understood it was over, but he kept on scrapping. On October 30, from Helen's bedside at the Cleveland Clinic, he said he could sense the momentum turning his way.[82] Perhaps in desperation, he promised he'd serve only one term if elected; it would take four years to clean up Celeste's mess, and then he'd be finished.[83] An overly optimistic Hughes was still saying in late October that Rhodes could win with a low voter turnout. "How many grand juries does it take?" Rhodes said on his campaign bus in late October, seeming to verify Ruvolo's accusation about campaigning by grand jury. "Seven? Twelve? Fifteen?" Rhodes would go down battling. "I came in this way," he said. "I can go out this way. I got a good business to go to." At one campaign stop in little Mount Gilead, Ohio, Rhodes was asked about his chances. "What should we be looking for?" he responded. "Maybe lightning, for want of a better term."[84]

On election night, the end came early. It was a landslide. The official results: Celeste 1,858,372; Rhodes 1,207,264.[85] The next day, Rhodes went back to his development office as if nothing had happened. He had projects to work on. He offered no apologies for his rough treatment of Celeste; in fact, he fired a closing shot: "You'll be able to write a 788-page novel about this [Celeste scandals].[86] There's gonna be some books written on this. Watergate was breaking in. They're already in."[87]

"After the election, there were a lot of people saying, 'We shouldn't have run him,'" recalled Jonathan Hughes, son of the Cuyahoga County Republican chairman. "Bob Hughes said there are always second-guessers. And he wasn't critical of Rhodes for raising the [antigay and Nazi] issues he did. His philosophy was, 'You throw everything at 'em in the campaign and when it's over, it's over.' Bob Hughes said dealing with Rhodes was like dealing with a meat grinder—when you throw in the meat, Rhodes can make it come out like hamburger. He was able to take something and turn it into a political advantage." This time, the meat grinder didn't work. "They knew at the end of the '86 election that it was the end of the line for Rhodes. That was the last hurrah."[88]

In victory, Celeste outspent Rhodes by 2 to 1—$5.93 million to $2.96 million.[89] Rhodes said the disparity showed "you can buy honesty and integrity."[90] Even though their candidate had far outspent his challenger, the Democrats had questions about Rhodes's campaign contributions. After the election, acting through Democratic Secretary of State Sherrod Brown, they accused Rhodes's main campaign committee of laundering $148,773 in campaign funds by funneling the dollars to seven minor campaign committees for the express purpose of attacking Celeste on a variety of fronts.

The main diversion of funds by Rhodes for Governor was $115,715 to Ohio Citizens for Decency and Health, the Cincinnati-based antigay group. That organization denied using the Rhodes donation to attack Celeste for supporting gay rights. Instead, it said, the donation went to programs to combat AIDS.[91] Ohio Citizens for Decency and Health had mailed letters to pastors throughout the state and placed ads in about twenty daily newspapers late in the campaign headlined "Why Homosexuals Support Celeste." Among the other Rhodes fund transfers, which campaign officials said were properly reported, were $7,000 to Citizens for Van Meter and $3,000 to Citizens for Responsible State Government to pay for *Richard's Poor Almanac.*

The case dragged through the Ohio Elections Commission until July 18, 1988, when the panel ruled the Rhodes committee did not violate the law forbidding dual campaign committees. The Elections Commission earlier had dismissed the complaint that the Rhodes committee had concealed the use of campaign funds.[92]

By this time, Jim Rhodes was back in the private sector, an elder statesman holding court in his development office, working on marketing his "invention," and spending more time with his growing swarm of great-grandchildren.

CHAPTER 14

Always Forward

WHEN JIM RHODES LEFT the governor's office in January 1983, he didn't go far. His destination was a suite of offices at 42 E. Gay St.—the next block north of the Statehouse—where he set up shop with his development corporation, James A. Rhodes & Associates. The location was less than two blocks from the private office he left in 1975 to go back to being governor. He brought along trusted associates Jim Duerk, who had served as his press secretary and then his state director of development; Chuck Shipley, a former state highway patrolman who had been on the governor's security detail; and Pauline Yee, who had been an administrative assistant in the governor's office.

His view of the Statehouse from the thirteenth-floor office was blocked by the office tower named for him, but he didn't need to look in the windows to spy on the current governor. He could rely on hundreds of longtime civil servants as well as loyal patronage employees the Celeste folks hadn't discovered. And he had a pipeline to the highway patrolmen, some of whom he knew personally but all of whom knew the popular Shipley.

The office suite had a glass-topped table, white carpeting, and walls decorated with a large photo of Rhodes golfing with Bob Hope, photos of his family, and drawings of outdoor scenes. There were bookshelves with pictures of his children and grandchildren and the sports trophies they'd won.[1] The former governor would cook up a pot of vegetable soup, and sometimes he'd make pancakes. Lunch might be the shredded cabbage and carrots he brought from home. He'd be popping grapes into his mouth, two at a time, while pursuing his dream of a 99 percent pollution-free atmosphere for an office building, an apartment complex, or even a community. Some folks noticed the irony that in the midst of this quest for clean air, Jim Duerk, an inveterate cigarette smoker, puffed away.

"He always had his deals going on," said Chan Cochran, Rhodes's aide who started his own public relations firm on the floor below. "It was a regular parade of people visiting the office."[2] If Rhodes wasn't handing out political advice to prospective candidates, he was mining for information.

Buck Rinehart, the feisty Franklin County treasurer, was one of the early recipients of the former governor's advice. Preparing to run for mayor of Columbus in 1983, Rinehart was Rhodes's kind of guy. "He would call me, some days every fifteen minutes, other days every hour," said Rinehart. "He was nonstop on advice. He never stopped with the advice."

When Rinehart won, the calls increased. Who wouldn't want counsel from one of Columbus's most popular mayors? "He called me the day after the election," Rinehart said. "I had been up until about five o'clock in the morning and he called me about 8:30. I was on the couch, and Carol handed me the phone and said, 'Governor Rhodes is on the phone.' He never offered me congratulations on my victory or anything like that. He says, 'Buckaroo! What in the hell are you doing?" I said, 'I'm sleeping.' 'Well, get your lazy ass out of that bed! You're the mayor of the greatest city in the country. Get moving!' I had to hold the phone away from my ear, he was yelling so loud.

"He says, 'You got a notepad?' I went and got a yellow legal-size notepad. 'Now start writing.' I filled up three pages of that yellow notepad with his instructions on what to do and what not to do, who to talk to and who not to talk to. It went on for an hour. He never let up. I was one of his kids, and he was going to make sure I didn't screw up."

Later, when Rinehart was preparing to name a city safety director, Rhodes wanted to know who he had in mind. It was Alphonse Montgomery, who had been with the Ohio Highway Patrol. "Rhodes said, 'Don't do it. Big-city cops and the Highway Patrol don't mix.' Later, after Rinehart had acted in spite of the former governor's advice, Montgomery did something great and Rhodes called up and said, 'That was great! I'm glad I recommended him for safety director.'"

Rhodes never lost his knack for getting things done, and on one occasion he passed his secret on to Rinehart. The city leaders in Columbus had been trying for more than twenty years to get a direct route from downtown to the airport to improve the business climate. They had the designs for what turned out to be the I-670 extension to the Port Columbus airport, but President Reagan had frozen the Highway Trust Fund, and the Columbus artery was 80 percent federally funded.

"You talked to Reagan?" Rhodes asked Rinehart.

"Governor, is the president of the United States going to listen to a two-bit mayor from Columbus, Ohio?" Rinehart responded. But, egged on by the former governor, he called the White House and got Donald Regan, the chief of staff. "He said, 'I can't get you a meeting with the president, but come on in, I'll talk to you. Be here Tuesday.' So I go in with [Congressman John] Kasich, and Reagan promises to talk to the president about our highway funding.

"The next morning, I get a call: 'The president has agreed to release [the money] from the Trust Fund for your project. That's how we got it. I said to the governor, 'Can I buy you lunch?' We had lunch in the Grill Room at the Scioto Country Club. He said, 'That's how you get things done. How do you think they win wars?'"[3]

Meetings with the former governor at the development office were arranged in one of two ways: Rhodes would call folks on the phone and invite them over, or they would ask for an appointment and come in. "He spent about half his time on politics," Duerk related. Kasich came in for advice. He wanted to know if he should run for the Senate. Rhodes said, 'Start working your way up to governor.' He never lived to see that come true." (Kasich was elected governor in 2010.) "He [Rhodes] never changed. He listened to people. He told people what he thought if they asked."[4]

Larry Householder, an up-and-coming Republican state representative who was charting a path to the speaker of the Ohio House, sought counsel from Rhodes. Householder was from Perry County, in southeastern Ohio, and he figured he had a lot in common with the Jackson County native. "I had told reporters that Governor Rhodes fished in my pond," Householder said years later. "That was a southern Ohio saying, meaning we were from the same area. He thought it was hilarious that the reporters believed Rhodes actually went and fished at my place. 'I guess they're not from around here,' Rhodes said. 'We're [people from southern Ohio] not supposed to get where we are.'"

Householder came to Rhodes recommended by the retired House speaker Vern Riffe, who also fished in the same pond. When Householder called,

Rhodes invited him to the Scioto Country Club, where he often entertained friends and politicos in the Grill Room. They hit it off. Rhodes had nicknames for everybody: "He called me Householder-Boy."

"We talked about people, we talked about policy, we talked about politics, we talked about jobs and development," Householder recalled. They developed a relationship and conversed frequently on the phone or in person, more than outsiders realized. "He'd call me when I was driving in [to Columbus from Perry County]. He would tell me places to go, who to talk to. He was helpful with business leaders in Columbus. He would say, 'I'm gonna talk to so-and-so. He knows about jobs. He'll call you.' And he did. He was scouting for what was ahead [for Householder]. He would say, 'Go see this business leader in Cleveland. Go see this church leader.'"

When Householder was elected Speaker of the House in late 2000, he wanted Rhodes to swear him in, but he was concerned that Rhodes, by then using a wheelchair, would look small next to the towering Householder, and it might be demeaning for him. Householder stewed over the idea until one day Rhodes called and said, "I hear you want me to swear you in. I'd like to say a few words before I swear you in." Now Householder was in a box. "I said, 'Governor, you're in a wheelchair.' He said, 'I can get out of this wheelchair and walk anytime I want. I could be lying flat on my back and swear you in better than anybody you could find.'"[5] But when the time came, Rhodes was not able to be there.

Contrary to the assumptions of many of his political rivals, Rhodes did not hold grudges against his adversaries. He was encouraging to friend and foe alike. Paul Pfeifer, who had tried to wrest the Republican nomination for governor away from him in 1986 and who narrowly lost a contest for attorney general before becoming an Ohio Supreme Court justice, said Rhodes enjoyed talking with him. "I would go over to his office on Gay Street and we'd swap stories," said Pfeifer. "He would urge me to set my sights on being chief justice: 'I don't think Tom [Moyer] is going to be there that much longer. You could be chief justice.'" As it turned out, Moyer set the record for length of service on the high court.

Even while making conversation with Pfeifer, a Bucyrus-area farmer-attorney in civilian life, the subject of air quality was not far from Rhodes's mind. "He told me that I should have a totally climate-controlled horse barn," Pfeifer said. "It was always my view that Rhodes understood and saw me somewhat as himself," he continued. "I came from a small place. The difference was that I didn't have any pals with deep pockets."[6]

But Rhodes also was willing to help even those whose views conflicted with his own. After he had retired from public life, he had a reserved suite in the press box at Ohio Stadium, right next to one occupied by another former governor—Democrat Dick Celeste. The two would chat, bitter days put aside. "He would tell old Woody Hayes stories and give me advice about my political future," Celeste said. "After 1990 [when George Voinovich got elected], he would say, 'Get back in there. You can win. I can help you.'" Imagine that! Jim Rhodes offering to help the guy he had savaged as unqualified to be governor in 1978 and 1986—and against the fellow who had been his own running mate! But that was Rhodes. And it was the reason Ray Bliss and some others who bled red Republican blood were driven mad by him.

"I had always liked Rhodes," Celeste said, in retrospect. "He was such an interesting guy." The Democrat said he thought he had earned Rhodes's respect by campaigning hard and using some of the tactics he had learned from Ohio's longest-serving governor. "I think he viewed me as a worthy adversary," said Celeste. "There were no hard feelings [on his part after the 1986 election]. If I had wanted somebody to help me carry on a political career, I think I could have called on him and he would have loved to do it. You had to pass a certain test with him to earn his respect."[7]

As Rhodes kept up with politics and counseled aspirants in his "retirement" from public life, he was constantly trying to market his plan to remove pollutants from the air in homes, stores, and offices and to create a planned, domed community with super pure air. Rhodes had gotten the idea when he took his family to the Super Bowl at the Silver Dome in Pontiac, Michigan, in early 1982. His grandchildren cavorted gleefully on the turf in the middle of a Michigan winter, and one of them inquired, "Po, wouldn't it be great if we could have something like this at home so we could play all winter?"[8] The lightbulb went on in Rhodes's head, and an invention was born. He put a local engineer to work combining existing air-filtration technologies, but it was slow going. He didn't get his patent on what he called the "HealthyLife" system until 1991. Still, the man who resisted clean air regulations as governor tried to sell the big idea—the Environmental City—to anyone who would listen.

Rhodes started by experimenting with a prototype in his own house. But he dreamed big. The full dome would encompass homes, parks, gardens, living units, and recreational areas. It would be contained in a glass-enclosed atrium; translucent material on the roof would screen out the sun's ultraviolet rays. Rhodes said he invested $2 million in the project.[9]

"I enjoyed public life," he said. "But I've never had anything as exciting as this! There's nothing else like it on Earth. These can make you live longer. They're not pills. They're buildings."[10] Rhodes said his vision was "25 years ahead of the times. When I mentioned the environmental city and got a trademark for it, some people thought insanity had set in. There are more can't-do people than can-do people. They stoned [Robert] Fulton when he invented the steamboat."[11]

In the late 1980s, Rhodes took his invention to some developers northwest of Los Angeles in hopes they would build a prototype house with the system in it. "They didn't understand it," related Duerk. "They didn't see how they could make any money with it."[12] Duerk said the ex-governor also took his idea to New York and met on one occasion with John F. Welch Jr., the chairman of General Electric, and on another with David Rockefeller, the brother of Nelson Rockefeller. "He was very interested," Duerk said of Rockefeller. "He said, 'I'll let you know'. We never heard anything. It was an awfully expensive proposal for developers to fit [into] their buildings. He [Rhodes] sent me to talk to Donald Trump in New York. I went to Trump Towers. They said, 'Mr. Trump isn't here.' I gave him the complete package and we never heard a thing."[13]

Later, Rhodes met with Mexico City businessmen interested in installing the system in a condo project in that smoggy city. But it never worked out.[14] "He was trying it on everybody to see if they'd bite," Duerk said.[15]

The plan was a complex melding of existing technologies—pressurized airlocks and multiple filters. It was designed to get rid of pollutants, including tobacco smoke, animal dandruff, and mites—anything that caused chronic bronchitis, sinusitis, emphysema, or asthma—even viruses. It combined the capabilities of methods already in use in industrial, commercial, and residential buildings into unprecedented efficiency, said Paul Steiskal, vice president of the Kahoe Air Balance Company, which tested the system.[16]

Outside air and recycled air within the home passed through six banks of filters. A pre-filter, two cartridge filters and an activated carbon filter rid the air of particles less than one micron (twenty-five microns is the smallest size that can be seen by the naked eye). The air then was directed through three modified industrial carbon filters—including a charcoal filter, a potassium permanganate filter, and a high-efficiency HEPA filter—that removed gases, odors, and chemical compounds.[17] That it was all existing technology was typical of Rhodes, the idea man: take somebody else's stuff and make it into something better. And have somebody else do the work—sort of like writing books, as he did with Dean Jauchius.

Raymond Meister, an engineer with Columbus Heating & Ventilating, designed the system and installed it in Rhodes's sixty-four-year-old, thirty-eight-hundred-square-foot home at a cost of $33,000. "The air being circulated inside the governor's home is probably the cleanest indoor air in the world today," Meister boasted. In 1992, a Cleveland company tested the system and declared the air 99.996 percent pure. It employed a pressurized filter system to draw out air; eliminate particulates, organic chemicals, gases, and odors; and pump in fresh air six times an hour. "I'm pleased with it," Rhodes said. "I enjoy it. The air is lighter in here."[18] In November 1993, Healthy Buildings International, headquartered in Fairfax, Virginia, conducted an air quality inspection and declared the air quality in Rhodes's home "matches the highest standards normally reserved for intensive care areas of hospitals."[19]

Less than a year later, Rhodes launched the next phase of his project, promising "the world's healthiest indoor air" in condominiums he planned for the affluent Columbus suburb of Upper Arlington, on twenty-two acres at the intersection of Henderson and Sawmill Roads on the Columbus border.[20] His patented pure-air system was to be installed in each of seventy-two condominiums and thirty-seven single-family homes in a development called Limestone Pointe. The configuration was eventually amended to include forty condominiums and fifty-nine single-family homes. Rhodes was ready to buy the farmland for the development, even though it was zoned for commercial use.

Shortly thereafter, however, the Board of Planning and Zoning for the city of Upper Arlington unanimously disapproved the proposed subdivision, saying it wanted to go after commercial development instead, to boost revenue for the city.[21] Rhodes's plan required a zoning change, and city council denied the change, even though Rhodes offered the city $200,000 to pay for widening roads and installing water and sewer lines.[22]

Rhodes scored a small victory a year later when an obvious ally—the American Lung Association—installed his system in its new 10,600-square-foot building in Upper Arlington. It was the first commercial use of the system. Meister, the engineer with Columbus Heating & Ventilating, which installed it, this time sounded pessimistic: "Companies are not going to spend money to correct a sick-building syndrome unless they have to. The last thing people will spend money on is the heating and air-conditioning and air-filtration systems."[23] Others have gotten patents on similar systems but, like Rhodes, never got them developed beyond the installation in a single home or office. "I think the reason it didn't go was that he didn't have the right people to bring about the execution," said son-in-law Richard Moore.[24] The system was subsequently installed in a medical office building at Sawmill and Henderson Roads.

Politics was still on the former governor's mind. Rhodes would talk campaigns and elections with little prompting when visitors to his office or home showed interest. He said he had gotten elected so many times with "hard work and a few tricks now and then," but he wasn't interested in running any more. His favorite campaign strategy: "Lie in the weeds and wait for the other guy to make a mistake."[25]

Helen Rhodes persevered through her ailments until December 1987. She was on the phone ordering Christmas flowers for the house when she collapsed.[26] She was discovered by housekeeper Carol Cooper, who was bringing her a glass of iced tea. Emergency medical technicians worked on Helen and took her to the hospital, but they couldn't revive her. It fell to Cooper to call Jim Rhodes at his development office and tell him his beloved Helen had died. "I got him on the phone and told him he had to come home right away," the housekeeper said. "He wanted to know why. I told him again to come home right away. 'Helen passed, didn't she?' Rhodes said. 'I want to know the truth, because I've got to face the public. I can't cry in public.' I told him the truth. He didn't put the phone down. He just sobbed. Later, at home, I came into the room and found him just sobbing and sobbing."[27] But the former governor got a grip, took over, got the family together, including daughter Sherry, who arrived from Florida; ordered carry-in food for dinner; and arranged for the funeral. "At a time like this, it's all about family," daughter Suzanne recalled her father saying.

One thing, however, took priority over Helen's services. When Rhodes found out his grandson Jason had a basketball game scheduled at 2:00 P.M., the time of the funeral, he called Overbrook Presbyterian Church and had the latter changed to 10:00 A.M. Rhodes made it a point never to miss a home game at Upper Arlington High School, where Jason, Ric, and Jamie, his grandsons, played for the Golden Bears.[28]

"It took a lot out of him when Helen died," Cooper recalled. "It broke his heart. He didn't have anybody to write love notes to anymore."[29]

After Helen's death, Rhodes had the whole house in Arlington to himself. He busied himself by growing tomatoes in the garden, attaching small American flags to the tops of the stakes.[30] He loved the neighborhood kids, and at Halloween he'd open his garage door, sit in a lawn chair and hand out candy to the little ghosts and goblins. Brian Ramey, a youngster who lived not far away, reported excitedly to his father, "The governor gave me a full-size candy bar and a guy took a picture of us!"[31] Carol Cooper, who had to haul the load back from the store crammed into her Oldsmobile 88, related: "At Halloween, he'd tell us to buy a thousand dollars worth of candy. The rules were that the teenagers got two candy bars and the little kids got one. The older ones got two because 'they're getting too big and they won't be back next year.'"[32]

In 1988, Rhodes campaigned for Vice President George H. W. Bush, who was trying to succeed Ronald Reagan. He was asked during an appearance at the Press Club of Ohio when he was going to retire from politics. "Ask the people in the cemetery," he retorted. "If you think I'm going to sit along the side of the Scioto River and fish and think about you guys [reporters], forget it!"[33]

For his eightieth birthday celebration the following year, he went to Joe Michael's ice cream store in Jackson, where he had had his first job, and passed out ice cream cones and bags of peanuts to youngsters. That night, friends hosted a $125-a-person gala reception with cake and ice cream at the Aladdin Shrine Temple in suburban Gahanna. Proceeds went to a scholarship fund for Jackson County students.[34] At the time of the birthday bash, he had stopped tinting his hair with a silver-lavender rinse for the first time in fifteen years and allowed it to go white. He lost weight by eating large quantities of tomatoes from his garden, and peaches. He'd have oats and orange juice for breakfast and maybe a tomato sandwich with vinegar for lunch. Any hamburger he ate was drained of fat when cooked, and his popcorn was devoid of butter.[35]

He wasn't out of ideas yet. He wanted the state to give $15,000 college scholarships to high school seniors proficient in science and mathematics who otherwise wouldn't be able to attend college. He said he would chip in part of his personal fortune to help pay the bill. He also wanted Ohio State and the Battelle Memorial Institute to collaborate on using the theory of superconductivity to store huge amounts of energy in small receptacles. "Stored energy will revolutionize the world," he said. "One power plant could light the whole state of Ohio."[36]

In the summer of 1991, Rhodes called George Voinovich, then governor for about six months, and asked to be appointed to the Ohio State University board of trustees. "I didn't think that was a good idea," Voinovich said. "He already had as much influence as anybody at Ohio State. He didn't need to be serving as a trustee with people he had appointed to the board.

"I wasn't going to deal with it over the phone. I thought I should talk to him face to face. So I called and asked if I could come over to his office. I went into his office and sat down and explained that from a public policy standpoint I didn't think it was a very good idea for him to be a trustee. The hard-of-hearing Rhodes said, 'Hah?'

"I went through the reasons again, and he said, 'Hah?' I explained again. Three times, he said 'Hah?' Finally he just looked at me, and he realized I wasn't going to appoint him. I got up and walked out. He didn't hold it against me. He didn't hold grudges, but he'd remember stuff and he'd take care of it quietly. If somebody did something he didn't like, he'd say, 'Just let 'em wander around outside the Statehouse in circles.' That meant they didn't have any access anymore."[37]

One other person who was in a position to know said Rhodes made another bid before Voinovich left his office that day, hoping the current governor would change his mind: "What about the $100,000 I gave to your campaign [in 1990]? I've got my checkbook here and I'd be happy to write a check."[38] Voinovich stoutly denied those sentences were uttered. "That was not part of the conversation," he said. "Even if he had [thought money would influence the appointment], I have to say that Jim Rhodes was smart enough not to mention it to me. That would really tee me off. He knew me well enough that he would never do that."[39]

Rhodes loved to assist Republicans during their campaigns. Actually, he loved to help anyone who would listen, including reporters when they didn't understand what he was talking about. "Let me help you out," he'd say. On an occasion in the fall of 1994, he took it upon himself to help state senator Nancy Chiles Dix, whose district included territory east of Columbus and who was engaged in a tough election campaign. Late one chilly October afternoon,

Rhodes wheeled up in his white 1992 Cadillac for the sale of champions in the swine barn at the Fairfield County Fair, the last one of the year in Ohio. Resplendent in a brown pinstripe suit, he greeted Dix, the mayor of Lancaster, and Congressman David Hobson: "I been here for an hour, canvassing. Go in and set right in front."

Rhodes then showed Dix how to bid on the champion goats and hogs belonging to the Junior Fair boys and girls. "Put your hand up!" he instructed, goading Dix into bidding $2,700—a record for a hog at the Junior Fair. Hobson, claiming he had no money with him and that he had another appointment, wriggled out of Rhodes's clutches after he and Dix split the cost and donated the hog to the Olivedale Senior Citizens' Center in Lancaster. Then, the payoff for Dix: photos were taken for various papers and newsletters showing her with Travis Queen, the Bloom-Carroll eighth grader who raised the hog. "There'll be more people remember you for this than anything you do," Rhodes crowed. "These people never forget."[40]

Dix wasn't the only one Rhodes helped that year. Auditor Jim Petro later recalled, "When I was running in '94, he would call me about every two weeks. He had lots of advice. I used to joke, he has a million suggestions, of which 20 percent are pretty good."[41]

Two weeks after the Fairfield County Fair, Rhodes took part in a reunion of three former governors at the Ohio Historical Center in honor of Kent State University Press's publication of the book *Ohio Politics*—a history of Ohio government and politics since World War II. Democrats Richard Celeste and John Gilligan were there, and Rhodes seemed to have reconciled with them. "I'm retired. I don't pay much attention to politics," he said to the horselaughs of the one hundred in attendance.[42] Rhodes, ever impatient, left abruptly before the event was over, walking out of a roundtable discussion with his fellow governors.

In 1995, Rhodes suffered a slight stroke, but it didn't affect his sharp mind. Housekeeper Carol Cooper told of the difficult time immediately afterward: "I usually got there [to the house] at 6:50 in the morning and he'd be in a chair. I'd bring him the newspaper and a cup of tea. This one day I came in and he was lying on the floor. I called Saunie and Sue. Sue and Dick [Moore] came over, and I said, 'Let me call 911.' He said, 'Gimme that newspaper,' and he started reading the paper while lying on the floor." Finally, he was persuaded to go to the hospital, but he wouldn't do his physical or occupational therapy. "I don't load no dishwasher," he told the occupational therapist.[43]

In downtown Columbus, there was talk that the Rhodes statue would move back to the Statehouse grounds from its position in front of the Rhodes Office Tower. "I think it ought to be on the Statehouse yard," Rhodes said. "But that's for the people in charge to decide."[44]

Senator Richard Finan, chairman of the Capitol Square Review and Advisory Board, said he thought the statue was in a logical place. "Some people think it's neat where it is," said Finan, who was in the middle of presiding over the complete restoration of the Statehouse. "People think it looks like he's coming out of his building and going to the governor's office." The $67,500 statue, which had been dedicated December 6, 1982, survived hits by a chocolate meringue pie and a car that drove up onto the Statehouse lawn in 1983.

One of Jim Rhodes's favorite haunts in retirement was the Scioto Country Club. His Tremont Road home backed up on the prestigious golf course, and he often played there until his body wore out. "He had a caddy swing," said his grandson Ric Moore. "It was a short, compact little swing but it [the shot] was always straight down the middle. And he could putt. He'd just jab at it, but it would go in."[45]

Another of Rhodes's golfing companions, Phil Hamilton, had a different take. "Anything within twelve feet was a gimme," Hamilton said, meaning Rhodes would concede putts within twelve feet of the hole and expect his playing partners to do the same for him. Moore said Rhodes's rules varied depending on the company he was keeping; that he played strictly by the rules with other adults, but "when it was just the two of us" he was not above using a "foot wedge" to improve the lie of his ball. "If I hit a bad shot, he'd roll a ball out there and say, 'Hit another one.' He was always giving lessons. He'd say, 'Keep your head down. I'll watch where it goes.'"[46]

Rhodes would play in celebrity tournaments and fund-raisers with folks like Bob Hope and Glen Campbell. His last year as governor (1982), he was in the Bob Hope Classic and was paired with Hope and Jack Nicklaus. "Next year," he told a couple of visitors to his office, "I'll be thirty-six foursomes back because I won't be governor." He was a realist.[47] Among his favorite local partners were Columbus developer Jack Kessler and Pandel Savic, the club pro who mentored Nicklaus in the early days. On Saturdays and Sundays, he would play Scioto with the Senior Swats. "He drove the cart," Ric Moore said. "That was the only thing we'd [the family] let him drive."

One day, when Bob Hope was visiting, the two of them wanted to go next door to play a few holes. Someone had given Rhodes a golf cart manufactured by Rolls-Royce, so he dusted it off and invited Hope to get in.[48] They were going to drive around the block and enter the club at the main driveway. But the highway patrol officer in charge of security told Rhodes he couldn't take the golf cart on a public road. Rhodes wasn't about to be deterred, until the officer told him, "If you do, I'll have to give you a ticket." So with Hope driving, they decided to just go through Rhodes's back yard. But first they had to negotiate four large steps. Cooper and the security officer hung onto the cart for dear life to keep it from tipping over while the aged golfers lurched down the steps.

Rhodes still hung out in the Grill Room at the country club, where he took cdining companions—politicians such as Bill Saxbe, friends and former cabinet officers like Hamilton, and family members. The room had a panoramic view of the golf course, plush appointments, and a large stone fireplace that created a cozy atmosphere in the winter. Rhodes's loud voice could be heard through nearby corridors, talking to friends or teasing the help.

He could wander down the halls and peer into the glass-enclosed trophy cases holding all manner of silver chalices from local and national golfing events. The wood-paneled walls were lined with photos of tournament action and trophy presentations. They dated back to the days of Bobby Jones, Walter Hagen, and Gene Sarazen and, of course, included many photos of Nicklaus in all phases of his career.

Among the saddest times for the former governor—aside from Helen's death—was the loss of their daughter Saundra, who died in March 1996 of cardiomyopathy—a weakened heart from which she had suffered for a year.[49] Suzanne heard first and had to inform her dad. She told him she was coming over to his house—but he didn't know why.[50]

"Daddy, I've got something very sad to tell you," Suzanne said.

"What's that?"

"Saunie has passed away."

"He just sort of sat there, shell-shocked, for about two minutes," Suzanne related. "Then, all of a sudden, he came alive and said, 'Get 'em all together. Get 'em all over to the house for dinner. We're all gonna talk about how good

Rhodes, a low-handicap golfer in earlier days, played golf with comedian Bob Hope at celebrity tournaments and when the comedian visited Columbus. Here they pose at the Memorial Tournament Pro-Am established by Jack Nicklaus in Dublin, Ohio. Fred Shannon, Columbus *Dispatch*, July 20, 1999.

Saunie was. We're in this together.'" It hearkened back to the days in Jackson when Susie Rhodes called the family together after her husband died. "Then at the funeral, he made plans for where everybody would sit and he ran the show." Rhodes took his daughter's death as part of life and, though saddened, he was philosophical during the calling hours.

The summer of that same year, Rhodes had partial hip replacement at Ohio State University Medical Center; he had fractured it when he fell while feeding the birds in the yard at his home. Earlier in the month, he had presided over the Sale of Champions livestock auction at the Ohio State Fair.[51] Phil Hamilton's son, John, was a paramedic with the Upper Arlington Fire Department when he was assigned to the emergency run to Rhodes's home. He found the former governor, whom he had known since he was a boy, lying in the driveway, saying, "John, I fell and broke my butt." John examined him and said, "Governor, I don't think it's your butt. I think you broke your hip." Recalled John's father, Phil: "They tried to get him to go in the pool and exercise, but he wouldn't. He didn't like to be told what to do."[52]

In 1997, Rhodes was invited to help Honda celebrate the twentieth anniversary of its first American manufacturing site, the motorcycle plant in Marysville. Rhodes called luring the Japanese firm to Ohio "the biggest thing we did" during his years as governor.[53] The plant then had thirteen thousand employees, far more than the estimate for the original plant of fewer than a thousand. But Rhodes, in his typical hyperbole, said: "I thought it'd be bigger than this."[54] Asked yet again if he would ever return to public life, he demurred. He was too old: "I was at the trough longer than anybody."[55]

His friends were dying. In August 1997, Rhodes attended the Statehouse funeral ceremonies for his southern Ohio buddy, the legendary former House speaker Vern Riffe. In a wheelchair because his legs had failed him—"blew my knee out," he told one old friend—Rhodes found himself in the south wing, near the former state auditor's office of his old nemeses, Joe and Tom Ferguson. It was late in the afternoon and as Rhodes glanced around, he saw that few people were left and he was about to close the place, as it were. "Well, I've done what I always wanted to do," he told a reporter. "Be the last one out of the Statehouse."[56]

Rhodes was front and center at the January 1999 swearing-in ceremony for Chief Justice Thomas J. Moyer, his former aide. He was conscious of well-wishers looking down on him in the wheelchair pushed by grandson Ric. "I have a bad leg from freshman basketball at Ohio State," he told people.[57] Other times, Rhodes would say he was incapacitated by "an old football injury." He accepted his limitation as part of the life cycle, telling his grandson, "It's just like you being in a stroller when you were a baby. It's something that happens."[58]

A few days later, on the evening of Bob Taft's inauguration as governor, boxing promoter Don King, his wife Henrietta, and the *Call and Post* newspapers of Cleveland, which King owned, sponsored a reception at the Columbus Athletic Club honoring Rhodes. It was an invitation-only affair, with George Forbes, the onetime president of Cleveland City Council, receiving responses. The sponsorship was revealing of Rhodes's ability to work with Democrats and help African Americans. Don King didn't show up, but Rhodes did, furnishing more stories from the past.

On his way out of office sixteen years earlier, Rhodes had pardoned Don King, who had served almost four years in prison for manslaughter in the 1966 beating of a man. In succeeding years, Rhodes called King to ask a favor for a friend. He was told King was not available. "Tell him I'm gonna rescind his pardon," Rhodes growled, knowing the person on the other end of the line didn't realize Rhodes had no power to do any such thing. King quickly came to the phone.[59]

In 1999, Rhodes sold his house in Upper Arlington. Despite its fabulous air purification system, the new owners wanted it demolished so they could build a more modern residence. After all the fine interior wood, fixtures, copper, windows, and roofing slate had been sold, a controlled burn was scheduled, to provide Upper Arlington firefighters with training.[60] Intentionally or not, Rhodes and his grandson Ric were driving down Tremont Road one day when they "noticed a big commotion with fire trucks."[61] They stopped and observed the conflagration from the car. Later, Rhodes was asked how he felt as he watched the flames devour the homestead that contained so many fond family memories. The inquiring reporter expected a twinge of emotion, perhaps a tear. But the dry-eyed man betrayed no sentimentality. "Fine," he said bluntly. "It gave 'em good training."[62]

About this time, the folks in Coalton decided they'd have a day for their native son. Steve Evans, the son of restaurateur Bob Evans, described it: "They called his grandson, and he checked it out and said, 'Grandpa would love to come.' They gave him a choice of two or three days, and he picked one. They got the fire department involved and organized a James Allen Rhodes parade down the middle of town. About three weeks before the day, another one of the grandsons called and said Grandpa can't come. He wasn't feeling well." So the event was called off. Recalled Evans, "On the very day we had set for the parade, here comes the limousine. He thinks we're having the parade. They had to tell him it was called off. He didn't let it bother him one bit. He spent two or three hours at the filling station sitting around telling stories."[63]

By March 1999, Rhodes had moved into The Forum at Knightsbridge, a retirement complex on the northwest side of Columbus. His condo had a rug with the Great Seal of the State of Ohio woven into it. One of his neighbors was Bob Thomas, a longtime executive at WBNS-TV and publisher of a series of three soft-cover books called "Columbus Unforgettables." Naturally, Rhodes was one of those. "I keep busy," he told a reporter. "I research quite a bit. I'm trying to put together a germ-free home. I'm about there."[64] Rhodes also said he was studying how improved blood circulation could allay the effects of Alzheimer's disease.

His thirteen great-grandkids would visit him and want to sit on his lap. "He had a huge drawer of candy bars," said daughter Suzanne. "And the minute those kids came in, he'd say, 'Get in the drawer! Get in the drawer!' And the parents would roll their eyes."[65]

And he was still the governor, always the governor. In his impressive PhD dissertation on Rhodes, William Russell Coil tells of a brief meeting he had with his subject in the lobby of his retirement community. Rhodes was in a wheelchair, but "his grip was firm, his eyes focused on the face of the visitor." During their conversation, Coil noticed a nurse pushing another resident in a wheelchair into the lobby where the poor fellow remained, alone, hooked to an oxygen tank and slumped over in his chair. As Coil departed, he noticed Rhodes rolled his chair over to the guy, "slung one arm around his neck, grabbed his hand and pushed his face to within a few inches of the man's ear.

"Suddenly the beaten, listless man was alive. His head jerked up, his eyes widened, a smile broke out on his face. Somehow Rhodes had summoned some of that old electricity, that elemental energy that forced him to always keep moving, that kept him from being another working-class kid in Springfield, Ohio. At ninety-one years old, Rhodes was still looking for the next hand to shake, joke to crack, and promise to make. At ninety-one years old, Rhodes was still campaigning."[66]

During the 2000 presidential campaign, Rhodes got a call from George W. Bush, who said his father told him to get in touch. When Carol Cooper, who was still with him, handed the phone to Rhodes, he was ready. "Look, I'm not telling you how to run your campaign," Rhodes opened. Then he told young Bush everything he needed to do to win Ohio.[67]

Chan Cochran, who hadn't worked for Rhodes since 1980, remembered getting a telephone call from his ex-boss early one morning in February 2000: "Chando, can you stop out here about one o'clock?" Sure, said Cochran, puzzled by the summons. Rhodes engendered fanatical loyalty from those who had ever worked for him, so Cochran rearranged his business schedule. When he got to The Forum, Rhodes opened the door, wearing the typical jacket and tie—this one was the Tabasco tie, fashionable at the time. "What can I do for you, boss?" asked Cochran.

James A. Rhodes prepares to celebrate his ninetieth birthday at the retirement center apartment he occupied in northwest Columbus during his last years. Rhodes almost always dressed up, and the carpeting reflected his love for his state. Eric Albrecht, *Columbus Dispatch*, September 9, 1999.

Rhodes reached in his pocket, pulled out a $100 bill and handed it to Cochran. "Go over to Der Dutchman and get me nine of those apple pies. I need 'em."

"Couldn't Ric [Moore] get 'em?"

"No, he's busy, and tomorrow's Valentine's Day. I gotta take care of all these widows," Rhodes replied, gesturing toward the entire complex.[68]

The former governor's generosity seemed unbounded, especially to Cooper, whose husband, Froud, had open-heart surgery in the early 1990s. Rhodes would get huge quantities of food from Der Dutchman, including cakes, pies, and rolls, and bring it to the Cooper household. If there was too much he would say, 'Give it to the neighbors.' We gave it to the neighbors and finally they told us to quit bringing any more food because they were gaining weight," Cooper recalled.

Jim and Helen Rhodes treated their housekeeper well. One year they paid for her round-trip flight to Colorado to visit her sister who was suffering from breast cancer, and they gave her an extra $500 to stock up on food. They thought nothing of paying for Carol's vacation flight to Nashville, along with hotel reservations, tickets to the Grand Ole Opry, and $125-a-head restaurant meals for herself and several relatives.

At home, Cooper would take Rhodes grocery shopping or to a restaurant. She recalled, "He'd see a woman with a couple of kids in the supermarket, and he'd say, 'Put her groceries on my tab,' or he'd be in a restaurant and he'd see a family and say, 'Put their bill on my card.' He did that because so many people helped him with food in the early days, and it was payback."[69] The sometimes out-of-control generosity became an inside joke among family members.

Rhodes was still phoning people, day or night. "He didn't care what time he called anybody," said daughter Suzanne. "He'd call me at 1:30 A.M. when he was at The Forum and say, 'Suziebelle, are you awake?' I'd say, 'No.' He'd say, 'Okay, go back to sleep.'"

While Rhodes enjoyed eating in the Grill Room at Scioto—because everyone knew him—he also patronized Bob Evans, Wendy's, and the Cooker in northwest Columbus. "He'd get on a roll and keep going back to one place," said Suzanne.[70] But his favorite of all was Der Dutchman, a sprawling banquet-style restaurant in Plain City on the outer reaches of Columbus's northwest suburbs. He took everyone there, from his family to business associates to out-of-town guests, including Bob Hope. At the end of each family-style meal came the pièce de résistance—the pies. There were apple crumb, shoofly, cherry, chocolate—you name it.

Phil Hamilton, a frequent visitor with Rhodes to "The Der," as they called it, remembered an evening when tornado-warning sirens sounded during a visit. Management ordered everyone to go back into the kitchen away from the glass windows. "I'm not finished eating," Rhodes growled. "I'm not goin' back there." They finally prevailed on him to retreat and pushed his wheelchair back into the kitchen.

The young Amish and Mennonite waitresses were wringing their hands and weeping, frightened by the prospect of the storm. Rhodes, to divert their attention, started asking about the pies. "Gimme that pie!" he said, marveling over its quality. He ended up buying a half dozen of them, mostly berry, which were taken out to his car.

When the all-clear sounded, the Rhodes party went back to the table, and he said, "I'm ready for dessert. I want some pie."

The waitress came back and said, "Sorry, Governor, we're out of pie. We sold it all."

"Go out to my car and get a pie." Back came the pie and he said, "Where's the ice cream?"

"Sorry, Governor, the power went out, and the mixer wouldn't work."

"Well," responded Rhodes, "Go over to Kroger and get some ice cream."

The ex-governor was so enamored of the pies at "The Der" that he took it upon himself to bring some back to the Scioto Country Club, saying, "Here's what *real* pie is like."[71]

It took a public ruckus over a road running past his beloved Der Dutchman to lure the old governor back into the public spotlight again, less than two years before his death. Rhodes had gotten stuck in traffic on busy Route 42, so he orchestrated a special meeting of the Plain City Council at Der Dutchman to hear from a representative of the Ohio Department of Transportation. Rhodes and some of his cronies were at the restaurant, along with many Plain City officials, developers, business community representatives, and area landowners. They wanted a bypass around Plain City to divert the semitrailer traffic.

The usual meal of chicken, beef, mashed potatoes and gravy, stuffing, and corn was served, prompting Ray Lorello, the Department of Transportation representative, to wryly observe that he thought *he* might be dessert. Rhodes was dressed in a sporty royal blue jacket, striped shirt, and no tie. "You're in the bottleneck business," Rhodes told the Plain City folk. "There's none worse." Lorello explained that the bypass was on the construction schedule for 2001. That wasn't quick enough for Rhodes. "You got to talk back to the poli-TEE-shuns," he said. "They don't hear very well. Get a delegation together and go in there and see 'em. Get the loudest guys in town." By now, Rhodes was warmed up. "Get the governor out here!" he shouted, slamming his hand on the table. "Have a little fund-raiser. That'll get his attention."

Someone asked Rhodes why, if the bypass had been requested in the 1970s and 1980s when he was governor, it was never started. "I was never aware of this until I came out here to eat, and it took me twenty-five minutes to get home," he said. It was typical Jim Rhodes, and it may have been one of his last public appearances. Subsequently, Route 42 was rerouted outside the village for through traffic, sparing the locals the congestion.[72]

At his ninetieth birthday party, held September 12, 1999, Rhodes was one of the last to leave, just as he had lingered at Riffe's funeral. Admirers gathered at—where else?—the Rhodes Center at the State Fairgrounds to celebrate. Bob Hope and former president George H. W. Bush—who wired: "You 90? No way!"—sent tributes. When Rhodes spoke, he was uncharacteristically humble. "We, you, every person in here has made a contribution to my success," he said. He greeted scores of the seven hundred well-wishers and enjoyed it so much that forty-five minutes after the salute ended, there he was, still at the head table, "a small, white-haired figure beneath a huge banner, signing autographs" as fairgrounds employees "retrieved colored streamers, harvested red, white and blue balloons and carted containers of melting vanilla ice cream and sticky toppings to the kitchen."

As pianist Marsha Peterson finished a medley of stirring patriotic and religious songs, including the "Battle Hymn of the Republic," Rhodes turned and led the applause. The *Dispatch* chronicled it: "Then the 90-year old historical marvel who doesn't know the meaning of the word *stop* went home to bed."[73]

Despite his activity, Rhodes's health was deteriorating. In late May 1999, the former governor broke his collarbone and was treated at the Ohio State Medical Center and sent home. His quality of life was slipping.[74] He was hospitalized in December 2000 and again in January, and visitors noticed the decline. He went to the hospital, at the Ohio State University Medical Center, for the final time on February 28, 2001.[75] "He never complained and never had a bad day," said daughter Suzanne. "When he was in the hospital for the last time, the nurses would ask him [how he was,] and he'd say, 'I'm fine.' Toward the end, he was having trouble breathing, and I said, 'Daddy, do you want me to call Pastor Paul?' He said, 'Hell, no, don't call him. I'm not gonna die.'"[76]

Carol Cooper had told Rhodes a personal story that profoundly affected the way he looked at life and death. When Cooper was about fifty, she had double pneumonia and was close to death. She had a dream about her late grandfather, who appeared at her bedside in a checkered shirt and jeans. He called her "Kelly" because he had so many grandchildren he couldn't get their names straight.

"I said, 'Am I gonna die?' and he said, 'No, Kelly, you're not gonna die. You've got too much in your life to do.'

"I asked, 'Are my mom and dad in heaven? And Aunt Lorraine and Carl?'

"He said, 'When you die, your family will greet you in heaven.' Rhodes loved to hear that story. He had me tell it over and over and over while he was at The Forum. When he was in the hospital for the last time, he couldn't eat but he could still talk. He said, 'If you find out I'm gonna die, tell me.' He wanted to say a prayer before he died."

One day while Cooper was trying to feed Rhodes his lunch at the hospital, Dr. Manuel Tzagournis, the attending physician, observed that the former governor could no longer swallow and his vital functions were shutting down. He told Cooper that Rhodes had three to six hours left to live, more likely three. She notified family members, and Rhodes asked her to tell him the story of her grandfather one more time. "I told him he was going to be in heaven with Helen," Cooper said, "and that family members would be there to greet him. He wanted to know whether Helen or his mother would greet him first. I said I didn't know."[77]

Jim Rhodes died peacefully at 2:45 P.M. on March 4, 2001, of complications from an infection and heart failure. He was ninety-one.[78] Family members were at his bedside when he breathed his last. The following day, another perennial politician, ninety-three-year-old Harold Stassen of Minnesota, a nine-time presidential candidate, also succumbed to advanced age.[79]

In Columbus's Statehouse rotunda, Rhodes's body, dressed in a dark suit with one of his favored flowered ties of the 1990s, lay in state in an open, maroon-lined casket for seven hours as hundreds of mourners passed by silently. He was only the fourth public official to receive that honor since Abraham Lincoln.[80]

Jim Rhodes had come a long way from his early days as a coal miner's son—the poor Jackson County boy who wanted to "be somebody."

Two Ohio Highway Patrol troopers attended the casket, which was adorned with sprays of roses. There was a large portrait nearby of Rhodes in earlier days. The bier was less than fifty yards from the scene of the former governor's sixteen years of triumphs and tragedies—the office where Rhodes had met with visiting dignitaries, set up a command post to help dig Ohio out of a blizzard, endured protests of furious property owners over high property taxes, and ducked reporters the day of the tragic Kent State shootings.

Columbus musician Arnett Howard, dressed respectfully in a black dashiki and matching African cap, selected a quiet moment to approach the coffin and play "Amazing Grace," the tones of his silver Severinsen Akright Bel Canto trumpet echoing throughout the building and drawing curious workers out of their offices. Howard's mother, Dolores, had helped Rhodes's campaign in 1962, and he helped her get a position in a Republican women's organization.

Howard said he and Rhodes used to talk about jazz and that Rhodes always wanted him to play "Woodchopper's Ball" and "Flyin' Home." Rhodes was a particular fan of the great vibraphonist Lionel Hampton. The bandleader had stayed at his home in Clintonville in north Columbus when he played gigs in Ohio while Rhodes was mayor; after there was no acceptable public lodging for black people.[81]

A memorial service was held March 7 in the Statehouse Atrium. Among the featured speakers were Senators George Voinovich and Mike DeWine, and Governor Bob Taft, who interrupted a two-week trade mission to South America to return for his mentor's funeral. Also speaking was Tom Moyer, who had become chief justice of the Ohio Supreme Court. "How Great Thou Art," one of Rhodes's favorites, was played along with "Amazing Grace," the latter by the Columbus Police Department Pipe and Drum Corps. The service had been preceded by a joint session of the General Assembly, called just to memorialize the late former governor.

Ohio House speaker Householder, who wasn't able to have Rhodes administer his oath of office, got to speak at the memorial service. He related that just two weeks earlier, Rhodes had called him to lobby for more research money for Ohio State University.[82] Even near death, he never stopped working.

Rhodes's death generated scores of newspaper columns, editorials, and compilations of humorous stories surrounding him, in addition to the normal news coverage. Tributes poured in from all directions, even from adversaries.

The following day there was a public funeral at Upper Arlington Lutheran Church, presided over by Pastor Paul Ulring. Speaking to Rhodes's large family in front of six hundred mourners, Ulring said: "'Family values' was more than a slogan for him, because Jim Rhodes valued families. . . . Governor Rhodes loved old hymns. If you see this [service] as an old hymn sing, that's what it is. The governor would tell you to sing loud."[83] Governor Taft quoted from a poem by Alfred Lord Tennyson, then said there should be no sadness that the boy from Jackson County was now with God. "James A. Rhodes has crossed the bar, and I know he is face to face with the Pilot that guides us all, who is telling him, 'Well done, my faithful and tireless public servant,'" Taft said.

Taft turned to Rhodes's family. "I also know what it's like to grow up in a political family and how difficult that can be," he said. "He loved his family more than anything else. I know you made sacrifices. You were his shelter against the stormy blasts." He added, to the amusement of all, that Rhodes would have recommended he not come back for the funeral; he would have said, "Stay where you are. Just bring home some jobs."

Rhodes was laid to rest alongside his beloved Helen in the Huntington Chapel at Green Lawn Cemetery on the West Side of Columbus. The funeral procession was an estimated three-quarters of a mile long. At the cemetery, Kenneth Morckel, superintendent of the Ohio Highway Patrol, presented Rhodes's daughter Suzanne Moore with the Ohio flag that had been draped over the casket of the state's longest-serving governor.[84]

Epilogue

JAMES A. RHODES was among the longest serving governors in the history of the United States. His sixteen years of service to his state were matched by Alabama governor George C. Wallace and exceeded in 2011 by Iowa governor Terry Branstad. New York's George Clinton served twenty-one years, but that was before the U.S. Constitution was adopted in 1789.[1]

In 2009, on the hundredth anniversary of Rhodes's birth, his friends, family, and admirers began gathering annually at his beloved Der Dutchman—where he would have wanted them to celebrate—to dine, enjoy fellowship, and tell stories.

His story—his legacy—is far reaching. In the northern corner of his beloved state, Lima Technical College officially changed its name to James A. Rhodes State College on June 24, 2002, at a ceremony featuring former U.S. senator and Republican presidential nominee Bob Dole, whose distant relatives lived in that part of Ohio. Rhodes received the honor because of his record of establishing a strong community and technical college system in Ohio.[2]

HIGHLIGHTS

James A. Rhodes left a rich heritage for his state. Often with the help of the Ohio General Assembly. He

- established the Ohio Board of Regents, coordinating state funding and programming for higher education.

- added six state universities, up to two dozen university branch campuses and created a system of twenty-one state-funded community and technical colleges. The new state-funded universities were in Cleveland, Akron, Toledo, Cincinnati, Youngstown, and the Dayton area. Central State College, historically welcoming black students, became a state-funded university on Rhodes's watch. His goal was to have a college within thirty miles of every young man and woman in the state.
- added Medical College of Ohio at Toledo; Ohio College of Osteopathic Medicine at Athens; and Northeast Ohio Medical University, a collaboration of Akron, Kent State, and Youngstown State Universities in Rootstown, Ohio.
- built forty-nine vocational and technical schools for students who wanted advanced training for jobs immediately after high school. His mantra was "a job in one hand and a diploma in the other."
- built eighty-five county airports, which he said were needed so corporate executives could easily fly their jets into all counties and make plans to open job-creating factories and stores.
- oversaw completion of the interstate highway system in Ohio and made progress on the Appalachian Highway system, linking rural areas in southern Ohio with major cities.
- added six state parks to the park system.
- created the Ohio Historical Center to store state records and serve as a state museum, complete with a mid-nineteenth-century historical village.
- established the Ohio Adult Parole Authority and began construction of the Southern Ohio Correctional Facility—a maximum-security prison housing death-row inmates in Lucasville.
- established the Ohio Youth Commission to remove wayward teens from the adult prison system and give them special accommodations and rehabilitation.
- established the Ohio Administration on Aging, later to become the Ohio Commission on Aging, which offers special services for senior citizens, including the Golden Buckeye Card retail discount.
- established the Senior Citizens' Hall of Fame, honoring the accomplishments of older Ohioans.
- created the Ohio Water Development Authority and the Ohio Air Quality Development Authority to regulate factory water discharges and air pollution.

The elder statesman—former governor Rhodes in June 1989. This is daughter Sue Moore's favorite photo of her dad. Photo copyright Michael Wilson, furnished by Suzanne and Richard Moore.

- established the Junior Fair Board; the Ohio Agricultural Hall of Fame; and the Sale of Champions at the Ohio State Fair, which allows young exhibitors to auction their livestock for college funds.
- boosted attendance at the Ohio State Fair and promoted it as the nation's largest.
- was a partner in the creation of the Arthur G. James Cancer Center at Ohio State University Medical Center.
- began phase-out of large mental hospitals and establishment of community mental health centers.
- established the Ohio Transportation Research Center in Logan County.
- attracted Honda Motor Company motorcycle and auto manufacturing plants to Marysville (near the Transportation Research Center), a Ford Motor Company plant to Batavia, and General Motors expansions in Moraine.
- established the Home Energy Assistance Program to assist low-income Ohioans in paying their winter heating bills.[3]

Lowlights

- Four individuals were killed and nine others wounded after Rhodes sent the Ohio National Guard to the Kent State University campus to quell a student antiwar demonstration.
- In May 1967 Ohio voters defeated a proposed constitutional amendment that would have established an Ohio Bond Commission to decide on all state capital improvements and sell the bonds to fund the projects, thus eliminating the need for voter approval of additional debt for such costly building plans.
- A plan to establish Golden Age Villages for low-income seniors, similar to today's independent and assisted living complexes, funded with revenue bonds, fell by the wayside.
- Voters soundly defeated Rhodes's three overly ambitious bond issues and a business tax relief issue in 1975. However, all or parts of them became a reality over the next twenty years.
- In the late 1970s, Rhodes promoted the development of the "fluidized bed" system of making Ohio's high-sulfur coal marketable by cleaning pollutants out of it. Thirty-five years later, the process had not gotten much beyond the experimental stage.

- To balance the budget, the governor had to persuade the legislature to raise taxes four times in the final two years of his tenure, going against his steadfast "no new taxes" political posture.
- Rhodes, seeking a fifth term, suffered a humiliating defeat in the 1986 election against Democratic governor Richard F. Celeste. He thus lost his first and last campaign for governor.

Former Ohio governor Bob Taft, who as Rhodes's running mate in the disastrous 1986 race saw the latter's faults and frailties up close, provided an honest and insightful historical appraisal of his political mentor. Taft comments from the perspective of his eight years as governor:

> I think Rhodes in his prime had a real feel about what people cared about—jobs, their communities, their schools, their parks and their campuses. He was totally nonideological. He would work with anybody who would work with him. He knew how power was organized, and he had his go-to people. Most of them were newspaper publishers and businessmen. His pro-jobs message was pro-business at the same time. He was nimble, quick in his heyday. He understood local pride. It fit with Ohio, which has a lot of big cities and small communities. Spreading it around works in Ohio. He was governor during an era of expansive economic growth. He was the antithesis of the ideological polarization that we have today. He would never lose sight of what mattered most. He would make it happen.[4]

In northeast Ohio, Edward W. "Ned" Hill, dean of the Levin College of Urban Affairs at Cleveland State University, offered a more detached view of the Rhodes era (although Hill said that in a way he owed his job to Rhodes, who in December 1964 helped create the urban university). In the short run, Hill said, it is difficult for any governor to counter national economic trends within his own state. But Rhodes transformed Ohio from "being a purely agricultural and blue-collar state" to one more in line with where the country was heading in the 1960s and '70s. The key was education, especially his determination to expand opportunity for higher education all over Ohio. Hill acknowledged that in his last term, in the 1980s, Rhodes was out of step with the structural changes remaking the U.S. economy. "But if you are thinking about the roots of the modern economy, it is his investment in education. He put in place an intellectual infrastructure [without which] we would look like Mississippi. That is his largest living legacy—and it will live forever."[5]

Notes

INTRODUCTION

1. George E. Condon Jr., "State Had Its Own Colossus in Rhodes," *Canton Repository,* Mar. 11, 2001.

2. "The Wonderful World of Ohio" was the name Rhodes bestowed on what had been a rather dull Department of Highways bulletin after he supervised expanding the publication into a lively and colorful, slick, tourist-oriented brochure.

3. Robert Howarth, interview by Richard G. Zimmerman and Tom Diemer, Dec. 3, 2004.

4. Paul Pfeifer, interview by Tom Diemer, in Pfeifer's Supreme Court chambers, Dec. 12, 2006.

5. Rhodes's denial resulted from a minor confrontation with Robert Burdock, an independent-minded reporter then working for the Ohio Press Service.

6. Ray Dorsey, "DiSalle Was Exciting Chief, Rhodes Is Politically Wiser," *Cleveland Plain Dealer,* June 16, 1963.

7. For a time, Zimmerman reported from Columbus for the one in a small chain of Ohio newspapers published by Harry Horvitz.

8. The Medical College of Ohio at Toledo, later the Medical University of Ohio, became part of the University of Toledo in 2006 and was rechristened the University of Toledo Medical Center.

9. Keith McNamara, interview by Richard G. Zimmerman and Tom Diemer, in his Columbus law office, June 13, 2006.

10. Duane St. Clair, "Governor Is Still Running Strong—But for What?" *Columbus Dispatch,* Feb. 24, 1980.

11. Condon, "State Had Its Own Colossus in Rhodes."

12. Thomas K. Diemer, "Rhodes Begins Fourth Term on Brief, Low-Key Note," *Cleveland Plain Dealer,* Jan. 9, 1979.

1. The Hustle from Coalton to Capitol

1. As most of those who knew Rhodes as a boy and young man preceded him in death, the authors primarily relied on several written sources to document much of Rhodes's early life, chiefly a PhD dissertation, "Gubernatorial Roles: An Assessment by Five Ohio Governors" (Ohio State University, 1971) by Rollin Dean Jauchius, a former Columbus newspaperman who knew Rhodes well, coauthored (or perhaps wrote) Rhodes's three historical novels, and worked in the state auditor's and governor's offices between 1957 and 1969. Jauchius's dissertation indicates he also interviewed Rhodes about his life at length on April 6, 1971, at Rhodes's Columbus industrial development office.

Jauchius also started a full biography of Rhodes, "Be Somebody: The Story of James Allen Rhodes," perhaps based on the 1971 interview and others he had with Rhodes, who was reluctant to speak with others about his personal life. Suzanne and Richard Moore, Rhodes's daughter and son-in-law, made that unpublished manuscript, which ended at the outbreak of World War II, available to the authors.

Also helpful was a lengthy profile of Rhodes ("A Man Named Rhodes"), which appeared in the *Akron Beacon Journal* on Sunday, March 5, 1978. Although that piece relied heavily on information from Jauchius's dissertation, its reporters—coauthors Brian Usher, Michael Cull, and other contributors—also developed several additional sources.

2. Richard G. Zimmerman, "Rhodes's First Eight Years," in *Ohio Politics,* ed. Alexander Lamis (Kent, Ohio: Kent State University Press, 1994), 353n1.

3. Usher et al., "Man Named Rhodes."

4. Jauchius, "Be Somebody," 9, 11. John L. Lewis, who became president of the UMW in 1919, was a Republican of Welsh ancestry.

5. Ibid.

6. Usher et al., "Man Named Rhodes."

7. Jauchius, "Gubernatorial Roles," 47–48.

8. Diemer's notes, as told by Rhodes in a meeting with reporters, c. 1980.

9. Rhodes seldom spoke of the period his family lived in Indiana but rather presented himself to voters as a product of Jackson County, Springfield, and Columbus, Ohio. He also seldom mentioned his two deceased siblings but often spoke of his two living sisters.

10. Jim Rhodes, interview by Lee Leonard, 1986. W. Bennett Rose, a former Ohio House member from Lima, also recalled Rhodes saying he once lived in a refurbished chicken coop.

11. Leonard's personal visit, July 14, 2012.

12. Jauchius, "Be Somebody," 40–41.

13. Ibid., 19–20.

14. Ibid., 48–49.

15. Usher et al., "Man Named Rhodes."

16. Jauchius, "Be Somebody," 19–20.

17. Suzanne Moore (Rhodes's daughter), interview by Mary Lou Crumley (niece of Helen Rawlins Rhodes), May 25, 2012.

18. Jauchius, "Be Somebody," 21–22.

19. Jauchius, "Gubernatorial Roles," 49. Jauchius also said that Susan Rhodes's confrontation with the county welfare officials had nothing to do with the move to Springfield and, in fact, took place in February 1919, five years before the move. "Be Somebody," 42.

20. Usher et al., "Man Named Rhodes." Sometime in late 1962, Zimmerman discussed Rhodes's career at Springfield High at some length with the always imperious, still presiding Springfield High School principal Charles Fox. Zimmerman also knew Pitzer as a coach and art instructor at Springfield South, where Pitzer often talked of his classmate Jim Rhodes.

21. Jauchius, "Be Somebody," 48, 56.

22. Usher et al., "Man Named Rhodes."

23. Zimmerman, "Rhodes's First Eight Years," 353nn1, 2; Jauchius, "Be Somebody," 55.

24. Suzanne Moore interview, May 25, 2012.

25. Jauchius, "Be Somebody," 25–26, 66.

26. Byrl R. Shoemaker, *Ohio's Greatest Governor James A. Rhodes: Politician of the Century* (Columbus: Shoemaker Enterprises, 2005), 15. Shoemaker writes that Ohio State coach Floyd Stahl offered Rhodes aid amounting to $25 a quarter—or $75 for a typical academic year.

27. Joe Eszterhas and Michael Roberts, *13 Seconds: Confrontation at Kent State* (New York: Dodd, Mead, 1970), 128–30.

28. Zimmerman notes that whenever Rhodes attended a national governors conference—often held at resorts—Rhodes usually could be found on the golf course whenever a formal meeting was not scheduled. He could usually hold his own against any of his fellow governors, and he shot his age at Scioto Country Club when in his seventies, according to his grandson Ric Moore.

29. Jauchius, "Gubernatorial Roles," 49.

30. Suzanne Moore interview, May 25, 2012.

31. Jauchius, "Be Somebody," 75–76.

32. Ibid., 53–54, 67.

33. Ibid., 66–67, 69.

34. Jauchius, "Gubernatorial Roles," 49.

35. Richard G. Zimmerman, "File Bares OSU Career of Rhodes," *Cleveland Plain Dealer*, Oct. 26, 1969.

36. Usher et al., "Man Named Rhodes."

37. Suzanne Moore interview, May 25, 2012.

38. Suzanne Moore, interview by Lee Leonard, July 16, 2012.

39. Jauchius, "Be Somebody," 77.

40. Jauchius, "Gubernatorial Roles," 50.

41. Usher et al., "Man Named Rhodes."

42. Jauchius, "Gubernatorial Roles," 51; Usher et al., "Man Named Rhodes."

2. Up Broad Street, Step by Careful Step

1. Usher et al., "Man Named Rhodes."

2. Jauchius, Be Somebody," 79.

3. Ibid., 80.

4. Ibid., 79.

5. Ibid., 80.

6. Usher et al., "Man Named Rhodes." See also the detailed outline of Rhodes's political career included in Stanley J. Aronoff and Vernal G. Riffe Jr., *James A. Rhodes at*

Eighty (Columbus: Privately published, 1989), 17–38. This paperback was produced by Republican Aronoff, then the president of the Ohio Senate, and Riffe, Democratic speaker of the Ohio House of Representatives, for Rhodes's eightieth birthday celebration. It is thought mostly the work of Thomas Dudgeon, a veteran Columbus lobbyist and political operative, with input from Dean Jauchius. While making no pretense at being balanced, it offers convenient references to key dates in Rhodes's long political career and authoritative versions of the precise wording of many of the oft-repeated quotations attributed to Rhodes.

7. Byrl R. Shoemaker, *A Good Guy Finishes on Top—Governor Rhodes at Ninety* (Columbus: Shoemaker Enterprises, 1999).

8. Ibid.

9. Jim Duerk, telephone interview by Lee Leonard, Nov. 8, 2013.

10. Jauchius, "Gubernatorial Roles," 51.

11. Harold A. Stacy, "6177 Votes Elects Green; Hauntz New Republican in Council; Levies Lose; Mrs. Johnson Nosed Out; Rhodes to Become Auditor Nov. 15; Blosser, Mathias and Miller Are Also Victorious," *Columbus Evening Dispatch,* Nov. 8, 1939.

12. Usher et al., "Man Named Rhodes"; Aronoff and Riffe, *James A. Rhodes at Eighty,* 15. The conflicting details concerning when and where Jim and Helen Rhodes met is rather typical of the often annoying (at least for biographers), if not always important, differences between Rhodes's recollections and others' accounts of his life. Rhodes, like many of us, but especially those in public life, sometimes recalled events as he wished they had taken place, not always as they actually did. Rhodes, always a bit puritanical and staid about family matters, may have thought it was more proper to have married his "childhood sweetheart" than a young woman he first met while slinging hamburgers at his campus restaurant. Then again, he may have regarded his brief time at Ohio State as an extension of his childhood.

13. Suzanne Moore interview, May 25, 2012.

14. Jauchius, "Be Somebody," 74.

15. Rumors of Helen Rhodes's overindulgence were never seriously pursued or overtly mentioned in print by reporters, but they did prompt the wife of a State-house newsman to say, in reference to Rhodes's often frenzied, peripatetic lifestyle: "If I were married to Jim Rhodes, I'd probably drink too."

16. Carol Cooper, interview by Lee Leonard, Columbus, June 4, 2013.

17. Suzanne Moore interview, July 16, 2012. Zimmerman notes that Rhodes's insistence on returning home to Columbus became a running gag among those who traveled with him. Rhodes always explained simply: "I sleep better in my own bed."

18. Carol Cooper, interview by Lee Leonard, Columbus, June 4, 7 (telephone), 2013.

19. Usher et al., "Man Named Rhodes."

20. Jauchius, "Gubernatorial Roles," 51.

21. Ibid.; Murray Seeger, "Rhodes Survives Democratic Landslide, State's Auditor-Author," *Cleveland Plain Dealer,* Oct. 11, 1959; Ohio Secretary of State, election results and data, Rhodes Office Tower, Columbus.

22. Aronoff and Riffe, *James A. Rhodes at Eighty,* 23.

23. "Fire Chief Ready to Let Men Quit," *Columbus Evening Dispatch,* June 29, 1948.

24. Zimmerman, "Rhodes's First Eight Years," 62. James Neff, *Mobbed Up* (New York: Atlantic Monthly Press, 1989), 151, 153, 215, 311. James Neff, interview by Richard G. Zimmerman, Mar. 3, 2004. And Rhodes was the subject of numerous informal conversations Zimmerman had with Wallace Quetch, a former DiSalle aide, in Washington, D.C., circa 2004. The *Columbus Citizen* story on Rhodes reelection to a third term as mayor is from November 9, 1951.

25. Zimmerman, "Rhodes's First Eight Years," 62.

26. Gene D'Angelo interview by Lee Leonard, June 11, 2013. See also Linda Deitch, "Uncrating Christopher Columbus, 1955," *Columbus Dispatch,* Oct. 10, 2011.

27. Ohio State University Official Proceedings of the One Thousand Two Hundred and Seventy-Eighth Meeting of The Board of Trustees, Columbus, Ohio, Dec. 6, 1991, Board's records, Bricker Hall, Ohio State University, Columbus.

28. Much of this information was contained in a sort of rogues' gallery of Rhodes's staff and supporters that the *Akron Beacon Journal* printed on March 5, 1978, in conjunction with Usher et al., "Man Named Rhodes."

29. Zimmerman, "Rhodes's First Eight Years," 63.

30. Ohio Secretary of State, election results and data, Columbus, Ohio.

31. Ibid.

32. Aronoff and Riffe, *James A. Rhodes at Eighty,* 26.

33. Jauchius, "Gubernatorial Roles," 52.

34. Aronoff and Riffe, *James A. Rhodes at Eighty,* 53–54. DiSalle also liked to repeat that Rhodes's historical novels also were written with the research assistance of "a little old lady" on the auditor's payroll.

35. Jim Duerk, telephone interview by Lee Leonard, Apr. 3, 2013.

36. Tim Miller, "Candidates Eager to Take Charge," *Dayton Daily News,* Sept. 21, 1986.

37. Suzanne Moore, telephone interview by Lee Leonard, May 20, 2013.

38. Aronoff and Riffe, *James A. Rhodes at Eighty,* 39, 41. Zimmerman covered the closing months of Rhodes's auditor term while reporting from Columbus for the Horvitz chain of Ohio newspapers.

39. Richard G. Zimmerman, *Call Me Mike: A Political Biography of Michael V. DiSalle* (Kent, Ohio: Kent State University Press, 2003), 57, 122–41.

3. The Telling and Fulfilling Campaign of 1962

1. Ray Dorsey, "Lausche, Locher, Taft and Rhodes Picked as Victors," *Cleveland Plain Dealer,* Nov. 4, 1962.

2. Aronoff and Riffe, *James A. Rhodes at Eighty,* 27; Zimmerman, "Rhodes's First Eight Years," 66.

3. Zimmerman, *Call Me Mike,* 242.

4. Ibid., 249.

5. It was always unclear whether the investigative report on Rhodes was commissioned by DiSalle or by his supporters. In any case, DiSalle always denied he had anything to do with it, and his supporters saw that copies were well circulated. Other than containing the allegation that Rhodes, while running Jim's Place near the OSU campus, had been charged with accepting "policy slips," that is, bets on the numbers

game, much of the report was of little consequence, filled with mostly conjecture and innuendo (see note 17, this chapter).

6. Aronoff and Riffe, *James A. Rhodes at Eighty*, 17–27. These highlights of Rhodes's political life up until 1962 have been augmented by Zimmerman's reporting on the candidates during the 1962 campaign.

7. Zimmerman, *Call Me Mike*, 236–40; Ohio Secretary of State, election results and data, Rhodes Office Tower, Columbus.

8. Zimmerman, *Call Me Mike*, 211–13. The often DiSalle-friendly *Akron Beacon Journal* was perhaps the only newspaper to emphasize that a Rhodes auditor prompted the Department of Mental Hygiene and Corrections collection program.

9. Ibid., 152–65.

10. Zimmerman, "Rhodes's First Eight Years," 67.

11. Ibid. Rhodes once vaguely alluded to the Mackler affair as the "odor" emanating from the DiSalle administration, according to the *Columbus Evening Dispatch*, Oct. 6, 1962.

12. Zimmerman, "Rhodes's First Eight Years," 354n13.

13. Usher et al., "Man Named Rhodes."

14. *Cleveland Plain Dealer*, Oct. 5, 1962.

15. Zimmerman, "Rhodes's First Eight Years," 67.

16. Ibid.

17. The accusation that Rhodes once was arrested for accepting bets on the numbers while proprietor of Jim's Place was about the only portion of the well-circulated investigative report on Rhodes's early life substantive enough to merit much interest. But reporters curious enough to pursue this accusation soon discovered that being charged with small-time gambling in Columbus during the 1930s was like being issued a parking ticket: the accused didn't even have to appear in court and fines were deducted from a court-approved fund contributed to by gamblers. (See also Zimmerman, "Rhodes's First Eight Years," 353n4.) Accordingly, no Ohio reporter was known to have traveled to Nitro, West Virginia, despite DiSalle's constant urging, to interview a retired Columbus vice squad officer who might verify that he had once charged Rhodes with gambling.

18. James T. Keenan, "Accuse Rhodes of Influence on U.S. Loan," *Columbus Citizen Journal*, Ohio Scripps-Howard Bureau, Oct. 17, 1962. For more on Rhodes-DiSalle campaign, see James Johnson, "DiSalle Seeking Probe of Rhodes," *Columbus Citizen-Journal*, Ohio Scripps-Howard Bureau, Oct. 17, 1962.

19. Zimmerman, "Rhodes's First Eight Years," 66

20. Zimmerman took part in the pools while covering the 1962 campaign. He did not recall if he ever won the pot, although he bet on the high side.

21. Zimmerman, "Rhodes's First Eight Years," 72–73.

22. There was a widely distributed and published news photo of Rhodes making such a speech in such a setting at least once during the campaign.

23. Ohio Secretary of State, election results and data, Rhodes Office Tower, Columbus.

24. Text of "Statement of Gov. Michael V. DiSalle, Nov. 7, 1962—9 A.M.," DiSalle Collection, Ohio History Center, Columbus. Most Ohio newspapers and television stations carried DiSalle's sour concession statement the same date it was delivered or the morning after.

4. First Term—Four Mostly Smooth Years

1. George W. Knepper, *Ohio and Its People* (Kent, Ohio: Kent State University Press, 1989), appendix, 470–71. According to Knepper's calculations, Rhodes was the fifty-fifth to serve as governor. Several of these individual governors, including John Brown (eleven days in 1957), served only briefly.

2. Perhaps Rhodes's only recorded public comment concerning capital punishment is "There ain't no votes in the electric chair," meaning, presumably, that no votes are to be gained by taking a public stand for or against the death penalty. According to information supplied by the Ohio Department of Rehabilitation and Corrections in 2000, from March 1963 until February 1999, there were no executions in Ohio. That would cover most of Rhodes's first two administrations (during his third and fourth administrations, a decision of the U.S. Supreme Court temporarily banned capital punishment nationally), along with those of Democrats John Gilligan and Richard Celeste, and Republican George Voinovich.

3. Zimmerman, "Rhodes's First Eight Years," 68.

4. That Rhodes and Rockefeller had become political bedfellows was made clear during the 1968 Republican National Convention, when Rhodes, again in control of the Ohio delegation's votes, withheld Ohio's support from Richard Nixon on the first ballot, apparently in hopes that his friend "Rocky" might win the nomination. But Nixon was nominated without Ohio's votes. It also was reported that during a governor's conference, Rockefeller, facing domestic difficulties, was given this sage advice by Rhodes on how to divert the attention of his political enemies: "The best way to keep flies out of the kitchen is to put a bucket of s——in the living room." The erudite Rockefeller was said to have been both appalled and rather enchanted by his friend's homey, if crude, counsel.

5. Knepper, *Ohio and Its People,* 403; Ohio Secretary of State, election results and data, Rhodes Office Tower, Columbus.

6. Zimmerman, "Rhodes's First Eight Years," 71.

7. Carl Stokes, *Promises of Power: A Political Autobiography* (New York: Simon & Schuster, 1973), 67.

8. Usher et al., "Man Named Rhodes."

9. George W. Knepper, "Ohio Politics: A Historical Perspective," in Lamis, *Ohio Politics,* 11–15; Ohio Secretary of State, election results and data, Rhodes Office Tower, Columbus.

10. Aronoff and Riffe, *James A. Rhodes at Eighty,* 44.

11. Ibid., 43.

12. Zimmerman was the "snoopy reporter" described. The caterer simply shrugged and explained that he could obtain California tomato juice at a better price.

13. Ohio Secretary of State, election results and data, Rhodes Office Tower, Columbus.

5. Four More Years, with a Few Bumps

1. Zimmerman, "Rhodes's First Eight Years," 73; Aronoff and Riffe, *James A. Rhodes at Eighty*, 29.

2. Zimmerman, "Rhodes's First Eight Years," 99; Mike Curtin, "The O'Neill-DiSalle Years, 1957–1963," in Lamis, *Ohio Politics*, 73, 74.

3. Ohio Secretary of State, election results and data, Rhodes Office Tower, Columbus.

4. Saxbe discussed his role in drafting his single-member legislative reapportionment plan on numerous occasions with reporters. Ohio Secretary of State's office, election results and data, Rhodes Office Tower, Columbus.

5. Zimmerman, "Rhodes's First Eight Years," 75.

6. Ibid., 74.

7. Editorial, *Cleveland Plain Dealer*, May 5, 1967.

8. Ohio Election Statistics, 1967–68, Report of Secretary of State Ted W. Brown, Columbus, Ohio, www.archive.org/stream/electionstatistics19671968mass#p44/mode/2up; www.uselectionatlas.org; Official Report of the Board of Canvassers of the State of Nebraska; www.state.nj.us; ourcampaigns.com; *1970 Wisconsin Blue Book* (Madison: State of Wisconsin, 1970), 828.

9. Jim Duerk, telephone interview by Lee Leonard, May 27, 2013.

10. Ben Rose, interview by Lee Leonard, Nov. 28, 2012.

11. Duerk, telephone interview, May 27, 2013.

12. Hal Duryea, interview by Lee Leonard, Oct. 26, 2012.

13. James Duerk, conversation with Richard D. Zimmerman in Columbus, date unrecorded. Duerk was a longtime Rhodes aide and later his business partner.

14. Ohio Secretary of State, election results and data, Rhodes Office Tower, Columbus.

15. Zimmerman, "Rhodes's First Eight Years," 76.

16. Ibid.

6. Kent State and the Day After

1. Except where specifically noted, details in this chapter primarily are based on Zimmerman's notes and recollections from 1970 and from his earlier knowledge of the Rhodes administration. He reported almost daily on the Rhodes-Taft primary for the *Cleveland Plain Dealer* from his post in the newspaper's Columbus Bureau.

In November 1964, according to the Ohio Secretary of State's election results and data records in Columbus, Goldwater lost Ohio to Lyndon Johnson by a whopping 1 million votes. Fortunately for Ohio Republicans, most state offices were not on the ballot. Besides Taft narrowly losing to Democrat Stephen Young, the only other partisan statewide race saw Democrat Robert Sweeney barely beating well-known Republican Oliver Bolton for the soon-to-be-abolished post of congressman at large. There also were four contests for the Ohio Supreme Court on the statewide ballot, but judges in Ohio ran without party designation.

2. John Kelley, telephone interview by Richard G. Zimmerman, Apr. 14, 2004.

3. Eszterhas and Roberts, *13 Seconds,* 134.

4. Michael DiSalle with Lawrence Blochman, *The Power of Life or Death* (New York: Random House, 1956), 121–34.

5. Eszterhas and Roberts, *13 Seconds,* 135 (emphasis added).

6. The *Plain Dealer* was among several Ohio newspapers to question Rhodes's statement on his income taxes soon after the release of his statement on the magazine article.

7. In several private conversations in Washington with Zimmerman, DiSalle hinted that the IRS had helped unearth details concerning his $54,000 Question, although he never named the source of the original tip. Also, any reporter who has worked in Washington has come to know that the IRS is not the bastion of confidentiality it publicly claims to be.

8. During the course of the campaign, Taft and his supporters twisted Rhodes's well-worn slogan "Profit Is Not a Dirty Word in Ohio" into "Integrity Is Not a Dirty Word in Ohio." See Eszterhas and Roberts, *13 Seconds,* 138. The *Columbus Evening Dispatch* supported Rhodes throughout the primary campaign and took Taft to task for his absenteeism and alleged conflict of interest when voting as a congressman on issues of financial interest to the Taft family; Rhodes also would mention these issues occasionally.

9. In addition to contemporary news reports, primarily from the *Akron Beacon Journal* (which won a Pulitzer Prize for its coverage of the Kent State shootings) and the *Cleveland Plain Dealer,* the authors depended on two books published soon after the Kent State shootings to chart events leading up to, including, and following the tragedy, which incorporated the Taft-Rhodes primary. Especially helpful was Eszterhas and Roberts, *13 Seconds.* Authors Joe Eszterhas and Michael Roberts were reporters for the *Plain Dealer* at the time of the events and were on site at Kent State during most of the troubles. Also of interest was James Michener, *Kent State: What Happened and Why* (New York: Random House, 1971). Although not on campus during the shootings, Michener arrived soon after and assembled his usual small army of researchers and interviewers to help him complete his manuscript. Zimmerman was a reporter and bureau chief for the *Plain Dealer* stationed in Columbus and reported on campus unrest at Ohio State, Ohio, and Miami Universities and attended three of the four Rhodes-Taft debates, including their final meeting in Cleveland.

10. Eszterhas and Roberts, *13 Seconds,* 138–39.

11. Ibid., 143.

12. Ibid., 111.

13. Michael D. Roberts, "4 Dead, 10 Hurt at KSU: Campus Is Evacuated, *Cleveland Plain Dealer,* May 5, 1970; Joseph Eszterhas, "Campus War—Troops 'Lost All Their Cool,'" *Cleveland Plain Dealer,* May 5, 1970; Michener, *Kent State,* 251–52.

14. Eszterhas and Roberts, *13 Seconds,* 145–76; Michener, *Kent State,* 340–42; *Akron Beacon Journal,* May 5–7, 1970.

15. John Kelley to Alexander Lamis, May 30, 1995.

16. Eszterhas and Roberts, *13 Seconds,* 144.

17. John Kelley to Richard Zimmerman, June 27, 1995.

18. Zimmerman, "Rhodes's First Eight Years," 82; Eszterhas and Roberts, *13 Seconds,* 127.

19. Ohio Secretary of State, election results and data, Rhodes Office Tower, Columbus.

7. Chasing Smokestacks, Dodging Democrats

1. Usher et al., "Man Named Rhodes." *Akron Beacon Journal* reporters Michael Cull and the late Brian Usher produced this authoritative series on Rhodes's wealth as he prepared to run for his fourth term as governor. David Hess of the paper's Washington bureau, Charles Lally, and Carol Bauer contributed. Significant information in this chapter about Rhodes's financial dealings was taken from the series and an October 5, 1986, *Beacon Journal* story.

2. The direct attribution for this quote is Usher et al., "Man Named Rhodes." But as an Associated Press reporter covering Rhodes's 1974 and 1978 reelection campaigns, Tom Diemer often heard the comment repeated. It was becoming Ohio political folklore, as would many of Rhodes's one-liners.

3. Usher et al., "Man Named Rhodes."

4. Joe Rice, telephone interview by Tom Diemer, Sept. 13, 2013.

5. Jim Duerk, telephone interview by Lee Leonard, Nov. 2, 2012.

6. William B. Saxbe with Peter D. Franklin, *I've Seen the Elephant: An Autobiography* (Kent, Ohio: Kent State University Press, 2000), 237, 238, 239.

7. Ibid., 239.

8. "Mrs. Onassis Backs Glenn," *Columbus Dispatch*, May 3, 1974.

9. Lee Leonard, United Press International, Jan. 29, 1974.

10. "Fred Rice Collapses, Dies at 62," *Columbus Dispatch*, May 3, 1974.

11. Hugh McDiarmid, "Columbus Comment, *Dayton Journal Herald*, Oct. 28, 1974, Kathy Gilligan grew up to be Kathleen Gilligan Sebelius, governor of Kansas and secretary of Health and Human Services under President Barack Obama. McDiarmid was a respected chronicler of the Gilligan years.

12. William Russell Coil, "New Deal Republican: James A. Rhodes and the Transformation of the Republican Party, 1933–1983" (PhD diss., The Ohio State University, 2005), 313, 314, 315.

13. "1934–1982: The Campaign History of James A. Rhodes," *Ohio Petroleum Marketer* (Jan.–Feb. 1982), 14. No author given, but Thomas H. Dudgeon is the likely writer. Various sources say Rhodes sometimes used saltier language: "Lead, follow or get the hell out of the way."

14. Dick Feagler, "Feagler Rides Vote Trail with Jim Rhodes," *Cleveland Press*, Oct. 22, 1974.

15. Shoemaker, *Ohio's Greatest Governor*, 69.

16. Chan Cochran, interview by Tom Diemer and Richard G. Zimmerman, Dec. 1, 2004.

17. Lee Leonard, *A Columnist's View of Capitol Square: Ohio Politics and Government 1969–2005* (Akron, Ohio: University of Akron Press 2010), 162.

18. An undated radio interview. Gilligan's wisecrack is part of Ohio political folklore. Diemer used a paperback vanity book by R. Dean Jauchius and Thomas H. Dudgeon, *Jim Rhodes' Big Win!* (Columbus, Ohio: PoliCom, 1978), 17.

19. Jauchius and Dudgeon, *Jim Rhodes' Big Win!*, 12.

20. Coil, "New Deal Republican," 232.

21. Jim Dudas and Roy Meyers, Ohio Press Service report of the *Cleveland Press*, Oct. 18, 1974.

22. Adrienne Bosworth, "Gilligan for Ohio" press release, Oct. 17, 1974, copy in Leonard Collection, box 12, folder 4, Ohio History Center, Columbus.

23. Feagler, "Feagler Rides Vote Trail with Jim Rhodes."

24. Robert Bennett, interview by Tom Diemer and Richard G. Zimmerman, Dec. 1, 2004.

25. Jauchius and Dudgeon, *Jim Rhodes' Big Win!,* 138.

26. Dick Moore, interview by Tom Diemer, Dec. 4, 2005.

27. Lee Leonard, "Rhodes's Second Eight Years," in Lamis, *Ohio Politics,* 128.

28. John T. Kady, interview by Lee Leonard, June 27, 2012.

29. Abe Zaidan, "Jack Gilligan at Ninety: The Tribute to a Special Person, *Grumpy Abe,* http://grumpyabe.blogspot.com/2011/04/jack-gilligan-at-90-tribute-to-special. html, Apr. 17, 2011.

8. The Third Term: Divided Government

1. Brad Tillson, "Rhodes Aide Martin Prefers to Work behind the Scenes," *Dayton Daily News,* Mar. 23, 1975.

2. Coil, "New Deal Republican," 199. See also Suzanne Moore interview, July 16, 2012.

3. Celeste e-mail to Tom Diemer, Mar. 5, 2001.

4. Lee Leonard, conversation with Tom Diemer and Richard G. Zimmerman, Dec. 3, 2005. Later, he joined them as a coauthor.

5. Jay Wuebbold, "Moyer Operates behind Scenes," *Lake County News-Herald,* (Willoughby), Apr. 9, 1978.

6. Jon Kelly, telephone interview by Tom Diemer, July 22, 2013; Craig Zimpher, telephone interview by Tom Diemer, Sept. 15, 2013. Rhodes, who enjoyed giving people nicknames, called "Slide" Kelly, after the late-nineteenth-century baseball legend Mike "King" Kelly, the inspiration for the poem and song, "Slide Kelly Slide."

7. Fred Mills, telephone interview by Tom Diemer, Mar. 6, 2014.

8. Over the years, Rhodes's inner circle in government and close associates outside of it widely told this story—without contradiction. It was repeated so often it became part of capitol folklore. No one, however, has produced a transcript.

9. Robert Teater, interview by Tom Diemer and Richard G. Zimmerman, Nov. 30, 2004.

10. All comments of William Wilkins (then Governor Taft's tax commissioner) in this section are taken from an extensive interview by Tom Diemer and Richard G. Zimmerman, twenty-second floor of Rhodes Tower, Columbus, June 12, 2006.

11. C. Luther Heckman, telephone interview by Lee Leonard, Dec. 30, 2012.

12. John Mahaney, interview by Tom Diemer and Richard G. Zimmerman, Nov. 30, 2004.

13. Robert Howarth, interview by Tom Diemer and Richard G. Zimmerman, Mar. 6, 2001.

14. Tom Diemer, Rhodes's appreciation, "Friend, Foe Alike Sum Up Rhodes Success," *Cleveland Plain Dealer,* Mar. 8, 2001.

15. Terry Casey, interview by Lee Leonard, Jan. 10, 2013.

16. Tom Moyer (chief justice of the Ohio Supreme Court), interview by Tom Diemer and Richard G. Zimmerman, Moyer's chambers, Columbus, Dec. 1, 2004. Moyer died on April 2, 2010, at age seventy, during his twenty-third year on the court.

17. McNamara interview, June 13, 2006.

18. Brad Tillson, "$2.5 Billion Asked for Cities," *Dayton Daily News,* Feb. 14, 1975.

19. Brad Tillson, "Rhodes Undaunted, Undeterred," *Dayton Daily News,* Apr. 27, 1975.

20. McNamara interview, June 13, 2006.

21. Thomas Suddes, "Ohio's 67: From the First Edward Tiffin to Bob Taft, the State's Governors Have Been a Varied Lot," *Cleveland Plain Dealer,* June 8, 2003.

22. Robert Howarth, interview by Tom Diemer and Richard G. Zimmerman, Dec. 3, 2004.

23. Jauchius and Dudgeon, *Jim Rhodes' Big Win!,* 138.

24. Shoemaker, *Ohio's Greatest Governor,* 121. Bill Cohen retired in 2013 after more than four decades covering the Statehouse for WOSU public radio. When he left his beat, he was one of the most respected and well-liked journalists in Ohio.

25. Diemer's files from coverage for the Associated Press.

26. Wilkins interview, June 12, 2006.

27. Joseph D. Rice, "Gov. Rhodes Is Nonchalant at Republican Convention," *Cleveland Plain Dealer,* Aug. 19, 1976.

28. Shoemaker, *Ohio's Greatest Governor,* 109.

29. Tom Diemer, "Meet the Ohio Campaign Chiefs for Ford and Carter," *Lorain Journal,* Sept. 9, 1976.

30. Tom Diemer, "'The People of Ohio Have Spoken,' Rhodes Says of Veto-Proof Assembly," *Dover-New Philadelphia Times-Reporter,* Associated Press, Nov. 4, 1976. "The people have spoken" was a line Rhodes often used after a political defeat. Riffe's sixty-two votes were two more than the three-fifths majority required to override. Democrats held a 21–12 majority in the Senate, one over the three-fifths threshold.

31. Teater interview, Nov. 30, 2004.

32. Bob Miller, "James A. Rhodes, Ohio's Governor for 16 Years, Dead at Age 91," *Gongwer News Service,* Mar. 5, 2001.

33. "Former Governor Rhodes Returns to Scene of One of His Greatest Triumphs 20 Years Later," *Gongwer News Service,* Oct. 8, 1997.

34. Teater interview, Nov. 30, 2004.

35. Mahaney interview, Nov. 30, 2004.

36. Wilkins interview, June 12, 2006.

37. Vernal Riffe Jr., interview by Tom Diemer, circa 1976.

38. See John McQuaid, "Mining the Mountains," *Smithsonian,* Jan. 2009, 74–85. The article notes that in his 2008 campaign Barack Obama had "backed investing in 'clean coal' technology which would capture air pollutants from burning coal—especially carbon dioxide, linked to global warming. But such technologies are still experimental, and some experts believe they are unworkable" (32).

39. Brown made the remark during his 1982 Democratic gubernatorial primary campaign. He finished second, losing to Celeste. Jerry Springer, then a Cincinnati politician, was third. Authors Leonard and Diemer covered the race.

40. Condon, "State Had Its Own Colossus in Rhodes." Tom Diemer witnessed the incident and wrote about it exclusively for the Associated Press. A tipster phoned

one morning with the advice, "Get over to the Wendy's on High Street in a hurry. The governor is entertaining his Japanese guests." Rhodes didn't flinch when he saw the AP reporter. He didn't think he was doing anything unusual, but the story got wide play.

41. Roger Dreyer, interview by Richard G. Zimmerman and Tom Diemer, June 13, 2006.

42. James A. Rhodes, "How Ohio Landed Honda: Hard Work, 'Providence,'" *Ward's Auto World,* Mar. 1, 1990.

43. Shoemaker, *Ohio's Greatest Governor,* 89.

44. Usher et al., "Man Named Rhodes."

45. Shoemaker, *Ohio's Greatest Governor,* 119, 114.

46. Moyer interview, Dec. 1, 2004; Shoemaker, *Ohio's Greatest Governor,* 119.

47. Text of Tom Moyer's remarks at Rhodes funeral, Mar. 7, 2001, Diemer's files.

48. Cochran interview, Dec. 1, 2004. By early 2013, Honda was the largest automobile manufacturer in a state recovering from the Great Recession. The Ohio employment number stood at fourteen thousand (it had risen to nearly sixteen thousand earlier in the decade) as Honda announced another expansion, this time in its sales office. See Dan Gearino, "Honda Restructures; Shift Brings Fifty Jobs to Ohio," *Columbus Dispatch,* Feb. 22, 2013.

49. Usher et al., "Man Named Rhodes."

50. Mahaney interview, Nov. 30, 2004.

51. McNamara interview, June 13, 2006.

52. Tillson, "Rhodes Undaunted, Undeterred."

9. "Give It to Jim Again since He Wants It. They Did!"

1. Celeste e-mail to Tom Diemer, Mar. 5, 2001.

2. Miller, "James A. Rhodes, Ohio's Governor for 16 Years, Dead at Age 91."

3. Gerald Austin, interview by Tom Diemer, Dec. 11, 2006.

4. Thomas K. Diemer, "Rhodes Campaign Low-Key, but Not Candidate," *Cleveland Plain Dealer,* Apr. 30, 1978.

5. George Voinovich, interview by Lee Leonard, June 27, 2012.

6. Robert E. Miller, "Time Will Tell: Rhodes Selection of Voinovich May Lead to Ohio's First Hand-Picked Governor," Associated Press, Mar. 12, 1978; Voinovich, telephone interview with Tom Diemer, Jan. 9, 2014.

7. Voinoich interview, June 27, 2012.

8. Dave Allbaugh, "Saxbe as Next Governor? 'I Quit a Better Job,'" *Dayton Daily News,* Dec. 1, 1976.

9. Mahaney interview, Nov. 30, 2004.

10. Thomas K. Diemer, "Kurfess Prods Rhodes to Bare Financial Deals," *Cleveland Plain Dealer,* May 9, 1978.

11. Thomas K. Diemer, "Kurfess on Victory: 'Close to Our Grasp,'" *Cleveland Plain Dealer,* June 2, 1978.

12. Thomas K. Diemer, "Rhodes Takes Long Way, Drops in on Kurfess Rally," *Cleveland Plain Dealer,* Sept. 23, 1978.

13. Amos A. Kermisch and Thomas K. Diemer, "Far from Last Hurrah, Rhodes Approaches 70 Years at Full Speed Ahead," *Cleveland Plain Dealer,* Sept. 9, 1979.

14. Thomas K. Diemer, "Campaign Trail Has Many Rough Spots," *Cleveland Plain Dealer,* Nov. 12, 1978.

15. "Campaign History of James A. Rhodes," 15.

16. George Voinovich, telephone interview by Lee Leonard, June 27, 2012.

17. Thomas K. Diemer, "Celeste Game Plan Holds No Surprises," *Cleveland Plain Dealer,* July 23, 1978.

18. Ibid.

19. Austin interview, Dec. 11, 2006.

20. Thomas K. Diemer, "School Taxes Heat Up Campaign," *Cleveland Plain Dealer,* Oct. 12, 1978.

21. Leonard, *Columnist's View of Capitol Square,* 267.

22. Thomas K. Diemer, "Celeste Accuses No-Show Foe of Lies," *Cleveland Plain Dealer,* Nov. 4, 1978.

23. "Campaign History of James A. Rhodes," 15.

24. Diemer's reporting notes, Nov. 1978.

25. Thomas K. Diemer, "Celeste Camp Weighs What to Do Next," *Cleveland Plain Dealer,* Nov. 10, 1978.

26. George Condon Jr., e-mail to Tom Diemer Nov. 8, 2012.

27. Thomas K. Diemer, "Celeste Loss Has Dems Asking Who's in Charge," *Cleveland Plain Dealer,* Nov. 16, 1978.

10. Gathering Storm

1. Thomas K. Diemer, "Let Rhodes Resolve to Keep His Promises," *Cleveland Plain Dealer,* Dec. 31, 1978.

2. Thomas K. Diemer, "Gov. Rhodes Is Convinced: Nobody Does It Better," *Cleveland Plain Dealer,* Jan. 7, 1979. Tracy made his comment in a breakfast interview at a Columbus hotel overlooking Capitol Square on December 13, 2006. The Riffe quotation is from Diemer's reporting notes, circa 1982.

3. United Press International, "Ex-KSU President Glad of Settlement," *Cleveland Press,* Jan. 6, 1979. See also Herb Kamm, "The Kent State Deal," *Cleveland Press,* Jan. 6, 1979.

4. Editorial, *New York Times,* Jan. 8, 1979.

5. James A. Rhodes, interview by Tom Diemer, Dec. 1981. In "Rhodes Comments on Criticism, KSU," a sidebar to Celeste's inauguration on January 11, 1983, the *Plain Dealer* reported that Rhodes said this about the tragedy: "The mayor wanted the town saved. There was nothing else you can do."

6. Thomas K. Diemer, "Rhodes Begins 4th Term on Brief, Low-Keyed Note," *Cleveland Plain Dealer,* Jan. 9, 1979.

7. Thomas K. Diemer, "Thomas Moyer, Long-Serving Ohio Chief Justice, GOP Political Figure, Dead at 70," *PoliticsDaily,* http://www.politicsdaily.com/2010/04/03/thomas-moyer-long-serving-ohio-chief-justice-gop-political-fig/, Apr. 3, 2010.

8. Howarth interview, Dec. 3, 2004.

9. Thomas K. Diemer, "Trail of Elusive, Aloof Rhodes is Tough to Follow," *Cleveland Plain Dealer,* Mar. 25, 1979; Thomas K. Diemer, "Low-Tax-Hike Vow Expected from Rhodes," *Cleveland Plain Dealer,* Apr. 18, 1978.

10. Dave Shutt, "17.7 Billion Budget Is Detailed by Rhodes," *Toledo Blade,* Feb. 8, 1979.

11. Thomas K. Diemer, "Rhodes' Address Gets Favorable Response," *Cleveland Plain Dealer,* Feb. 7, 1979.

12. Diemer, "Celeste Accuses No-Show Foe of Lies."

13. Howarth interview, Dec. 3, 2004.

14. Thomas K. Diemer, "State School Funds Boost Wins OK," *Cleveland Plain Dealer,* Mar. 30, 1979.

15. Howarth interview, Dec. 3, 2004.

16. Thomas K. Diemer, "Budget Talk Bursts Rhodes' Balloons as He Ends Trip to China," *Cleveland Plain Dealer,* July 18, 1979.

17. Paul Schroeder, telephone interview by Tom Diemer, Feb. 3, 2013.

18. Miller, "James A. Rhodes, Ohio's Governor for 16 Years, Dead at Age 91." Schroeder returned to China in 1980 and discovered that Chinese officials were charging an admission fee at some sections of the Wall.

19. Amos A. Kermisch, "Easy Does It, Chinese Tell Eager Rhodes," *Cleveland Plain Dealer,* July 4, 1979.

20. Chan Cochran, interview by Lee Leonard, Mar. 26, 2013; Duerk telephone interview, Apr. 3, 2013.

21. Diemer, "Budget Talk Bursts Rhodes' Balloons as He Ends Trip to China."

22. Thomas K. Diemer, "'Part-Time' Voinovich Still Practices Law," *Cleveland Plain Dealer,* Jan. 25, 1979.

23. Thomas K. Diemer, "Voinovich Refuses to Lead Inflation Parley in Ohio," *Cleveland Plain Dealer,* Mar. 15, 1979.

24. Voinovich telephone interview, June 27, 2012.

25. Thomas K. Diemer, "Voinovich Tells Why He Chose to Run," *Cleveland Plain Dealer,* Aug. 19, 1979.

26. Voinovich telephone interview, June 27, 2012.

27. Office of the Governor, news release, Nov. 7, 1979, in Diemer's files.

28. For more on the Morrow County Boom, see Jeffrey E. Fort, "Ohio Oil Boom—Why It Will Be Different This Time," *Lexology,* www.lexology.com, Aug. 24, 2012.

29. Taken from full text of speech in Diemer's files.

30. Howarth interview, Dec. 3, 2004.

31. Teater interview, Nov. 30, 2004.

32. Thomas K. Diemer, "A Face-Off on Pollution," *Cleveland Plain Dealer,* Oct. 29, 1979.

33. Douglas Martin, "F. Herbert Bormann, 90, Dies; Documented Acid Rain," *New York Times,* June 15, 2012.

34. Marissa Weiss, "Acid Rain Has Waned, but Its Effects Remain," *Washington Post,* July 3, 2012.

35. Diemer, "A Face-Off on Pollution."

36. Rick McGahey and Teresa Ghilardjucci, "Myths about the Unemployed Onerous Regulations Cause Jobs to Disappear," *Washington Post,* Dec. 9, 2012.

37. James A. Rhodes, "Environmental Extremism Is Root of Crisis," *Columbus Dispatch,* Aug. 9, 1979.

38. Diemer, "Face-Off on Pollution."

39. Office of the Governor, news release, Sept. 16, 1979.

40. Thomas K. Diemer, "GOP Governors Throw Down Fuel Gauntlet," *Cleveland Plain Dealer,* Nov. 21, 1979.

41. Iver Peterson, "E.P.A. Show on the Ohio, Floats Warnings," *New York Times,* Aug. 19, 1979.

42. "Economic Pearl Harbor," *Youngstown Vindicator,* Nov. 28, 1979.

43. Office of the Governor, news release, Nov. 28, 1979.

44. Robert L. Shaffer, "Plant Closings to Idle Thousands: Frustration, Anger Mars 'Last Big Christmas' for Many of Youngstown's Steelworkers," *Associated Press, Youngstown Vindicator,* Dec. 25, 1979.

45. Leonard and Diemer's notes, circa 1980. An updated version of this anecdote appears in the text of Rhodes's December 15, 1980, speech to a joint session of the Ohio General Assembly.

46. Thomas K. Diemer, "Panic Threatens Economy, Rhodes Says," *Cleveland Plain Dealer,* Nov. 28, 1979.

47. Thomas K. Diemer, "Help for Shutdown Victims," *Cleveland Plain Dealer,* Dec. 1, 1979.

11. Recession!

1. Thomas K. Diemer, "Wife Sees No Retirement for Rhodes," *Cleveland Plain Dealer,* July 22, 1979.

2. Wilkins interview, June 12, 2006.

3. Ro Khanna, "Myths about Manufacturing Jobs," *Washington Post,* Feb. 17, 2013.

4. Karen M. Mills, "Congressional Apportionment: Census 2000 Brief," *U.S. Census Bureau,* www.census.gov/prod/2001pubs/c2kbr01-7.pdf, issued July 2001.

5. Howarth interview, Dec. 3, 2004. Bob Howarth, a graduate of Denison University and the Ohio State University College of Law, also served thirty years in the military as an officer in the Air National Guard. He was on Guard duty at Ohio State on the day of the Kent State shootings in 1970.

6. Moyer interview, Dec. 1, 2004.

7. Howard Wilkinson, "Rhodes at 90: Very Little in Ohio He Didn't Have an Impact On," *Cincinnati Enquirer,* Sept. 12, 1999.

8. Thomas K. Diemer, "Rhodes Proposes State Bonds to Aid Industrial Expansion," *Cleveland Plain Dealer,* Nov. 14, 1979.

9. Jerome Cahill, "Inflation Roars at 18% Annual Rate," *New York Daily News,* Mar. 26, 1980.

10. Associated Press, "Worst Is Yet to Come, Experts Warn," *Cleveland Plain Dealer,* May 17, 1980.

11. William Carlson and Thomas K. Diemer, "Pinched State Hoping for a Washington Bail-Out," *Cleveland Plain Dealer,* June 15, 1980.

12. Doris Kearns Goodwin, *Team of Rivals: The Political Genius of Abraham Lincoln* (New York: Simon & Schuster, 2005), 308, 309.

13. James A. Rhodes, text of speech to joint session of legislature, Dec. 15, 1980, Diemer's files.

14. George Bush, with Victor Gold, *Looking Forward: An Autobiography* (New York: Bantam, 1988), 204.

15. McNamara, interview, June 13, 2006.

16. John McDonald, "Campaign Advice from 1980 Still Holds Message for Bush," *Hartford Courant,* Sept. 5, 1992.

17. Zimpher telephone interview, Sept. 15, 2013.

18. Office of the Governor, news release, Mar. 10, 1980, Diemer's files.

19. Thomas K. Diemer, "Earth Day Statement by Rhodes Slips Issues," *Cleveland Plain Dealer,* Apr. 27, 1980.

20. Thomas K. Diemer, "Triumphant Reagan Tours Ohio, Rules out Meeting with Carter," *Cleveland Plain Dealer,* May 29, 1980.

21. Thomas K. Diemer and Amos A. Kermisch, "Rhodes Is Waging 'Holy War,'" *Cleveland Plain Dealer,* Oct. 19, 1980.

22. Cochran interview, Dec. 1, 2004.

23. Thomas K. Diemer, "Reagan Borrows Rhodes' Rhetoric," *Cleveland Plain Dealer,* Aug. 28, 1980.

24. Leonard, "Rhodes's Second Eight Years, 1975–1983," 149.

25. Tim Radford, "Do Trees Pollute the Atmosphere?" *Guardian,* May 13, 2004.

26. Howarth interview, Dec. 3, 2004.

27. Diemer and Kermisch, "Rhodes Is Waging 'Holy War.'"

28. Thomas K. Diemer "Reagan: Many Believe This Is His Year to Win the Role of 'Leading Man,'" *Cleveland Plain Dealer,* June 1, 1980.

29. Amos A. Kermisch and Thomas K. Diemer, "Rhodes Savors Being Reagan's Favorite Governor," *Cleveland Plain Dealer,* Nov. 9, 1980.

30. Thomas K. Diemer, "At 71, Rhodes Plans to Expand His Influence," *Cleveland Plain Dealer,* Jan. 4, 1981.

31. Thomas K. Diemer, "Rhodes Pushes Gas Tax Hike, Jobs to Lift a 'Wounded' Ohio," *Cleveland Plain Dealer,* Feb. 5, 1981.

32. Thomas K. Diemer, "Rhodes Hits Brown on Oil Drilling," *Cleveland Plain Dealer,* Aug. 11, 1981.

33. Thomas K. Diemer, "Governors Fretted over Depth, Range of Reagan Slashes," *Cleveland Plain Dealer,* Aug. 16, 1981.

34. Thomas K. Diemer, "Rhodes Campaigns for School Tax Hike," *Cleveland Plain Dealer,* July 23, 1981.

35. Leonard, "Rhodes's Second Eight Years," 156; William Carlson, "Legislature Split on Tax Call," *Cleveland Plain Dealer,* Sept. 9, 1981.

36. Thomas K. Diemer, "Permanent Tax Hike Only Reasonable State Cure," *Cleveland Plain Dealer,* Sept. 13, 1981.

37. Thomas K. Diemer, "Riffe Stakes Political Future on Tax Pack," *Cleveland Plain Dealer,* Sept. 27, 1981.

38. William Carlson and Thomas K. Diemer, "State Nears Brink of Tax Crisis over Budget Financing," *Cleveland Plain Dealer,* Oct. 18, 1981.

39. Thomas K. Diemer, "How New Tax Hike Hits You," *Cleveland Plain Dealer,* Nov. 15, 1981.

40. Thomas K. Diemer, "Rhodes Clears up Death Law Statement," *Cleveland Plain Dealer,* July 26, 1981.

41. Zimmerman, *Call Me Mike,* 280.

42. John Byrne, telephone interview by Tom Diemer, Apr. 15, 2013.

43. Thomas K. Diemer, "Honest, Folks, Rhodes Is Running for Senate," *Cleveland Plain Dealer,* May 31, 1981. For more on Senator Metzenbaum, see Tom Diemer, *Fighting the Unbeatable Foe: Howard Metzenbaum of Ohio, the Washington Years* (Kent, Ohio: Kent State University Press, 2008).

44. Thomas K. Diemer, "No Decision Yet on Senate, Rhodes Says," *Cleveland Plain Dealer,* Dec. 16, 1981.

45. Diemer, "Wife Sees No Retirement for Rhodes."

46. Leonard, "Rhodes's Second Eight Years," 156.

47. Ibid., 157, 158.

48. United Press International wire report, June 25, 1982.

49. Robert Howarth, telephone interview by Tom Diemer, Apr. 30, 2013.

50. Howarth interview, Dec. 3, 2004.

51. Mary Anne Sharkey, *Cleveland Plain Dealer,* Mar. 6, 2001.

52. Wilkins interview, June 12, 2006.

53. James Drew, "Rhodes Recalled as Different Kind of Republican," *Toledo Blade,* Jan. 9, 2005.

54. Robert Schmitz, telephone interview by Tom Diemer, Nov. 17, 2013.

55. Rice telephone interview, Sept. 13, 2013.

56. Mahaney interview, Nov. 30, 2004.

57. Dick Kimmins, "Rhodes Steers Jobs Plan," *Columbus Citizen-Journal,* July 22, 1980.

58. "Rhodes Shows No Emotion as Successor Is Sworn In," *Cleveland Plain Dealer,* Jan. 11, 1983.

59. Wilkins interview, June 12, 2006.

60. Diemer, "At 71, Rhodes Plans to Expand His Influence."

12. How Does He Get Away with That Stuff?

1. Howarth interview, Dec. 3, 2004.

2. Leonard, *Columnist's View of Capitol Square,* 156.

3. Gerald Tebben, "Columbus Mileposts: Praise, Protest Greet Rhodes at Statue Unveiling," *Columbus Dispatch,* Dec. 5, 2012.

4. Leonard, *Columnist's View of Capitol Square,* 153.

5. Leonard witnessed, strictly by accident, the letters going up by looking out the windows from across the street in the Statehouse as he passed through the Senate chamber one day.

6. Lee Leonard, United Press International, Sept. 9, 1982.

7. Aronoff and Riffe, *James A. Rhodes at Eighty.*

8. "Rhodes Fronts Fountain," *Toledo Blade,* Sept. 6, 2002.

9. "No Mistaking Jim Rhodes," *Toledo Blade,* Sept. 15, 2002.

10. David Shutt, "James A. Rhodes, 4-Term Governor, Dies," *Toledo Blade,* Mar. 5, 2001.

11. Drew, "Rhodes Recalled as Different Kind of Republican."

12. Leonard's notes from the dedication.

13. Bennett interview, Dec. 1, 2004.

14. Leonard, *Columnist's View of Capitol Square,* 151, 152.

15. Lee Leonard, United Press International, July 16, 1978.

16. Miller, "James A. Rhodes, Ohio's Governor for 16 Years, Dead at Age 91."

17. Lee Leonard, United Press International, July 16, 1978.

18. Reginald Stuart, quoted in ibid.

19. Cochran interview, Dec. 1, 2004.

20. James A. Rhodes to Nancy Reagan, Apr. 16, 1981, Rhodes Papers, Ohio History Connection Collection.

21. Miller, "James A. Rhodes, Ohio's Governor for 16 Years, Dead at Age 91."

22. Cochran interview, Mar. 26, 2013.

23. Ibid.

24. Moyer interview, Dec. 1, 2004.

25. Paul Gillmor, telephone interview by Tom Diemer, Mar. 4, 2001.

26. Condon, "State Had Its Own Colossus in Rhodes."

27. Rice, telephone interview, Sept. 13, 2013.

28. Mahaney interview, Nov. 30, 2004.

29. Wilkins interview, June 12, 2006.

30. Dreyer interview, June 13, 2006.

31. Teater interview, Nov. 30, 2004.

32. Moyer interview, Dec. 1, 2004.

33. Teater interview, Nov. 30, 2004.

34. Dreyer interview, June 13, 2006.

35. Thomas Green, telephone interview by Lee Leonard Oct. 26, 2012.

36. Ed Michael, telephone interview by Lee Leonard, Feb. 17, 2013.

37. Casey interview, Jan. 10, 2013.

38. John Mahaney, interview by Lee Leonard, Oct. 10, 2012.

39. Dana Rinehart, telephone interview by Lee Leonard, Jan. 16, 2013.

40. Green telephone interview, June 17, 2013.

41. Steve Evans, telephone interview by Lee Leonard, Nov. 20, 2012.

42. James A. Rhodes to Richard Celeste, Apr. 22, 1983, Leonard Collection, Ohio History Center, Columbus.

43. Robert Bennett, interview by Lee Leonard, Jan. 31, 2013; and Cochran interview, Mar. 26, 2013.

44. Suzanne Moore interview, July 16, 2012.

45. David Shutt, "James R. Rhodes, 4-Term Governor, Dies," *Toledo Blade,* Mar. 5, 2001.

46. "The 9th Most Embarrassing Moment in Ohio History Is . . . ," *Ohio Historical Society Collections Blog,* http://ohiohistory.wordpress.com/2010/03/04/now-for-number-9/, Mar. 4, 2010.

47. Lee Leonard, United Press International, July 16, 1970.

48. Ibid.

49. Ibid.

50. Governor's office press release, July 16, 1970.

51. Adrian Burns, *Business First,* Mar. 8, 2010.

52. Ben Rose, interview by Lee Leonard, Nov. 28, 2012.

53. Duerk telephone interview, Apr. 3, 2013.

54. Jim Ruvolo, telephone interview by Lee Leonard, July 19, 2012.

55. Aronoff and Riffe, *James A. Rhodes at Eighty.*

56. Except as otherwise noted, the source of these quotations is Aronoff and Riffe, *James A. Rhodes at Eighty.*

57. Miller, "James A. Rhodes, Ohio's Governor for 16 Years, Dead at Age 91."

58. Ibid.

59. Lee Leonard, United Press International, Jan. 6, 1983.

60. Lee Leonard, United Press International, Sept. 17, 1982.

61. Miller, "James A. Rhodes, Ohio's Governor for 16 Years, Dead at Age 91. "

62. The accurate quotation was "The people have spoken and *we* will abide with their decision."

13. The Last Roundup

1. Lee Leonard, United Press International, Jan. 25, 1981.

2. Lee Leonard, United Press International, Mar. 14, 1982.

3. David Lavelle, interview by Lee Leonard, Oct. 18, 2012.

4. Lee Leonard, United Press International, Mar. 10, 1982.

5. Jonathan Hughes, interview by Lee Leonard, Dec. 21, 2012.

6. Curt Steiner, interview by Lee Leonard, Nov. 28, 2012.

7. Rose interview, Nov. 28, 2012.

8. Leonard notes, undated, Leonard Collection, box 37, folder 14, Ohio History Center, Columbus.

9. Rose interview, Nov. 28, 2012.

10. Lee Leonard, United Press International, Sept. 23, 1984.

11. Teater interview, Nov. 30, 2004.

12. Dreyer interview, June 13, 2006.

13. Karen Gillmor, interview by Lee Leonard, Sept. 5, 2012. Paul Gillmor went on to become a U.S. representative and died September 5, 2007, in his suburban Washington, D.C., townhouse.

14. Bennett interview, Jan. 31, 2013. The chain-smoking, coffee-slurping Hughes was a favorite with reporters, partly because he had been a reporter and partly because he cut through political rhetoric and gave lively quotes: "Rhodes is nuts! But he wins!" He died late in 1991.

15. Ibid.

16. Lee Leonard, United Press International, Oct. 20, 1985.

17. Casey interview, Jan. 10, 2013.

18. Miller, "Candidates Eager to Take Charge."

19. Lee Leonard, United Press International, June 20, 1984.

20. Paul Pfeifer, interview by Lee Leonard, Aug. 22, 2012. Pfeifer went on to narrowly lose a race for state attorney general but later became an Ohio Supreme Court justice.

21. Lee Leonard, United Press International, Nov. 10, 1985.

22. Lee Leonard, United Press International, June 21, 1982.

23. Lee Leonard, United Press International, Nov. 17, 1985.

24. Pfeifer interview, Aug. 22, 2012.

25. Lee Leonard, United Press International, Nov. 24, 1985.

26. Lee Leonard," Lesson of Challenger Ignored in Workers' Comp Legislation," United Press International, Feb. 2, 1986.

27. Pfeifer interview, Aug. 22, 2012.

28. Bennett interview, Jan. 31, 2013.

29. Lee Leonard, United Press International, Dec. 8, 1985.

30. Lee Leonard, United Press International, Apr. 27, 1986.

31. Lee Leonard, United Press International, Mar. 30, 1986.

32. Lee Leonard, United Press International, Apr. 20, 1986.

33. Pfeifer interview, Aug. 22, 2012.

34. Karen Gillmor interview, Sept. 5, 2012.

35. Lee Leonard, United Press International, Mar. 16, 1986.

36. "Primary Foes Hop on Rhodes Express," *Columbus Dispatch,* May 20, 1986.

37. Karen Gillmor interview, Sept. 5, 2012.

38. Pfeifer interview, Aug. 22, 2012.

39. Lee Leonard, "Age Catching Up? Rhodes Mistakes Steubenville for Youngstown," United Press International, Apr. 13, 1986.

40. Bob Taft, interview by Lee Leonard, Oct. 30, 2012.

41. Hughes interview, Dec. 21, 2012.

42. Ohio Election Statistics, 1985–86; Report of Secretary of State Sherrod Brown, Secretary of State's Office, Rhodes Office Tower, Columbus; Ohio Secretary of State official vote totals for 1986 primary election.

43. Lee Leonard, United Press International, May 11, 1986.

44. Karen Gillmor interview, Sept. 5, 2012.

45. Casey interview, Jan. 10, 2013.

46. Green telephone interview, Oct. 26, 2012.

47. Neil Clark, interview by Lee Leonard, Feb. 21, 2013.

48. Diemer, working as a Capitol Hill reporter, witnessed the event, circa September–October 1986. After the exchange with Heather Gradison, Rhodes turned to him and said, "You've got your story."

49. Heather Gradison, telephone interview by Tom Diemer, Jan. 19, 2014.

50. Lee Leonard, United Press International, May 11, 1986.

51. Green telephone interview, Oct. 26, 2012.

52. Richard F. Celeste, telephone interview by Lee Leonard, Jan. 18, 2013.

53. James Ruvolo, telephone interview by Lee Leonard, July 19, 2012.

54. Steiner interview, Nov. 28, 2012.

55. Taft interview, Oct. 30, 2012.

56. Bennett interview, Jan. 31, 2013.

57. James Ruvolo, "Jim Rhodes, 25 Years of Witch Hunting," Leonard Collection, box 5, folder 15, Ohio Historical Society, Columbus.

58. Roger K. Lowe, "Celeste, Rhodes Debate Corruption Charges in People's Court, *Columbus Dispatch,* July 11, 1986.

59. Celeste telephone interview, Jan. 18, 2013.

60. Lee Leonard, United Press International, Oct. 5, 1986.

61. Taft interview, Oct. 30, 2012.

62. Casey interview, Jan. 10, 2013.

63. Celeste telephone interview, Jan. 18, 2013.

64. "Rhodes Pledges Tax Deduction for Child Care, *Associated Press, Akron Beacon Journal,* Aug. 27, 1986.

65. Lee Leonard, United Press International, Sept. 14, 1986.

66. Tim Miller, "Candidates, Eager to Take Charge." *Dayton Daily News.*

67. Mary Beth Lane, "Environment: Split in Campaign Trail," *Dayton Daily News,* Sept. 26, 1986.

68. Lee Leonard, United Press International, Sept. 21, 1986.

69. "Rhodes' New TV Ads Star Local Officials, Rinehart, Voinovich and Robert Taft III," *Columbus Dispatch,* Sept. 27, 1986.

70. Michael Curtin, "Rhodes Just Keeps on Rolling," *Columbus Dispatch,* Leonard Collection, box 37, folder 14, Ohio History Center, Columbus.

71. Recap of federal income tax returns, E. C. Redman, CPA, Columbus.

72. Leonard had sparred with Rhodes before when the governor criticized Celeste for spending his entire adult life on the public payroll. "Governor, you've spent all your life in public office," Leonard observed. "You were only in the private sector for the last four years." Without missing a beat, Rhodes retorted: "Yes, and did forty years of work!"

73. Duane St. Clair, "Wife in Hospital, Rhodes Halts Race," *Columbus Dispatch,* Oct. 24, 1986.

74. Suzanne Moore telephone interview, May 20, 2013.

75. Robert E. Miller, "James A. Rhodes, Ohio's Governor for 16 Years, Dead at Age 91."

76. Leonard notes, Oct. 9, 7, 1986.

77. Melissa Johnson, "Rhodes, Celeste Run Long and Hard," *Akron Beacon Journal,* Oct, 21, 1986.

78. John Kostrzewa and David Adams, "AIDS Program Riles Rhodes: He Would Fire Homosexual Sympathizers," *Akron Beacon Journal,* Oct. 28, 1986.

79. Kurt Waldheim obituary, *New York Times,* June 14, 2007.

80. John Kostrzewa, "Rhodes, Celeste Spar for Hour: Issues Range from Homosexuality to Home State," *Akron Beacon Journal,* Nov. 3, 1986.

81. Celeste telephone interview, Jan. 18, 2013.

82. John Funk and John Kostrzewa, "Rhodes Says He's Gaining: TV Ad Blitz Begins Today," *Akron Beacon Journal,* Oct. 31, 1986.

83. John Kostrzewa, "As Vote Nears, Rhodes' Magic Seems Missing," *Akron Beacon Journal,* Oct. 26, 1986.

84. Leonard notes, Oct. 21, 1986.

85. Ohio Secretary of State, official returns for the 1986 general election.

86. Lee Leonard, United Press International, Nov. 9, 1986.

87. Leonard notes, Oct. 21, 1986.

88. Hughes interview, Dec. 21, 2012.

89. Michael Curtin and Roger K. Lowe, "Celeste Spent Twice as Much as Rhodes in Race," *Columbus Dispatch,* Dec. 13, 1986.

90. Leonard notes, Oct. 21, 1986.

91. Roger K. Lowe, "Rhodes Group Sought Grass-Roots Aura, Report Says," *Columbus Dispatch,* Sept. 12, 1987.

92. James Bradshaw, "Rhodes Campaign Backed Gay Foes, But It Was Legal," *Columbus Dispatch,* July 19, 1988.

14. Always Forward

1. Sue Gorisek, "The Colossus of Columbus," *Ohio Magazine,* Aug. 1989, 71.

2. Cochran interview, Mar. 26, 2013.

3. Rinehart telephone interview, Jan. 16, 2013.

4. Duerk telephone interview, Nov. 2, 2012.

5. Larry Householder, interview by Lee Leonard, Mar. 14, 2013.

6. Pfeifer interview, Aug. 22, 2012.

7. Celeste telephone interview, Jan. 18, 2013.

8. Ric Moore, interview by Lee Leonard, June 20, 2012.

9. Joseph D. Rice, "Retirement Not in His Vocabulary," *Cleveland Plain Dealer,* Sept. 9, 1989.

10. Lee Leonard, United Press International, Sept. 9, 1989.

11. Rice, "Retirement Not in His Vocabulary."

12. Duerk telephone interview, Apr. 3, 2013.

13. Duerk telephone interview, Nov. 2, 2012.

14. Jack Willey, "At 85, Ex-Governor Rhodes Too Busy for Age to Catch Up with Him," *Columbus Dispatch,* Nov. 21, 1994.

15. Duerk telephone interview, Apr. 3, 2013.

16. Robert E. Miller, "No More Smoke-filled Rooms for Rhodes," Associated Press, Nov. 9, 1992.

17. Ibid.; Healthy Buildings International Inspection Summary Report, Nov. 1993, 2.

18. Miller, "No More Smoke-filled Rooms for Rhodes."

19. Healthy Buildings International Inspection Summary Report, 6.

20. James A. Rhodes & Associates press release, Sept. 26, 1994.

21. Matthew Marx, "Arlington Board Rejects Rhodes Housing," *Columbus Dispatch,* Nov. 22, 1994.

22. Matthew Marx, "Rhodes Offers Arlington $200,000 for Project Vote," *Columbus Dispatch,* Dec. 13, 1994.

23. David Lore, "Lung Group Offers Whiff of Clean Air; Agency Will Open to Public Its Building Equipped with Rhodes' Air-filtering System," *Columbus Dispatch,* Apr. 14, 1996.

24. Richard Moore, interview by Lee Leonard, July 16, 2012.

25. Willey, "At 85, Ex-Governor Rhodes Too Busy for Age to Catch Up with Him," *Columbus Dispatch,* Nov. 21, 1994.

26. Suzanne Moore telephone interview, May 20, 2013.

27. Cooper interview, June 4, 2013.

28. Suzanne Moore interview, July 16, 2012.

29. Cooper interview, June 4, 2013.

30. Miller, "James A. Rhodes, Ohio's Governor for 16 Years, Dead at Age 91. "

31. Dennis Ramey, telephone interview by Lee Leonard, Feb. 1, 2013.

32. Cooper interview, June 4, 2013.

33. Sandra L. Latimer, "Former Governor Says Bush Will Take Ohio," United Press International, Sept. 21, 1988.

34. Lee Leonard, United Press International, Sept. 9, 1989; Joseph D. Rice, "Retirement Not in His Vocabulary," *Cleveland Plain Dealer,* Sept. 9, 1989.

35. Ibid.

36. Lee Leonard, United Press International, Sept. 9, 1989.

37. Voinovich telephone interview, June 27, 2012.

38. The source of Rhodes's quotation requested anonymity during an interview with Leonard.

39. George V. Voinovich, telephone interview by Lee Leonard, May 31, 2013.

40. Lee Leonard, "Livestock Lesson Shows Rhodes Remains Master Politician," *Columbus Dispatch,* Oct. 17, 1994.

41. Andrew Welsh-Huggins, "Rhodes Family Values Recalled," Associated Press, Mar. 9, 2001.

42. Steve Stephens, "Ex-Governors Hold Their Own Talk Show," *Columbus Dispatch,* Oct. 30, 1994.

43. Cooper interview, June 4, 2013.

44. Doug Caruso, "Rhodes Statue May Move Back to Statehouse," *Columbus Dispatch,* Dec. 29, 1995.

45. Ric Moore interview, June 20, 2012.

46. Phil Hamilton, telephone interview by Lee Leonard, Jan. 19, 2013. (Hamilton's family believed its lineage could be traced to Alexander Hamilton, information that Rhodes, the historian, no doubt treasured.)

47. Casey interview, Jan. 10, 2013.

48. Cooper interview, June 4, 2013.

49. "Saundra Jacob, Daughter of Former Governor, Dies," *Columbus Dispatch,* Mar. 24, 1996; Suzanne Moore telephone interview, May 20, 2013.

50. Suzanne Moore interview, July 16, 2012.

51. Associated Press, Aug. 22, 1996, copy in the Leonard Collection, box 37, folder 14, Ohio History Center, Columbus.

52. Hamilton interview, Jan. 19, 2013.

53. James Bradshaw, "Gilligan, Rhodes, Recall Their Finest, Worst Hours as Governors," *Columbus Dispatch,* Oct. 28, 2000.

54. Lee Leonard, "Rhodes Visits What He Started 20 Years Ago," *Columbus Dispatch,* Oct. 14, 1997.

55. Gongwer News Service, "Former Governor Rhodes Returns to Scene of One of His Greatest Triumphs 20 Years Later," Oct. 8, 1979.

56. Lee Leonard, "James Rhodes Lingers at Statehouse, Just Like Old Days," *Columbus Dispatch,* Aug. 5, 1997.

57. "Rhodes' Quick Wit Keeps Them Laughing," *Columbus Dispatch,* Jan. 7, 1999.

58. Suzanne Moore interview, July 16, 2012.

59. Hamilton telephone interview, Jan. 19, 2013.

60. Cooper telephone interview, June 7, 2013.

61. Ric Moore interview, June 20, 2012.

62. Donna Glenn, "Rhodes' Old Home to Serve Arlington," *Columbus Dispatch,* May 4, 1999.

63. Evans telephone interview, Nov. 20, 2012.

64. Lee Leonard, "Ex-Governor, Now in Senior Citizens' Home, Refines His Research," *Columbus Dispatch,* Mar. 9, 1999.

65. Suzanne Moore interview, July 16, 2012.

66. Coil, "New Deal Republican."

67. Suzanne Moore interview, July 16, 2012.

68. Cochran interview, Mar. 26, 2013.

69. Cooper interview, June 4, 2013.

70. Suzanne Moore interview, July 16, 2012.

71. Hamilton telephone interview, Jan. 19, 2013.

72. Lee Leonard, "Rhodes Serves Up a Lesson in How One Goes about Getting Things Done," *Columbus Dispatch,* May 31, 1999.

73. Lee Leonard, "Even at 90, Rhodes Can Deal Happily with Democrats," *Columbus Dispatch,* Sept. 17, 1999.

74. "Former Governor Breaks Collarbone," *Columbus Dispatch,* June 1, 1999.

75. "Former Governor in Hospital; Rhodes' Friends Report His Health Has Declined," *Columbus Dispatch,* Mar. 3, 2001.

76. Suzanne Moore interview, July 16, 2012.

77. Cooper telephone interviews, June 4, 7, 2013.

78. "Former Governor James A. Rhodes Dies," *Cleveland Plain Dealer,* Mar. 5, 2001.

79. "Former Minnesota Governor Stassen, 93, Dies; He Sought Presidential Nomination 9 Times," Associated Press, Mar. 5, 2001.

80. Lee Leonard, "Farewell to a Dreamer and a Man of Action," *Columbus Dispatch,* Mar. 8, 2001.

81. Lee Leonard, "Local Musician Remembers Rhodes as a Jazz Aficionado," *Columbus Dispatch,* Mar. 13, 2001; Arnett Howard, telephone interview by Lee Leonard, June 6, 2013.

82. "Former Governor James A. Rhodes Dies," *Cleveland Plain Dealer,* Mar. 5, 2001.

83. James Drew, "Taft Remembers Political Mentor as a Man of Impact," *Toledo Blade,* Mar. 9, 2001.

84. Welsh-Huggins, "Rhodes Family Values Recalled."

Epilogue

1. Robert Sobel and John Raimo, The Biographical Directory of Governors of the United States, 1789–1978 (Westport, Conn.: Meckler Books, 1978); Lee Leonard, United Press International, Sept. 9, 1982.

2. Lee Leonard, "Lima Technical College Renamed to Honor Ex-Gov. Rhodes," *Columbus Dispatch,* June 25, 2002.

3. Sources for highlights include plaques at the James A. Rhodes courthouse plaza in Jackson, Ohio; Shoemaker, *Ohio's Greatest Governor;* Tom Dudgeon, "Ohio's Governor of the Century" (Columbus: Ohio Editorial Enterprises, 1991), copy in the Leonard Collection, box 37, folder 8, Ohio History Center, Columbus.

4. Taft interview, Oct. 30, 2012.

5. Ned Hill, telephone interview by Tom Diemer, Oct. 21, 2013.

Selected Bibliography

As WORKING PRINT REPORTERS who covered James A. Rhodes up close and personal, the authors often relied on the first drafts of history—that is, daily newspapers. But they also fleshed out their story with fresh reporting and the sources included in this bibliography. Richard G. Zimmerman reported for the *Cleveland Plain Dealer* and Horvitz Newspapers; Lee Leonard followed the Rhodes trail first with United Press International and later with the *Columbus Dispatch,* and Tom Diemer was on the Statehouse beat for the Associated Press and the *Plain Dealer.*

Reports from the *Dispatch,* the *Plain Dealer,* and the two wire services cover the breaking news in *Ohio Colossus.* The authors also wish to acknowledge the *Akron Beacon Journal,* the *Dayton Daily News,* the *Dayton Journal Herald,* and the *Toledo Blade* as frequently cited sources.

PUBLISHED SOURCES

Aronoff, Stanley J., and Vernal G. Riffe. *James A. Rhodes at Eighty.* Columbus, Ohio: Privately published, 1989.

Bush, George H. W., with Victor Gold. *Looking Forward: An Autobiography.* New York: Bantam, 1988.

"The Campaign History of James A. Rhodes." *Ohio Petroleum Marketer* (January–February 1982): 4–15.

Condon Jr., George E. "State Had Its Own Colossus in Rhodes." *Canton Repository,* March 11, 2001.

DiSalle, Michael with Lawrence Blochman. *The Power of Life or Death.* New York: Random House, 1956.

Eszterhas, Joe, and Michael Roberts. *13 Seconds: Confrontation at Kent State.* New York: Dodd, Mead, 1970.

Goodwin, Doris Kearns. *Team of Rivals: The Political Genius of Abraham Lincoln.* New York: Simon & Schuster, 2005.

Jauchius, R. Dean, and Thomas H. Dudgeon. *Jim Rhodes' Big Win!* Columbus, Ohio: PoliCom, 1978.

Knepper, George W. *Ohio and Its People.* Kent, Ohio: Kent State University Press, 1989.

Lamis, Alexander, ed. *Ohio Politics.* Kent, Ohio: Kent State University Press, 1994.

Leonard, Lee. *A Columnist's View of Capitol Square: Ohio Politics and Government 1969–2005.* Akron, Ohio: University of Akron Press, 2010.

Michener, James. *Kent State: What Happened and Why.* New York: Random House, 1971.

Miller, Robert E. "James A. Rhodes, Ohio's Governor for 16 Years, Dead at Age 91." *Gongwer News Service,* March 5, 2001.

Neff, James. *Mobbed Up.* New York: Atlantic Monthly Press, 1989.

Saxbe, William B. with Peter D. Franklin. *I've Seen the Elephant: An Autobiography.* Kent, Ohio: Kent State University Press, 2000.

Shoemaker, Byrl R. *Ohio's Greatest Governor James A. Rhodes: Politician of the Century.* Columbus, Ohio: Shoemaker Enterprises, 2005.

Sobel, Robert, and John Raimo. *The Biographical Directory Governors of the United States.* Westport, Conn: Meckler Books, 1978.

Stokes, Carl. *Promises of Power: A Political Autobiography.* New York: Simon & Schuster, 1973.

Usher, Brian et al. "A Man Named Rhodes." *Akron Beacon Journal,* March 5, 1978.

Zimmerman, Richard G. *Call Me Mike: A Political Biography of Michael V. DiSalle.* Kent, Ohio: Kent State University Press, 2003.

Unpublished Sources

Coil, William Russell. "New Deal Republican: James A. Rhodes and the Transformation of the Republican Party, 1933–1983." PhD dissertation, The Ohio State University, 2005.

DiSalle, Michael V. Governor's statement, November 7, 1962. DiSalle Collection. Ohio History Center, Columbus.

Jauchius, Rollin Dean. "Gubernatorial Roles: An Assessment by Five Ohio Governors." PhD dissertation, Ohio State University, 1971.

Index